WATCH
WHERE
YOU
STEP

Jenepher Field

WATCH WHERE YOU STEP

Going to the Dogs

Jenepher Field

— Hal — in return for more stories!

Outskirts Press, Inc.
Denver, Colorado

Outskirts Press, Inc.
http://www.outskirtspress.com

PB ISBN: 978-1-4327-6929-1
HB ISBN: 978-1-4327-7509-4

Library of Congress Control Number: 2011931618

Outskirts Press and the "OP" logo are trademarks belonging to Outskirts Press, Inc.

PRINTED IN THE UNITED STATES OF AMERICA

Dedication

TO LOUIS

WITH MY LOVE

AND THANK YOU FOR LEAVING THE COMPUTER TO ME
AND FOR TAKING ON SUCH JOBS AS THE SEPTIC SYSTEM,
THE LANDSCAPING, THE MAINTENANCE, AND WALKING
THOSE LITTLE DOGS LATE AT NIGHT.

Acknowledgements

So many people were involved in this endeavor that the list of those we would like to personally thank is long. It would include all those who helped with the planning, building, and advising as well as those who have worked and those who are still working at Sagemoor Kennels, providing the quality care we know to be important.

All family members in this story are real people. They may not always identify themselves, but the author will put them straight if she is contacted.

The pets are real. Some of their names have been changed to protect the innocent. Other characters -- clients, friends, staff, and colleagues -- have fictitious names, or may even be fictitious, but are suitably covered up as to be unidentifiable.

Erratic *adj.*

1. deviating from the usual or proper course in conduct or opinion
2. having no certain or definite course; wandering; not fixed; erratic winds
3. Geol. Noting or pertaining to a boulder or the like carried by glacial ice and deposited some distance from its original place of origin
4. (of lichen) having no attachment to the surface on which it grows
5. – n. an erratic or eccentric person

- Syn. 1. unpredictable, unstable, capricious
- Ant. 1. consistent, regular, stable

Webster's Unabridged Dictionary 1998

"A rolling stone gathers no moss" – old proverb

Contents

Prologue

"LOOK OUT, WATCH out for that stuff out there – watch where you're stepping."

What a great piece of advice when dealing with dogs and cats! Louis spoke those words to me often, just as I was about to step into some smelly stuff...animal or human or organizational.

Louis grew up on a farm, knew more about animals than I did, and knew about watching where you put your feet, but we both had a great deal to learn about watching our steps when we started a boarding kennel for dogs and cats. Just a small business as a retirement project – that was all it was supposed to be -- a small retirement project to keep us from joining the traveling and bridge-playing crowd.

This book is not just about retirement. And it's not just about building and running a small business. It's not just about all the pets who became our boarding guests. All of these things are in it, as well as our family and ourselves.

It's not a "how-to" story; it's a "how we did it" story. Looking back, there are some things we might have done differently. We didn't always agree about doing some of what we chose to do. We certainly didn't agree about when to do it.

But it worked out for us both, and when you get two people as completely different as Louis and I, that's saying a great deal. Our differences were probably what made it work. I always went along with Louis's plans and he said he always did what I wanted.

What do two people think lies ahead when they say those two simple words "I do," and agree to live together "till death do us part," or whatever promises they make? On that memorable day in September 1957 when Louis and I made those promises, I don't think either of us thought beyond getting away from all the people who had come to wish us luck and a good life together. After that, there were jobs and children and making some money. Perhaps we thought of traveling, getting more education. But did we (does anyone?) starting off down that slow-moving, predictable stream of marriage see the rapids and snags that lie ahead as the stream widens and deepens? What about when the river slows down, and your feet hit bottom? What about the retirement years? Did we talk about them way back then? No, that came much later. We never thought about what new challenges we might face, and we never imagined becoming owners of a small business, boarding dogs and cats. Two people in a marriage are like two rocks in a river being tumbled around by the currents. Sometimes they are together, moving in a slow current; other times the current is faster and one rock may be tumbled ahead of the other for a while. With luck, both rocks will land up in about the same place when the current slows down and the rest of the debris that's flowing along in the river passes on. Retirement comes along with some dreams unfulfilled, new concerns beginning to show up, and a great many scars left from all that tumbling around in the water, leaving the individuals smooth in some places, rough in others. Retirement is the time in your life when you suddenly stick your head out of life's currents and look around to see what else is out there waiting for you. The business of the cats and the dogs was out there, waiting to grab hold of us, but when we were newly-weds, we didn't think beyond living together in America.

Open for Business

A SHIVER OF...SOMETHING...RAN through me. Excitement? Anticipation? Anxiety? I didn't know. There was so much to look forward to; it was probably a little of each. Here we were, behind the desk: Louis, Mary and I, waiting for the first customer to arrive. We were like three sheepdogs sitting at the ready, heads up, noses raised, ears pricked, and waiting for the signal to go into action. Sagemoor Kennels was ready to open for business. For the past few days, even weeks, we had been on the run, sometimes in circles, rounding up all the last-minute items we were sure we couldn't do without: pens, a receipt book, staples and a stapler, toilet paper and disinfectant soap.

Now we waited. How many years had this enterprise been waiting for the signal to take off? We weren't counting. We just wanted to get it off the ground and into orbit.

We declared opening day to be October 14th 1995, because that was the day our first boarder was due to arrive. It was fall, and those long summer days when we worked late were over. It was still warm, but the cool wind made us put on jackets.

"Are we ready for this?" Mary asked, as we watched a car

come around the corner and head toward the parking lot. I thought its approach was cautious. But that might have been my imagination, or because it was carrying our first boarder and we didn't know what to expect. This one was somewhat more than we had expected.

He was large and hairy. He was built like a tank, a black and white fur-covered tank, and his name was Jake. Jake was a Newfoundland -- to be accurate, a Landseer Newfoundland. They're the biggest variety of the breed. The sort the artist painted rescuing a small child from the ocean's tumbling breakers somewhere far away from where we were today.

Jake arrived in a small, elderly Jeep, the sort built like a box. Jake sat in the passenger seat, up front, with his head out the window, to provide the driver with another guidance system. There might indeed be some need for caution when driving this load. The driver was a young woman, small in stature, though not in authority when it came to Jake.

"Jake, sit!"

When she gave the command to sit, Jake sat, like a new recruit coming to attention when addressed by the commanding officer. Jake, we were told, was very friendly -- we should have no trouble from him, and he was staying for two weeks. We reviewed his paperwork.

"How much does Jake eat?" I asked.

"Just don't feed him too much – a couple of large bowls twice a day should do him." She held her hands out to show me how big a bowl she thought would hold enough for this very large dog. "And any treats you want to give him."

We agreed with his owner that the best room for Jake was in one of the outside Barn Kennels where he would have the most space. We all walked out with Jake to his vacation house and he promptly sat down, outside the kennel door, as though to say, "This is not what I had in mind. Let's go home."

Jake was not going home, as his owner explained to him, giving the simple command to "Kennel up!" And he did. He promptly walked in, turned around, and sat down, waiting for whatever came next. She gave him a pat on the head and told him to be a good boy and she would be back in two weeks. He seemed to understand, but he was very large, and he might have other plans!

Jake was just what his owner had said – very friendly, and we had no trouble with him. Soon we found out just how friendly he could be. His favorite trick was to wait until someone was taking him on a walk and not paying any special attention to him -- then, choosing exactly the right moment, he would rear up and place his front paws on the walker's shoulders. This put him eyeball to eyeball with whoever had the assignment to exercise him. The first time he tried this attention-getting strategy was with Louis, who went down backwards, Jake on top of him, licking his face.

"I'd have been fine if I hadn't got my foot stuck in the furrow and couldn't step back easily," Louis explained when he had found his feet again and was trying to push Jake back, adding, "Won't happen again, I can tell you."

It was a warning. We would take action any time Jake was seen to start to lean back a little and lift his paws off the ground. If you waited any longer, it was too late. It was impossible to keep your balance under this loving embrace. The only thing to do was to aim a knee or a foot at his chest, and he would immediately drop down again.

His owners had requested that Jake have a daily brushing. It took two of us to do this. While Mary held him, I would curry his formidable coat. Jake loved this. He would roll over for us to do his tummy and he would groan with delight as we brushed his shoulders. The fur flew. There was enough to knit a sweater, if we had known any knitters.

We were sad to see our gentle giant go. We learned a great deal from our first boarder. His owners assured us that they too had fallen under his embraces, and that their house was well- covered with dark fur.

The next two boarders were as unlike Jake as night and day: small and black and trembling with fright. Jacques and Mimi were two toy Poodles who went into the Homestyle Room, where they shared a doghouse. The Homestyle Room was reserved for the very little dogs – the sort that sit on your lap and will fit in carry bags under seats in planes. Hotels welcome them. We had realized early in the planning phase that very little dogs might feel threatened if boarded near some of the larger ones. Certainly their owners might not want to think of their tiny little canine family member being exposed to the loud noise and vigorous behavior of some of the larger dogs. Mimi was the more friendly of these two. She would come out of her doghouse when invited. Jacques would not. Jacques was terrified, and he dealt with his fear by attacking whatever appeared to be a threat – especially an outstretched hand. He retreated to the back of his doghouse and made it clear to everyone that if a hand came any closer, he would sink his small sharp teeth into it. Dogs in the Homestyle Room did not have a run of their own, but were taken out to the exercise yard five times a day to do their "doings."

Jacques had to come out of his doghouse one way or another. Louis treated the problem with some cold roast chicken brought over from the house to tempt Jacques. Louis was Jacques's friend for life after that. To make sure, Louis always brought a treat from the house. He didn't trust that Jacques might one day forget the agreement they had made – you bring me roast meat, and I'll let you pick me up and carry me outside. But a slight growl, a curl of the lip, a narrowing of Jacques' eyes, and one of us would rush to bring him some goodie. Then, and only then, would he consent to prance out of the doghouse and, along with Mimi and whoever else was in Homestyle, he would trot down the hallway, through the office, and out the heavy back door to the grass beyond.

Louis loved Jacques. And he loved a Chihuahua named Buddy, another Homestyler who, like Jacques, didn't want to come out of his doghouse and go out with the others -- not until Louis enticed him with some roast beef. Buddy came over to the house with Louis one day at lunch time and when Louis patted his knee and said "up," Buddy jumped up onto Louis's lap. You can't do that with an English Pointer or Setter or a Labrador – or even a Welsh Corgi. Buddy was the right size for lap-sitting, and Louis had the roast beef. Louis decided that if the time came when he could no longer ride a horse and take his dogs to run in American Field or shoot-to-retrieve trials, then he would get a small black Poodle, like Jacques, or a Chihuahua like Buddy.

There were still a few details to take care of, but with those first boarders, we declared ourselves finished with the construction phase of the kennels, barn, and house. Louis and I had been living in the house for almost three months. Mary had moved into the apartment with Max, her Australian cattle dog. Bob, our adopted handyman – or did he adopt us? – had been living in the barn for longer than that. And the barn held the tractor.

Perhaps we were not as ready as we thought, but here we were, already boarding pets, taking in money, paying bills, ordering more supplies. The inquiries for boarding were increasing.

I surveyed the place one day soon after opening. Behind me was the house, backed by the Columbia River; the barn was to my right, and there in front of me was Sagemoor Kennels. The sun was shining, but the wind was cold and I could see clouds to the east. They wouldn't bother us, but the general appearance was not to my liking. I wanted blue sky, warm breezes, and green lawns. None of that was there. Our business venture – or perhaps adventure would be a better word – would have to do some maturing. There was no lawn in yet, no paths, no shrubs, in fact, very little was green except the alfalfa in the field beyond. But the parking lot was paved, its parking spaces marked, and there was even a handicapped sign up over the one closest to the kennels, adding a professional touch, I thought. There were still landscaping ideas to consider and lawns, paths, and more signs to do. The only lawn was in the exercise yard, complete with a seven-foot-high fence to keep the jumpers and climbers contained. *Looks like a prison yard,* I thought. *Just hope the clients don't see it that way.*

Had we thought of everything? We'd made so much progress in two years. Sagemoor Kennels had grown from a wild dream we'd had years before, thinking retirement might be the opportunity to try another challenge. Here we were about to launch a small business housed in a new facility, complete with indoor kennels, exercise yard, a barn, and our home.

"Is this going to be another Christmas production?" Louis asked. He had survived many Christmases that had just missed being "perfect" according to my standard. He had a point. I made lists for Christmas, for birthdays, for anything that needed some planning. I had made lists for this project too. Was I becoming too involved in the details? I took another look at the view. I couldn't do much about the weather. We'd just have to wait and see.

Meeting Down Under

IT ALL STARTED back in 1957, when Louis Field from Almena, Kansas, USA, asked Jenny Fitzgerald to go for a drink after work at the Royal Albert, the pub around the corner from the Medical School in Dunedin, New Zealand. A ridiculous invitation. Didn't he know that girls didn't go into pubs out here in New Zealand? He used that fake Southern accent too. But it was a tempting invitation. What kept me from accepting? In my mind I could hear my mother's voice, "Don't be silly, Jenepher!"

"Miss Jenny, ma'am, would y'all care to join me for a beer after work?"

His voice was low, the smile warm, and those brown eyes held a welcoming glow. Most attractive, but still, there was that warning.

"No, thanks, I don't drink beer and women don't usually go into pubs here."

That was about as much of our first conversation as I remember. Even then, I was never sure when he was teasing and when he was serious.

Louis was doing research for the Chairman of the Department of Internal Medicine at the University of Otago Medical

School. He said he hadn't been ready to settle down into a surgical residency back in the States. He'd graduated from the Medical School at the University of Kansas, and he liked to try new places. So he applied for a fellowship on the other side of the world in New Zealand. He knew little about the place, except that there was fishing and hunting out there, and those were of great interest to him.

"I usually just fall into things and this was one of them," he would say later on.

What about me? Did I have a habit of falling into things too? Looking back, I saw I had allowed other people to arrange my life, and sometimes I'd fallen into situations I might have been wiser to stay out of.

"It sounded good at the time," could have been my motto for the past few years, and who knew? Life might be about to take a new turn.

Margaret Jenepher Fitzgerald was born and grew up in Dunedin, New Zealand. I had interests that included skiing, travel, meeting interesting men, and was, at that time, in need of money, but not sure how to find it. My skills were varied though minimal in expertise. My dad found me a job in the same research lab where Louis hovered over his research equipment. Dad's intention was probably to get me out of the house and into supporting myself. Both my parents were medical doctors – Dad was an orthopedic surgeon, and Mother worked for the government as a school medical officer. They didn't need a young twenty-something hanging around the house. If Dad had only been able to look into some crystal ball and see just how far out of the house this job would take me, he might have considered continuing to support my living at home, arguing with my mother about money and how late I was allowed to return from dates.

You could say that Louis and I fell into our jobs and later fell in love in much the same way. One day we were just going out, and the next we were making plans to get married. Proximity had a lot to do with it. I had a small corner cell in the laboratory where Louis did his research. My job as a technical editor, administrative assistant, and general secretary to the Boss, - the Chairman of the Department of Medicine - consisted of cleaning up the grammar and researching references for a book the Boss was writing. There were other chores, such as ordering supplies and writing letters to other research professors, but the book was the big one, and the whole department knew it. Its subject was malignant hypertension and its treatment. There were other research labs and professors racing to find the right treatment and to be the first to publish their findings. My boss was out in the lead, but there were one or two others and it was a close race. This was to be the book to end all books on the subject. The Boss wrote in longhand on legal-sized pads of yellow lined paper, and he appeared to have an aversion to capital letters, commas, and periods. I was to insert them where necessary.

My office had been a storage closet and now contained two filing cabinets, a desk ,and my typewriter, an old Royal which took a great deal of finger power to move any key. The rest of the room -- tall ceilings and sash windows that stuck if opened -- had a pronounced chemical smell. It was on the second floor of the old medical school building on King Street, across from the hospital, and probably dated back over a hundred years. Besides my cell, the room housed three research fellows sitting on stools at counters that held black box-like machines and whatever else they needed. Their heads were bent and their eyes attached permanently to their microscopes. There was not a great deal of conversation. Louis had a corner spot near a window and as far away from anyone as he could get. He wore a white lab coat, and in many ways was indistinguishable from all the other research fellows. Except he had this accent, and was labeled as the "Yankee." It was reported that he spent his weekends fishing, hunting, and drinking. He had dark hair, good looks, a quiet manner, and wore the same tweed jacket all the time he was there, when not wearing that old white lab coat. I had dated several men in England during the past two years. Some had jobs, others might one day be employable when, and if, they decided between a medical degree or skiing and scuba diving, one had a degree in mathematics and did the Times Crossword every morning. Louis was certainly the most interesting man I had met in a long time. Being an American, he spoke with an accent. He had never skied or scuba dived, had a paying job, and in addition to his weekend hunting and fishing, spent his evenings reading classic American authors, none of which I had read. He drank with the other men from the department every evening after work at the local pub.

At that time in New Zealand, pubs closed at 6 p.m. and the drinking customs were something a cultural anthropologist might have found worth studying. Work ended at five o'clock, and so from five until six o'clock pub drinkers tried to drink as much beer as possible. They did this by the "school" method. Each member of a "school," or group, would buy a round of beers for everyone in the group. At fifteen minutes before six o'clock, the barman would call out "Time, gentlemen, please," which was the signal for all "school" members to look at each other and ask, "Shall we have another each?" This was code for "shall we each buy another round of drinks?" If there were six men in the group, that meant each would have six beers to drink in about fifteen minutes. This certainly contributed to

New Zealand's reputation at that time for the country with the greatest consumption of beer on the planet.

Women back then didn't frequent bars. We might go to the "lounge bar" in a hotel and drink something called a "shandy" which was a mixture of beer and lemonade. Wine hadn't hit the country at that time. That came later.

Back to Louis's invitation to have a drink with him at the Captain Cook. Certainly I might consider going out with him, though not to the five o'clock beer swill. I tried it once and that was one time too many. New Zealand beer was strong and their pints were Imperial-sized. I could hardly manage a half. So dating Louis was not something I considered long-term. Not back then...but he grew on me.

The Boss's book was not one with a great story line, so when I came out of my cell I wandered around the lab to see what others were doing. I would walk over to Louis, stand behind him, and watch what he was doing. I had met few Americans, so I asked questions about the States, probably showing some prejudice. Looking back, I see that I never appreciated how tolerant he was of my ignorance. I was also curious about the research he was doing.

"Why are you cutting those rats in half? I hope you gave them a shot of something first."

"I'm studying the effects of shock," Louis replied without looking up.

"You certainly shocked that rat -- he's never going to get over it!"

Louis was impervious to my sarcasm, and charm wasn't having any effect. However I had an effect on him. He always said it was my low-necked peasant blouse and the way I leaned over him to look at the rats that grabbed his attention. I firmly maintained I never had a peasant blouse but I certainly had some low-necked dresses that I probably wore to work. Back then I liked to dress to be noticed. I even bleached a wide streak of my hair. I'd hoped for a nice pale blond, but it came out a sort of reddish yellow. It was hard to miss. Louis took one look at me and said loudly and clearly – and in words I would never forget.

"Good God, woman, what have you done to your hair!"

I had caught his attention with that one, but I was a little afraid I might have overdone it.

I'm not sure when Louis asked me out for a date that did not involve going to the pub with the boys. Eventually he made the right steps, and I agreed to go to a university dance and later to a party. There was probably a great deal of drinking and since neither of us had a car, driving was no problem. Louis walked me home and then walked himself back the four or more miles to where he boarded with a good-natured, but thrifty, old Scottish landlady, Mrs. Johnson, who kept a watchful eye on this Yankee.

"She believed in not wasting valuable resources," Louis told me, having never met anyone quite like this Scot before. "She put one log on the fire in the evening for heat and we would hunch around this to keep warm, which was a challenge since the space at the bottom of all the doors let the Antarctic southerly winds blow through." One night when she was away, Louis decided to get some more heat in the house and built up a roaring blaze in the fireplace. The chimney quickly caught on fire and Louis had to call the fire brigade. Mrs. Johnson had good reason to keep an eye on "those Yanks."

We continued in this way for some time. We'd walk to a movie, a party, the beach, and we'd talk. Louis had grown up on a farm in the Midwest during the Dustbowl Depression days. He would tell me about seeing the old cars and trucks piled high with all a family's possessions as they started the trek to California. I had read Steinbeck's *The Grapes of Wrath*, but here was the real thing. His family stayed, and Louis remembered the dust clouds that rolled up from Oklahoma, sometimes red dust and sometimes it was black, but it covered everything. He had driven a team of five horses abreast and run greyhounds after jackrabbits. Then there were the locusts that died and rotted in the fields. He and his brothers had shot pheasants and ducks in and out of season. As soon as he was old enough, he had enlisted in the Army and found himself in Korea. When he returned with the G.I. Bill and enough money saved to buy a car, he decided to go to medical school and become a doctor.

"At the time I didn't even know where the university was, let alone the medical school."

I felt I was watching several movies at once as I listened to his stories. I had no stories to match his, but I kept asking questions and then there would be another story. Like that proverbial rolling stone, Louis hadn't let any moss, or grass, grow under his feet. I never gave a thought to what it might be like trying to keep up with him.

At the same time, my parents were doing a great deal of talking -- about us, that is, though we were not aware of any concerns they might have had at that point.

"When are you going to bring this young American friend home for dinner?" Mother asked me one day. A harmless sort of question, though I should have known better. In the past whenever Mother showed any interest in my boyfriends -- "your young men" as she put it -- I seemed to lose interest in them. Perhaps she hoped for a similar reaction this time, too.

Louis came to dinner. He came many times. He brought

gifts of freshly caught trout and salmon, carefully gutted, and venison steaks and roasts. Mother appreciated the fish, though she declared all venison "too gamey," but did her best with it. My parents found him "charming, most interesting." We had family fishing trips and my father was impressed by Louis's fly fishing skills.

One day, Dad appeared in the department to talk to my boss. I had an uncomfortable feeling they were not discussing the relative merits of treatments for malignant hypertension or Dad's specialty of fractures of the hip. I was sure they were discussing the future prospects the American research fellow might have. Mother and Dad were beginning to show some anxiety about Louis's and my relationship. Mother would ask questions about Louis's family back in the States.

"Does he have any brothers and sisters?

"What does his father do?"

Innocuous questions, but I knew there was more to them than innocent curiosity on Mother's part.

By now Louis and I had passed the point of just "going together." Our plans included marriage and a move to the States. I was, however, terrified of telling my parents, especially Mother, who had other plans for her daughter.

Mother was English. She never stopped calling England "Home" with a capital "H," in spite of all the years living in New Zealand. She had spent a great deal of time and money on my education so that I could speak without that "New Zealand accent," and with the hope that I might find an English husband. I had recently returned from two years in England. I had a degree in history, some small acquaintance with journalism, shorthand in three languages and typing at fifty words a minute. I had skied whenever and wherever I could from Austria to Scotland, and had met many attractive men, but none who fitted into a list of possible husbands, either hers or mine. I was out of funds, jobs and boyfriends. It had been time to come home.

That was the point at which my father found me the job working for his old friend, the chairman of the Department of Medicine. And that was the point at which I met Louis.

While doctors were high on Mother's list of future sons-in-law, American ones barely made the bottom of the list. Louis's only redeeming feature in my mother's eyes was that he had been brought up in the Methodist Church, though the Methodist church in rural Kansas was very different from the one Mother had known in England. But I had decided that Louis fitted everything I needed in a husband: he was fun, had great ideas of things to do, he liked trying new things, and we loved each other. What was more, we would move to the States. I don't think at the time I contemplated what that last point might entail. It sounded exciting, new, and full of endless possibilities…and I'd never been there. So in spite of my parents' reservations, at which they would hint though never state outright, we got married. Dad warned me that there were some strong feelings in the States about Communists and that the views I frequently voiced at the dinner table might not go down so well over there.

"And don't tell anyone you ever went to the University Congress," he advised. He referred to a summer student gathering I had attended several times which had a reputation for its more liberal views.

Louis had to return to the States to start his general surgery residency in Texas, and my parents thought it wise if we waited a few months. Then he could return for the wedding. I don't remember why we agreed to this, but I was used to following my parents' wishes, as were most of my girl friends.

Weddings took some planning, and I didn't know anyone who rushed into such things without a great deal of organization and preparation. I think my parents had the hope that distance would put an end to what they saw as their daughter's latest outrageous idea. In the past I had been known to undertake some crazy projects. They had also seen a great many boyfriends come and go. They probably had breathed a sigh of relief at those departures. I knew Louis was different, but was never able to explain that to my parents. They were not of a generation who held deep "meaningful" conversations with their children.

We were married in September, 1957. In New Zealand, that is early spring. There was still snow for skiing in the mountains, but in Dunedin the cherry blossom trees were blooming, the daffodils and tulips were adding color to the gardens, and my wedding veil had a crown of cherry blossoms picked from our front garden. The wedding went off as planned, though Louis almost missed his plane from Houston to New Zealand – something to do with a farewell party the night before – and his luggage didn't arrive till the day of the wedding. He was caught by his best man about to go into the pub for a beer and a mutton bird – a particularly foul-smelling variety of smoked sea bird Louis had taken to eating. His best man wisely took the future groom back home for a cup of tea and cake instead. Meanwhile I was struggling with veil and floral hair piece. Mother was on her way to the church and Dad thought it a good idea to open a bottle of champagne. The two of us had a long toast to the future. I would have thought the smell of champagne left one's breath quickly. However, in spite of a long Episcopal wedding service, on our way to the reception and sitting close together in the car, Louis leaned close and announced:"You've been drinking!"

The poor man explained he had been denied a beer and mutton bird by his best man. It just wasn't fair to find his bride had been given champagne.

"And you were late. My best man and I were on our knees in the church all the time waiting for you!" Louis found it convenient to remind me of this many times since.

We went wild pig hunting on our honeymoon. Some might think this a strange way to spend a honeymoon, but it made sense to us. Louis didn't ski; the fishing season hadn't started, nor had the deer hunting season. That left just pig hunting, and Louis believed in always having something to do. It sounded an interesting spectator sport to me, since I had never shot anything more than an occasional tin can off a fence post.

"If I'm not up doing something, then I'm lying down sleeping," Louis would say.

I should have read the writing on the wall. The pattern for our lives was being set. Activity of some sort was always important to Louis and he preferred an activity that would present a challenge. He fished to catch fish and strove to do so with skill; he would consider a hike only if there was a river or stream at the end of the hike in which he might catch a fish. When he eventually agreed to join me skiing, he took lessons so he could become a better skier. It was the same with table tennis, water skiing, dog training and horseback riding. I had never met anyone who set goals as Louis did. I certainly hadn't considered setting any high level of achievement for myself before meeting him, and it was only over time that I learned the excitement that went along with achieving a personal challenge.

First Steps

LOUIS AND I started married life in Galveston, Texas.

As an introduction to America, Galveston and Texas were hard to beat. I arrived in November and the weather was warm and wet, but there was talk of winter and cold "blue northers" though I never saw frost or snow. People talked so slowly that I wanted to finish their sentences for them, yet they would shake their heads at me when I spoke and ask me to repeat what I'd said. I found it an exciting and challenging place to live, where I could walk to the shrimp boats and buy -- for under ten dollars -- enough shrimp and crab to last a week. I had had little interest in cooking before this, but now the diversity of food and cooking methods introduced me to a love of cooking that I never lost.

Louis completed his general surgery residency at the University of Texas Medical Branch located there, and was appointed to the faculty as an instructor in general surgery. I worked as a librarian in the public library and later in the medical school library. In no time we had two children, a boat for fishing and water skiing, and those jobs helped support these choices. But we had no plans or challenges for the future. We survived two hurricanes. During the last one,

Hurricane Carla, our daughter Catherine was born at about the time the power in the hospital failed due to the high water flooding the hospital basement. I had warm chocolate milk and bologna sandwiches for my post-delivery meal. I've never liked either since.

My parents visited us several times. I well remember Dad asking Louis what his next plans were – more training, perhaps?

"Trauma -- I'm interested in trauma." Louis had been caught off guard by my father's question and that was the best answer at the time. He added that we would like to travel as well. My father made inquiries about where the best residencies were for trauma, came up with names and addresses for Louis to contact, and as a result we went to England for two more years of training in trauma for Louis.

We lived first in Reading and Louis worked at the Battle Hospital. We lived in an apartment complex built for the residents and interns, and I had a baby buggy I could put the two children in and push them to the neighborhood parks. The next year we were in Oxford and Louis worked at the Nuffield Hospital. We lived in an old Victorian brick house, which had been divided into three apartments. Ours was the ground floor. It was midwinter when we moved in. The snow lay all around us and it took many trips in our small Austin van to move our stuff from Reading to Oxford. We learned that each winter, the English would announce that there had never been a winter like this one. We agreed with them about this winter. The house had four main entrances to our apartment and all had spaces beneath the doors to allow for the passage of air. I remember lying in the bathtub and watching the ice slowly melt and slide down the inside of the window next to the tub!

It was so cold that our car wouldn't start. Louis could walk to the hospital but I was stuck when it came to grocery shopping and the daily diaper wash. This was in the days prior to disposable diapers! I would put the two children in the baby buggy, stack the sack of clothes on top of them, and walk the mile up to the Headington shops where there was a launderette. I had a choice then. I could stay and do the laundry, or I could leave it for a friendly attendant to do for me. I could collect the washed and dried laundry later on – but it would be afternoon before it would be ready. So that meant another walk, pushing the baby buggy with two children in it. I certainly got my exercise. When spring came and the snow melted, I still continued this routine, though by then Henry, our eldest, was in a preschool close by and I would drop him off in the morning and pick him up later. That baby buggy got its workout, as I did.

I was pregnant with number three when we went to Oxford, and Elizabeth was born on a warm summer evening in June. So now we had three children to fit into that baby buggy. I found it a heavy load to push, but Henry solved that problem by riding his tricycle next to me and the buggy. There was a seat across the end of the buggy for Catherine to sit on and, as usual, the laundry was piled around the baby, Elizabeth.

By the end of 1963 Louis's training in trauma was over. We moved back to the States with three children, little money, and one old car. It was time to find somewhere to settle down and for Louis to start in practice.

We moved to Washington State. We chose Washington because we had already been in Texas and wanted somewhere new. The Midwest didn't interest either of us even though Louis had come from Kansas. The East seemed a long way off, and California too crowded. Washington and Oregon appealed to me because they were both on the Pacific Ocean, and Louis liked them for the mountains and the apparent lack of large populations. So we looked at several places, visited many medical clinics that assured us they were just dying for a general surgeon with orthopedic and trauma background, and eventually chose Richland, one of three towns on the Columbia River in eastern Washington. I had imagined Washington State to be tree-clad, but the eastern half of the state was at that time dry desert, and Richland was the gateway to the Hanford Atomic Works and the Manhattan Project of World War II. With such a background, we found the place to be full of scientists from all over the world. Louis started in private practice in orthopedics. I met women from England, Ireland, Australia, and other parts of the world. I enjoyed this cosmopolitan background to the place.

Our housing situation hadn't improved much. We rented a house complete with a basement, a garage, and spacious yard. But it was small, and it wasn't long before Michael was born. We became a two-car family and saw we needed more space than our little two-bedroom one-bathroom rental provided. We took the financial plunge and built a house with swimming pool, tennis court, and large vegetable garden. I practiced my cooking skills and joined whatever volunteer group sounded interesting, from the women's church guild to reading nursery rhymes to kindergarteners. Our life together became busy, if predictable, and looking back we probably felt we had settled down as a family at last.

It was a long time before we again contemplated anything new or unusual.

Living Alone

MY FATHER DIED in July 1974. He had written to me in March of that year to let me know of the diagnosis. He was ill for only a short time. In fact, we hoped that he and Mother would still be able to visit Louis and me and the family later in the fall on their way to England as planned. He and Mother were thinking of moving permanently over there. It didn't happen that way. In June he had to be hospitalized, and I flew over to Dunedin at once. He and Mother and I had about ten days with him before he died peacefully one morning. I never realized how much I would miss his gentle ways and thoughtful suggestions. Our children loved him, especially for the time he took with them to build model cars, boats, and airplanes.

My brother Tony came out from England for the funeral. He stayed only a short while and I stayed for almost a month. I don't know about Tony, but I couldn't bear to leave Mother and home and all that seemed to have gone with Father's death. In silence, Tony and I took his ashes down to Waitati and scattered them in the bush and on the waters of the outgoing tide. It was a difficult time to talk about anything except perhaps plane flights back to England or to the States. When it came time for Tony to leave, Mother and I drove him out to the airport, and in silence watched the plane lumber down the runway, gaining speed and finally leaving the ground to climb up into the clouds that were sweeping in from the south, carrying their load of rain to add to the dreariness of the day.

For the first time since Father's death I thought of Mother, now completely alone. As we walked through the airport back to the car I watched her, almost seeing her for the first time. She had always been a small woman. Now she seemed to have shrunk as she walked, bent slightly forward as though to ward off anyone who might approach her. Her grey hair was carefully waved in a style that had stayed the same for probably forty-two years of marriage. She looked like many a sturdy elderly British woman. Sensible walking shoes and a brown raincoat added to her air of invisibility. If one looked long and hard, however, one might notice the telltale signs of grief and stress in the way she carried that familiar old crocodile-skin handbag in front of her, both hands tightly clasping the handles.

I drove slowly back home, their home, not wanting to go into that now-empty house. Neither of us spoke, just watched the rain pelting down and the windshield wipers trying to keep up with the job of keeping the windshield clear to see through. I reminded Mother that the windshield wipers needed replacing. She just nodded, mouth set in a straight line. The car heater wasn't doing a very good job either, but one thing at a time. The heater could wait. I thought of all that still had to be done: letters to be written, Father's belongings to be gone through, the bank, the solicitor, and goodness knew what else. Tony and I had gone over a great many things with Mother, but the bulk of it still had to be done.

The house was warm when we got home, but I lit the fire to put some life in the silent room. Then I put on the kettle for tea and went to see if there was any milk, or if I should go to the shop up the hill. It looked as though there was plenty of all we needed till the next day. No need to go out. We sat by the fire and drank tea, and listened to a bell bird chime its four solitary notes somewhere in the bush behind the house. Wax-eyes were dancing around the empty bird feeder. I needed to put out something for them. Mother broke the silence.

"I think I may go home to England, Jenepher. Don't know when. Walden and I had planned to go, you know, but he got ill so we couldn't. But it's just an idea."

New Zealand had never been her country. It had always been his. It was his family who had lived there for four generations, not hers. They had always been kind, loving, but even after all this time I think Mother always felt the outsider: accepted, but different. But she had never felt alone. Even when Father had been away for five years at the War, Mother had had us children to care for and do things with. She had always told me that had been a good time. Had she told him? Probably not; just having him home with her again was the most important thing. Now he was gone and it felt as though some presence was no long there – an emptiness seemed to settle like some dark cold blanket on the house.

I found myself looking around at the room. It was dark outside now, and the rain might have let up a bit. This house was the one they had planned and built together after Tony and I left the nest, he to Cambridge and I to the States. I thought of how Father had found the lot, one at the end of a road backed by some of the loveliest of native bush and full of the sounds of birds. He had surprised Mother with the purchase, but she was delighted. The two of them had planned the house, just the way they wanted it to be, and it had been perfect for them...windows all around, a circular stair leading up to the loft where Father had his desk and did his dictating, or where the two of them would drink their sherry, sitting in the late evening sunshine, before Mother prepared dinner.

I think now of Louis and me. How later we did much the same thing: retired from our professions and moved to the country, building not only the new house, but also a small business. While we don't have the native New Zealand bush around us, we have the Columbia River, the sagebrush and rabbit brush, orchards and vineyards and an openness with wonderful clouds climbing like castles up from the horizon or scattered in drifts across the sky. It reminds me of my beloved Central Otago. A familiar feel, but at the same time, not the same place.

Back then, it was time to draw the curtains, to turn on the television and watch the six o'clock news, to have that ritual glass of sherry. I went to the corner cupboard and found the bottle of Amontillado, three glasses, and the little silver tray. I turned to look at Mother. She was looking at me as I held the three glasses between my fingers. Outside birds twittered their evening calls. I raised my eyebrows in question.

She shook her head. "Let's not pretend," she said firmly. I replaced one of the glasses.

I poured the sherry and we raised our glasses in a silent toast. To whom? To what? Mother and Father had had so many plans and dreams. Would she still be able to do some of the things she wanted to do? Her eyes were closed as she slowly sipped her drink. Was she thinking of some of those things?

I picked up the embroidery I had brought with me. I'd been doing it when Mother and I sat with Father those last days in the hospital. It is with me now here, finished as a cushion cover, and it sits on the sofa in our living room, reminding me of how time seems to stand still at these moments. The bright colors of the wool threads show two pheasants and flowers, seed heads, grasses. If I touch it I can feel the quiet stillness of that living room, those many years ago, smell the wood smoke from the fire, taste the sherry, and almost hear Mother's slow breathing as she leans head back against the cushions of her chair.

The next year Mother moved back to England to live in Cambridge.

"I have so many friends there still," she reassured my doubting, questioning silence. How would she do, living by herself there after almost fifty years on the other side of the world? She had always preached personal freedom, the rights of individuals to choose for themselves, that women should have their own bank accounts, their own careers, jobs, and educational opportunities. She lived by that mantra "Anything the boys can do Freda can do, too," told to her by her father and repeated to her children and grandchildren many times. At the same time, a core principle for her was that one must always think of the other person, of how one's behavior might affect others. So another phrase I heard many times was "Don't be a bother to people." It seemed ironic that the first opportunity she had for personal freedom and the opportunity to make her own choices came when she was seventy-two years of age, with the death of her beloved husband.

In a few weeks she went from being her husband's principal support to someone who now was in need of support herself and, what was new to her, to someone who was being looked to for directions. Walden had always known just what she would want – and he had never been wrong. Now he was not there to tell her, and the terror of "being a bother" did battle with her need to ask questions, to gradually decide what she might do with the rest of her life, one in which she quickly realized she would have to make her own choices.

"I'm quite good at being on my own," she had often said, little realizing that there had always been someone there for her, either to support her or for her to support, to feel needed. She came from a generation of women who considered men to be the breadwinners, the ones who set examples, who gave their lives for their country, and yet she had earned a degree from Cambridge University, practiced medicine, and believed "being a wife and mother are the most important roles a woman can fulfill." Her educational successes seemed always to be discounted by her.

"I have only a small flat, so I don't need all this furniture. I'd like you and your brother to choose some of the larger pieces. Better now, than waiting till I die." Mother made her announcement in her usual matter of fact way. No nonsense about her. She had lost her husband and no longer wanted to live in New Zealand. It was that simple.

"I've decided to buy a flat in Cambridge. One next to Malcolm. It's so easy to get up to London from there or over to Oxford to see Molly." Molly was an old Cambridge friend, also a medical doctor, who had lived in New Zealand almost as long as Mother had, and now lived with her husband, in Oxford.

How did she feel about such a bold move? As usual, she never spoke of how she felt, but I wondered if she had had such a plan in mind if she were ever left on her own. Certainly she and Father had planned a long visit to England, cut short by his illness and death. Though they had never said, I had picked up hints that they might move permanently back to England. Mother had long dreamed of living again in England.

My brother was there, and I was only an eight-hour flight away from Heathrow.

She made a visit to England during that year after Father died, to scope out the situation there. She found an apartment available near her brother Malcolm. The pieces were falling into place, though she said little to anyone, except her brother, about her plans.

I was unaware of her decision until she wrote asking my brother and me what pieces of furniture we wanted her to send to us. It was not difficult to decide which pieces I wanted, and Tony seemed to come to his decision easily. There was no family bickering. At least not then.

What about me? She was pulling up my roots with this move. I was only dimly aware of my own loss with Mother moving to England. Back to the place she had always called "Home." But I felt as though something was being taken from me. It was much later that I discovered just how deep those roots lay for me in New Zealand. That sense of "place" is so strong...the pull to return is almost physical. Was it like that for Mother? Was there no alternative but to pull up what roots she had in New Zealand and return to the place imprinted deeply in her unconscious?

Did I ever say anything to her? Of course not. But years later I remembered that feeling of loss when my husband and I moved, after twenty-eight years, from the house we had built, home for our four children, to build another house and a business. It was close by, just across the Columbia River, but it was very different from the one where they had grown up, swam in the pool, played tennis and basketball on the tennis court, hunted lizards and scorpions in the desert. Would they have that same sense of loss? I asked, but never trusted their answers that were meant to reassure me.

"Just the swimming pool, Mom."

At least I wasn't moving to the other side of the world. It would be several years before I fully understood the pull those "usual and accustomed places" of my childhood had on me.

In pulling up her colonial roots for the move "Home," she sent my "roots" to me. For the next twenty-six years, she visited not only me, but also these many items, large and small, her connections to other times and other places, and to people who played important roles in her life. There were antiques from her family, or ones she and my father had collected over their years together. And there was the silver tea service, china and porcelain, copper and brass pitchers and cooking pots, mahogany and oak chests, dresser, table and chairs.

She came every Christmas and stayed three weeks or more. During that time she undertook certain housekeeping tasks she could see had been neglected since her last visit -- namely, cleaning the silver, the brass, and the copper; polishing the furniture, mending the fringes on the old oriental rugs.

"In another life," she told me each visit, "I would have been an excellent front parlor maid."

I had no idea what a front parlor maid was, let alone what it took to be a "very good one." Mother had grown up at a time when there were front parlor maids. I soon saw what might have been some of the duties of a front parlor maid.

The day after she arrived, Mother would start her instructions to me.

"Now it's time to get out the cleaners and rags for me to do the silver and the copper. I shall need rubber gloves and lots of newspaper."

I learned the routine. I was prepared with Goddards Silver Cleaner, the Brasso and several pairs of rubber gloves. The dining room table was declared out of bounds for anything except the tray of cleaners, the rags saved from old undershirts, the rubber gloves and the newspapers. Mother spread out the newspapers, several layers thick, so that nothing would leak through and mark the old oak table. She sat, apron-clad, a strand of hair falling over one eye, the head front parlor maid in her chosen place in the Sheraton armchair that had once been her father's – a fact she was sure to tell me.

My job was to stay close by, though not actually at the table, so I could fetch the items as she called for them. Later I returned them, paying close attention to the history of each piece. Copper jam pans and molds, a large fish cooker, water pitchers for carrying the hot water to an early morning riser back in the mid-nineteenth century... all were covered with cleanser, rinsed, and polished. As she rubbed the shine into them, she brought something of her family history into this Eastern Washington home.

"We'll do the brass knobs on the Welsh dresser next. That dresser came from Oswestry, you know. Your grandmother bought it there when I was very little."

I passed Mother the Brasso and watched as she applied it with a rag, now green from cleaning. Then each of the fourteen brass knobs was lovingly polished with a clean rag as Mother told me of the vacations – she called them holidays – she and her two brothers spent with their parents, aunts, uncles, and numerous cousins in the old Welsh farmhouse in the mountains of north Wales.

"We all went off every day for walks, whether it rained or not. We took picnics with us. Bread, fresh baked by the farmer's wife, meat pies, venison spreads, fruit cakes, and thermoses of tea." Mother was back climbing the hills, stopping off for "high tea" at a farm before the long walk back again. I watched her old arthritis-thickened fingers stroke the dresser knobs into a high shine, and was transported to those green rain-soaked slopes and smoky kitchens, rich with cooking smells.

Morning tea was declared promptly at eleven o'clock.

"Don't use the good china, Jenepher -- we have such dirty fingers, and can't stop for long, there's the silver yet to do." But she would wash her hands before sitting down at the unused kitchen table for three cups of hot tea and cookies. Then came the stories of the maids she remembered in her home back in Cheshire. There had been Irish Annie and Welsh Jenny, who cried all the time. Mrs. McGinnes, who did the laundry, had once stolen something and "had to be let go, though I don't remember all the details. Things like that were kept from children, and I was very little at the time."

There had been Florence who had indeed been the one to clean the silver and who had let Mother do the polishing. No one cleaned silver or polished furniture the way Florence had. Mother was intent on carrying on the Florence tradition; indeed, she was probably hoping to instill some of Florence's cleaning knowledge and skills in me.

Silver grape scissors, an ornate candle snuffer, a treasured silver teapot, sugar bowl and creamer, teaspoons, fish knives and forks were polished to a high shine. Next came a small tray that sat on a table in the front hall and had been used for visiting cards.

"Your grandmother's visiting day was always a Thursday. Friends and acquaintances knew that was her afternoon for visitors to come to tea. I was allowed to pass the sandwiches – cucumber usually." I imagine Mother tasting the sandwiches as she spoke.

"What happened to the visiting cards?" I asked.

"Oh, I expect your grandmother kept them somewhere in her desk."

The desk had come to me when Mother moved back to England. At that time we lived in the house we had built in Richland, and it sat in our guest room which served as my office between guests. It held my computer and unpaid bills. It still does, sitting in my office in the loft above our main living room. When Mother was staying with us, I always moved the computer away. She loved that desk. It had been in our living room when I was a child, and I remember Mother writing at it to Father during the War, and to friends all over the world. She was a great letter writer, though she disdained the computer. The desk has numerous little drawers and a secret compartment. What had Grandmother put in that secret compartment? And what had Mother used it for, I asked. She just shook her head.

"Probably our passports."

Mother's cleaning took us into the afternoon. The brass, the copper, and the silver were all polished and carefully put away when Mother rose slowly out of her father's high armchair and announced it was time for a glass of sherry.

"Before you start dinner. Don't you agree, Jenepher?"

I was quick to agree. I knew she would tell me that my sherry glasses were too big and should be used only for port.

"Does anyone drink port anymore?" she would say, adding that port was for men and only after dinner.

The next day Mother concentrated on polishing furniture. She brought with her from England two different furniture polishes, insisting they were not available in America. I watched each time with a growing understanding that an old carved armchair was more than something to sit on. I pictured my great-grandfather sitting there, bent over the mahogany desk, writing to his son in Canada, asking questions about the price of corn. A long oak stool, its upholstery faded and worn, had once been a warm place to sit in front of the fireplace in the nursery. If turned upside down, it made a boat for a little girl, her long brown hair tied back with a wide blue ribbon and wearing a blue pinafore over her white dress. She was sailing to India or the Far East in search of the spices that Cook told her about. Two more generations of children, boys and girls, sailed in that boat, either across the Pacific, following the trade winds to Chile, or down the Columbia River in search of ducks or salmon.

More stories came out as Mother rubbed away at the oak chest that had once stood in the front hall of her parents' home.

"Good thing I took it out to New Zealand, or it would have been lost in the bombing. Your grandmother's house in Wallasey was bombed when the Germans bombed the Merseyside docks."

What had it been like for her, on the other side of the world, husband away in the Middle East with the New Zealand Army hospital, knowing how close her family back in England came to death back then? She just shrugged her shoulders.

"News took so long to reach us. It didn't do to worry too much."

But it was time to finish the work of restoring Mother's memories. She had grandchildren demanding she play cards with them

"Grammy, can we play Pounce?"

Of course she could. I looked for the packs of cards, one pack for each player, that were kept in the old oak chest of drawers that once lived in a cottage in Wales. Mother had taught her children and grandchildren this cut-throat game.

"Never use good cards for Pounce. They'll only get bent." Her instructions never changed.

With the years, however, Mother's memory failed. There were times when she would stare off into space.

"Just where am I – in the States, or New Zealand? Is this Wallasey, or just where am I?" she questioned with a shake of her head.

The years were taking their toll and I knew one of these Christmases would be the last for this excellent front parlor maid. Would we be ready, when it came?

Looking at New Roads

WHENEVER ANYONE ASKED why we did it, I always said we'd been planning for years to build a boarding kennel for people's pets. The first time the subject came up was on a trip to Seattle at least thirty or more years before we took any serious steps toward building a boarding kennel. We were somewhere on the road near Vantage, just me and Louis, no children demanding potty breaks, and we started talking about what we'd do when we retired. The four children were still in grade school and I was busy driving them to this or that and trying to keep up with the laundry and the chicken pox and how to keep Louis happy. Retirement must have seemed a safe subject. We weren't talking about how to bring up kids, my habits with regard to spending Louis's hard-earned money, or keeping up with our friends. Those were not always safe subjects. So I don't remember how we got on to retirement and then on to running a boarding kennels as a retirement project. But we agreed it would be a great thing to do.

"You have to have something to do when you retire." Louis was adamant about that. He had to keep busy, have some project to plan and execute, something that answered the question of "Are you having fun?" with "I'm working." His favorite position when not up and busy was lying on the sofa, feet up, perhaps just watching television or reading a book, and he'd be asleep in two minutes. Even watching television, unless it was the news, his eyes would close and in seconds he'd be asleep. I'd have to grab for the coffee cup before it slid out of his hand.

At that time, with small kids, a busy practice and a mortgage, talking about what to do when we retired was like telling each other a fairy story, each adding another piece to the plot.

"We'd need to buy some land in the country. We don't have enough room where we are now." Louis nodded his head to emphasize this insight.

"We'd need quite a bit of land – then we could have a lot of kennels and that would bring in some money." I was treading on a slippery slope bringing up the subject of money. We both had very different backgrounds when it came to financial planning and Louis didn't always think some of my purchases were really necessary! Louis had grown up in the Depression when money was short for farm folk in Kansas.

"Each of us four boys got one pair of shoes and one pair of overalls beginning of the school year. Things were tight for everyone around and our mother used to bake bread for the neighbor family who lived in a dugout over the hill. But that's another story." Louis had some wonderful stories. I could never match them. Even growing up during the War my mother and my brother and I were never hard up for money and it was never a subject that came up for discussion, so some guidelines on how to live thriftily were missing for me.

"You're right, we'd need quite a bit of land. We could invest in farmland and then lease most of it out to someone who wanted to farm it." Louis was sounding enthusiastic. "Think of those kennels where we board our mutts! We could do better."

Sometimes the dogs came home with what we called "That Kennel Smell." One boarding facility we tried we weren't sure our dogs hadn't been sharing space with dogs from another family.

We envisaged, that afternoon in the car, how we would visit kennels, ask around, see who does what. We discussed all the things we could think of that would make our kennels something that people would want to use for a home away from home for their family pets.

"And cats. Louis, we need to have a special room for cats. Think of the place we've left Mouse and Muffy – the one with the room where the cats all get together and watch the birds outside. We could have a fish tank and a bird feeder outside a window."

I could see the cats lined up, watching the outdoor activity, sitting on a window ledge, tails twitching eagerly.

"It would be better than playing golf or going to coffee klatsches or bridge parties," I added. Though I sometimes had a secret yearning to learn how to play golf just as soon as the children were old enough to be left alone without fear of any damage being done to the furniture or to each other, or leaving the water running and flooding the floors. But Louis wanted to hear about practical suggestions. He was raised on a farm in the Midwest and you were expected to be doing something that had some outcome – playing was not an option, unless it involved dogs or fishing. Hence the kennels option.

I couldn't think seriously about retirement. It was too far off. I wondered what else life would bring, other than the weeks filled with children and school and meals and the occasional get-together with friends. We skied and spent vacations at a lake. Sitting there in the car with Louis, both of us became lost in some personal world. Retirement would mean no more children running in and out of the house -- having birthdays, needing kisses and Band-Aids for their cuts and bruises, telling me their woes. Perhaps Louis was right. We should make plans, think ahead, so we wouldn't one day discover we were retired and had nothing to look forward to. But what if our plans didn't match? What if what Louis's plans didn't match mine?

"Cheer up Jenny, don't look so gloomy. Retirement is a long way off, and the kids are still very young. They need all the attention you can give them. I wish I had more time for them." He sighed.

How did he do it? How did he read my mind? Scary! But of course, I wasn't one to hold back on speaking my mind. He knew how much I liked doing the "mother thing," as I called it, and how much I got bored to tears doing the "housekeeping thing." Cleaning toilets and the "ring around the bath" never turned me on. Cleaning was of no interest to me -- except peanut butter off faces and, of course, cleaning dirty bottoms.

Once upon a time doctors' wives were used to keeping dinners warm, children quiet, having schedules for weekends and vacations changed at a moment's notice, and managing problems on their own. Such problems might range from plugged toilets to the third notice from school of a misbehaving child. I had grown up in a medical family, so none of this was new to me when I married Louis. I knew it was all part of the deal. Families of firemen and ambulance drivers probably had it the same. So I didn't complain. One just learned to work around them, keep quiet about the little things, and find the right moment to bring up the big ones. Doctors believed they were experts at solving problems. That's why they became doctors. But not all the problems in a family had to do with broken legs and ailing tummies. Mending broken hearts and recovering lost dreams were usually outside of their expertise. At one time doctors were not supposed to be married until well-established in their practices. Nowadays it was unusual for medical students not to be married. Their wives worked to "put hubby through" the training. Doctors in training were meant to dedicate themselves to their patients, and a doctor's wife was expected to dedicate herself to supporting her husband in every way possible. Did that mean when they retired, too? I asked myself.

We didn't talk about retirement again for a long time. Mostly we talked about the children and about the practice. But something Louis had said stuck in my mind. It was about buying some land, building the kennels and a house, and moving to the country. I couldn't envisage such a thing. We had a wonderful house, one we had had designed together and had built specially for us. I loved it. No one was going to get me to move. I must have thought nothing would change. Had I changed? I used to be up for anything new and exciting. Hadn't I married someone from another country and moved there, knowing nothing about the place? Even my mother had done that when she married my dad. I knew she had always hoped to return to England with my father and her children, but the most she could do was spend long visits in England. I had no intention of returning to New Zealand to live, but I felt uncomfortable talking about moving from our wonderful home. I wasn't ready for that.

When I thought seriously about the retirement business idea of caring for other people's pets and running a boarding kennels, it was stretching things. Neither of us had any experience with running a business and when it came to pets, my experience growing up was close to zero. I remembered the Labrador puppy my father had sent us when he left for Egypt and the War in 1939. That dog, a black Labrador, had driven my mother crazy, though as children my brother and I loved him. Louis had much more experience with animals, having grown up on a farm. My experience was mostly in my imagination.

When we settled down in Richland we acquired our first family pet, a dog. Rika was a Viszla, and like several other dogs, she was a given to us by some friend who was moving away and couldn't keep her. She was mostly a hunting dog for Louis, but turned into a much-loved member of the family. We frequently went out of town for vacations and skiing weekends. Rika spent that time at a boarding kennel close to home. She was always pleased to see us and seemed to have put on some extra pounds while we were away; even if she smelled a bit more "doggy" than usual, we assumed she was being well-cared-for in our absence. I don't think either of us ever personally observed how she was being cared for.

Retirement was a long way off and I had plenty to occupy my time without worrying about the distant future. I was an expert at keeping track of the children's homework assignments and vaccination records, or driving an entire swim team to practice. Keeping the checkbook balanced was not the high priority for me that it was for Louis.

The Dream

THE BOARDING KENNEL retirement project was shelved, but not forgotten. I would get the idea out now and then, dust it off, and examine it. Louis might bring it up and say something about the boarding kennels at which we left our dogs or cats when we were away from home. I would mention it to friends and family -- testing the waters, you might say. People seemed to think it a funny idea, kind of crazy.

"You're going to do what? Retire and board dogs? You mean you're going to let Louis just live out in the desert and train his old hunting dogs?" Smiles and laughter. "You're joking!"

"No, but he'll do that as well. We're thinking of building and running a boarding kennel. A business -- you know, taking care of people's dogs and cats. Like where we all take our pets when we're away." I'd try to make it sound like a serious proposition, even if I didn't take it all that seriously myself.

"But you'll never be able to get away; you'll be stuck there. No more skiing, Jenny, think of that! And where will you do this crazy thing?"

A good question, and one we had not really answered.

Our friends knew we both had undertaken some unusual

projects. Louis had taken off to New Zealand for a two-year research fellowship in internal medicine and come back with me. I was often asked why I married an American and left my home country – "…such a beautiful place, Jenny – you must miss it." I could never think of a good reply to the question except to say that it seemed a good idea at the time and still did – I had no regrets. Louis spent hours out in the field quail hunting – dawn to dusk was his standard hunting day. These were not really crazy things, but a little off-center in the minds of some of our friends.

When it came to retirement planning, most of our friends planned to travel and then do more travel. None of our friends was going to venture into small business ownership, and certainly not in the field of pet care. The conversation might move to a safer subject, such as hospital politics, comparing our children's progress in school or college, or where the snow was best for skiing that winter. No one mentioned anything that prevented us from continuing with the idea. Even our children, as they grew older, never gave any indication they might be against it. Either they didn't really believe we would go through with the plan, or they had come to accept it.

"We'll help. We'd love to play with the dogs, and take them for walks." Their enthusiasm was encouraging.

No one said it wouldn't work, and no one said they didn't like it. I began to realize that no one took the idea seriously. Probably neither did Louis or I. Not back then, when retirement was still some time away.

Of course we were not prepared to admit that neither of us knew anything about running a business. We never questioned whether we knew anything about taking care of other people's pets, and if I thought about it, I wasn't sure I liked dogs and cats – some, perhaps, but I had not had that much experience with any except the family pets. But, like so many things we did, it sounded great at the time. We had yet to consider the reality.

One thing for sure was that these two rolling stones were not about to gather any moss.

Other Roads Less Traveled

I DON'T KNOW if it was my father's death and mother's move to England, Louis becoming more involved in his orthopedic practice, the children needing less of my time, or the feminist movement hitting the area, but I decided to try my hand at something new. Here in Richland where we now lived, the University of Washington Richland branch offered a master's degree program in library science. I had worked in bookstores and libraries in the past, so this sounded just the thing I needed. It might even lead to a job, and between the women's movement and feminism I was beginning to have dreams of someday having a job again. The children were not going to need me forever, and this retirement dream of Louis's was still a long way off. So I enrolled, and about halfway through the course it was moved back to its home base in Seattle and I was left wondering if I should ask the family to move to Seattle for the sake of my degree. I could not do that. So I turned to volunteer jobs. The first one was working with first graders and kindergarteners at the grade school my children were attending. I would read and tell stories and play games with the slow learners in these classes. I loved it, but that was only two mornings a week. I had plenty more time.

The Mental Health Center wanted a volunteer to help with checking in and checking out books and researching questions asked by library users. Again, this was just what I wanted. I had the qualifications and it was only a couple of mornings a week or even afternoons, whatever time I could give. In that environment I learned about some other interesting directions that seemed to call me. One was the Rape Relief Program that had been started by a group of women to give assistance and support to victims of sexual assault as well as provide information to police, the justice department, and anyone else who would listen. I took the training and was then on call for phone calls. I found myself pulled into new directions by what I was learning through these opportunities. Working with disadvantaged children, with victims of sexual assault, taking classes, I discovered I wanted a lot more – I wanted to go to university and get a degree – not in library science, but in counseling. I enrolled in and completed a master's degree in applied behavioral science, available in Richland through Whitworth University in Spokane. I found I was learning not only about the behavior of others and of groups, but of myself. This was one of the most important steps I had taken so far, and it took up a great deal of my time. I sometimes worried that my family were suffering from lack of attention from me. But I didn't let go, and when I finished this degree I was already to go on with another. A doctoral program would have meant leaving the area, and I was not prepared to do that. My family meant a great deal to me and I did not think Louis would go for leaving what was now a very busy and interesting orthopedic practice. Instead I enrolled in a master's degree program in clinical psychology from Eastern Washington University that was offered through the Mental Health Center. This gave me an excellent grounding in the clinical side of counseling that the first degree had not provided. I was ready to find a job. Louis encouraged me, as by now the children were well on the way to finishing high school and deciding on college. We had always had plenty to share, but now we could talk about the work I was doing too. He had had a good background in psychiatry during his medical training and I enjoyed sharing stories from work. I wondered what my mother thought of all this. I told her some of what I was doing, but she never seemed interested. I longed for her approval, or at least to show some interest. After all, she had had graduate training in Children's Health in Edinburgh when my brother and I were in boarding school in England after the war was over, and we spent almost two years in England. She used this training to good purpose when we returned, getting a full- time job as a School Medical Officer. But mental health and mental problems did not seem of any interest to her. I remembered psychology had not been high on the list of approved medical specialties in my family.

I found part time jobs at Catholic Family Services and later at Lutheran Social Services, and continued to take any class or educational program offered in the area of family and group counseling. I was especially interested in the dynamics of dysfunctional groups, whether it was the family group or a work group, and this understanding helped me get a full-time position as Employee Assistance Counselor out in the Hanford Area, first with Rockwell and later with Westinghouse Hanford. This was a job where I worked not only with individuals, employees, and their families, but also with management and work groups where I discovered the group dynamics were not unlike those in a family. Little did I appreciate that I might use these same insights much later on understanding the roles pets played in their human families.

Erratics

IT WAS IN that clinical psychology class that I learned an important lesson about myself and my mother. An insight, really, into why we both behaved the way we did. The object of that class must have been something to do with understanding personality. If we better understood ourselves perhaps we could also understand our clients. The instructor gave us the assignment to go home and look for a rock – any sort of rock – but it had to be a rock that would tell us something about ourselves. We received no more instruction than that. We were to bring the rock to class the next day and tell the class what the rock we'd chosen had told us about ourselves. I went home and found my rock. It was round and flattish, about the size of the palm of my hand, and approximately an inch deep. It had plenty of weight to it, and I thought that would be the point I would make to the class. We both carried some weight.

I showed it to Louis and explained my purpose for the rock. He studied it carefully and then handed it back, announcing that it was an "erratic."

"What's that?" I asked

"It's a rock that's come from somewhere else," was his significant reply. "Probably came with one of those Ice Age floods from way off – it's not a local rock. Probably it got a lot of polish and scarring," he pointed to the shiny side and to the rough indented side, "on its way down in that ice flood, sort of got knocked around a bit. Lot of force in those floods - powerful things."

So that was it. That rock said all I needed to know about myself. It had come from somewhere else and had been knocked around so that it bore some scars and also some smoothness.

And that was me. I'd come from a long way off and been given some polish and a few scars along the way. There had been a lot of force pushing me around too. I thought of Mother and of Louis. Two powerful people.

But weren't they both erratics too? There was one difference. Louis may have travelled overseas, but he came to settle in his own country. Both Mother and I had moved from our where we had grown up to another country and another culture. Those moves left some polish but also some deep scars.

Mother had grown up in England, had been to Cambridge and to medical school, her father had told her that anything "the boys can do, girls can do too." So she married my father and came out to New Zealand, a colonial country on the other side of the world where she had to deal on arrival with a lack of welcome from her future husband's family, since his mother had died only two weeks before her arrival; then on their honeymoon, her trousseau was stolen, her father-in-law didn't approve of women doctors, and then her father died suddenly and she returned to England for a brief period. On her return, she faced World War II and five years on her own with two small children when her husband was overseas. Later she returned to England to study and at the same time sent me to boarding school both there and later in New

Zealand so I could get the best education and perhaps learn to speak without that colonial accent. I hated boarding school and developed a rebellious attitude towards authority figures. I was certainly a challenge to Mother then and later when I fell in love with Louis and moved to the US to live with him. She had always hoped for a medical son-in-law, but not an American one.

I have come to believe that "erratics" are never sure where they belong and where is home. I know moving has always been a problem for me. So when I contemplated what exactly "retirement" might involve, I could sense this might be a struggle for me. Another scarring move for this erratic. But would it be? There might be some differences this time.

The Reality

THE CHILDREN WENT from kindergarten to elementary school, junior high school, high school. I cheered for swim teams, softball and football teams, track team, and drill team. I made dozens of cookies and cupcakes for numerous class celebrations and officiated at PTAs and other organizations that were generally parent-run. I even taught Sunday school, believing that the children should have something to rebel against at a later stage of life.

I was still a rebel at heart. When feminism came along, I embraced it with enthusiasm, though with some reservations about burning my bra. The dangerous waters of liberal opinion beckoned, and while we lived in the conservative area of Eastern Washington, I had not lost my disregard for personal safety. I had had little experience of the period when the country had been watching Senator McCarthy and the Un-American Activities Committee hearings, and looking for the "Red Under the Bed." I carried a Green Card for the first twenty-five years of our marriage and occasionally wondered if some little Justice Department man might pop up and deport me! I knew this was a ridiculous fear, but it was present nonetheless. After all, I was living in a foreign country now.

I had the children, the children had their pets, and Louis had his hunting dogs. There were guinea pigs in cages in the kitchen, a hamster or two, somewhere else a couple of cages of gerbils, and at one time there were at least eighteen tropical fish tanks all glub-glubbing. Each child had his or her own cat, and of course kittens would follow, together with lessons in salesmanship as we found homes for the kittens – or the guinea pig or hamster babies. We inherited a Poodle which we gave to one of our daughters. It turned out she was highly allergic to dogs and cats. I managed to avoid most of the responsibility for this massive family pet care industry, except for overseeing that all livestock, like the family, received food and clean bedding at the appropriate times. I was a believer in the delegation of duties. The children had to do most of the pet care.

"You'll feel bad if old Ginger dies because you didn't feed him." Guilt proved to be a great motivator.

Four children learned to drive, thanks to driver's education classes at school and Louis's great patience. I did my best to play the role of driving instructor, but found I was too nervous. I had a tendency to yell if I saw potential hazards looming up in the distance, such as red lights, dogs, and elderly ladies who might chose to cross the road at any moment. These hazards were followed by the horrors of prom dresses, tuxedoes, corsages and photographers, limousines and expensive dinners. High school graduations came and went. I cried buckets each time one of the offspring shuffled up the center of the high school gym to the old Pomp and Circumstance march. Then it was college, marriages, and grandchildren.

I remembered my mother's words about having a university degree: "It will give you something to talk about with your husband at breakfast." Those two Masters Degrees should keep my mind from degenerating into some teenage fantasy world. I got a part-time job. No more volunteering -- this one paid money.

Life seemed so settled then. I thought I knew what I was doing, though I didn't know where I was going -- not that I ever gave the future a second thought. There were meals to cook, dinners to plan, lectures to attend, books to read, papers to write.

I failed to notice that while many of the students in the classes I attended looked the same age as my children, or even younger, I, on the other hand, showed definite signs of age. Grey hairs were disguised by a most efficient hair stylist, and my figure rapidly came to resemble that of a pear. My friends and I agreed we didn't feel a day older than twenty-nine – or perhaps thirty-nine? But we were all involved in some form of exercise to keep our bodies and our minds as young as possible.

Louis cut back on his medical practice as he had always said he would. But to me it didn't seem time yet, not for quitting. We were too young for retirement. That was why I'd gone back to college – to stay young. And of course, getting a job was a sign that I was still part of the youthful workforce in the country. My part-time jobs led me into a full-time position as a Employee Assistance Counselor with one of the Hanford Contractors. This meant I had health benefits and pension to come. I took the big step and became an American citizen. Now I acquired a "Q" Clearance showing I was a responsible person who posed no security risk for the country. My self-confidence was growing; life looked good to me. Christmases were followed by the tensions of tax time, to be relieved by ski season, then summer vacations and Halloween and Thanksgiving and we were back the beginning again. I saw no reason for anything to change.

Louis Makes His Move

I SHOULD HAVE seen it coming, but it was still a surprise when Louis announced that he was ready for retirement. He'd had enough of people's ailments and dealing with medical insurance companies. He'd been in practice more than thirty years and he wanted a change; other things were beckoning him. His plan was to buy some land and keep his pointing dogs there -- train them, hunt them. The time had come for him to follow his dream.

The topic was discussed over and over. I told myself that this dream of a return to the land had to do with his early childhood growing up on a farm in that endless Midwest. Did he miss that land of his birth? I hoped not, because I had no intention of moving to the Midwest where the horizon stretches on and on for ever and the land is a quilt pattern of giant squares, but he assured me he didn't want to go back there.

I did not have the same dreams.

"Louis, I am not ready for any changes – at least not yet." I practiced those words, but had difficulty articulating them.

I had grown up on the other side of the world, with the sea, beach, rocky cliffs and rivers, mountains…all close by, and part of my life. Louis and I took the children on annual pilgrimages to the mountains to ski and to the beach where I would have my ritual paddle in the Pacific Ocean. As often as we could, we would spend a month with my relatives New Zealand. There the weather in summer might be wet and cold, but it was still better than January in Washington State.

I was not suggesting that we return to my country of origin. I loved living in Washington State. We had built a beautiful home, one I had never thought of leaving. The children had grown up there and we had lived in it for almost thirty years. Our children and grandchildren visited us, swam in the pool, played tennis, had their parties. This had been their home as much as ours. How could I cut them off from their roots?

We discussed the subject of retirement from all angles. Louis had one angle, and I had many. Question followed question, like a river in flood, full of debris and sharp objects.

"What will you do all day? Train dogs?" I questioned. "And what about the old kennel idea? Are we going to buy some land for you to do this dog training? Is that what you want to do with all our savings?" My tone became louder as I grew increasingly anxious. "You're thinking of selling this house and moving to the country, aren't you?" I could find more and more small details to pick at, ones that needed a thorough exploration. Louis usually lapsed into silence when I started in on the questions.

Our discussions always came back to the same thing. Sometimes the discussions were serious disagreements. Louis wanted to sell the house and move to the country. I did not. I could feel panic grow inside me. It was painful. I wanted to scream something like: "Oh, go and do your thing, just don't include me in any move to the country, I'm staying right here."

Instead I remained silent, not trusting myself to say anything constructive.

We might talk about the kennel idea, but when the discussion came around to moving, something deep inside me screamed out "NO!" When the word "retirement" came up, I always changed the subject. It sounded so final, so much the end of things. I could dredge up the most dismal pictures if given a chance.

For the first time in our married life, I did not want to follow along with Louis's plans. In fact, I wanted something quite different. I wanted things to stay the same as ever. "Yes, Louis," I'd have liked to tell him, "I know life moves on, and one day we'll all be dead, but in the meantime, can't we just slow things down a bit? I mean, I've got a job now. Just let me get used to the children not being around so much." But I couldn't say the words clearly enough.

We hadn't really mentioned these ideas to the children -- not for serious consideration --and I refused even to call them plans.

Louis must have seen I was becoming more and more resistant, so he came up with an alternative.

"We'll buy some land, put a building on it, hire someone to help, and I'll keep my dogs out there." This way he would have somewhere to train his dogs during the day and I could stay on at home and not have to move. It was a nice offer.

"And it's not you that's retiring, Jenny, it's me. I've had enough. But you keep on doing what you're doing and we'll just go on living here. I'll sort of commute."

But I knew Louis. Once he's out in the country he's not coming home till dark – whether he's hunting or fishing or training dogs. I would see little of him.

Louis was very firm in his intent to retire, and I knew he wanted that place in the country. *Is it such a bad idea?* I'd ask myself. Perhaps we should move to the country after all. We could build the kennel we had so often talked about – or was that just a dream? What if it meant selling the house? I almost choked on the words "sell the house."

"Look, we'll build another house, all modern conveniences and a great kitchen and room for the kids to come and visit. And we can do the kennels at the same time." Louis was being so reasonable. Why couldn't I be reasonable too?

I considered these suggestions from every angle.

"We'll find a nice piece of land, build a new house – and you can put all the ideas into it that you wished you'd had for this one. Promise." He'd look at me in the same way his dogs would look at him, waiting for a treat or to be allowed to run. Longingly, lovingly, persuasive.

"And we could do the kennels too?" I'd ask.

"Of course. That's the point of living out in the country. We build a house, the kennel, and a barn."

What was this about a barn? Barns house animals -- cows and such. What was Louis holding back from me now?

"Why the barn? The dogs are going in the kennel, aren't they?" I asked.

"The barn is for the tractor and the truck, and we would still need somewhere for the boat and supplies and all our stuff. There'd be stalls and corrals for the horses too." He was using his "let's be reasonable and listen carefully" voice.

"Why a tractor? What are you going to do with a tractor?" This was getting more complicated and more expensive than I had imagined. And Louis was not one to spend money easily. I was getting suspicious. What else was he keeping from me? The tractor was a new item.

"Well, if we build a house and a kennel, then I want to do the general contracting. Be in charge so that we get exactly what we want. And, being retired, I should have plenty of time to supervise." He had a dreamy look in his eye as he said that. "The tractor is so I can dig foundations, haul things, and plenty more. And I can look busy while personally seeing that the work is being done to my specifications."

Louis sat back in his chair, his arms crossed, looking pleased with his explanation; there was nothing more to be said. I couldn't fault him on it. A tractor? He'd obviously thought way ahead of me. But that was Louis. His mind would be miles ahead of me and I'd be frustrated with the effort to keep up. His mind was already into building the house and kennel – and a barn. I still found it easier to picture the home we had than the imaginary one we might build.

I was beginning, however, to see the possibilities change might present. Louis was very good at persuading me to see things his way. I began to admit to myself all the plans he'd had for us in the past had worked out well.

I thought more and more about the plan. I looked for books on dogs, cats, boarding kennels, and small business management. Since I knew little about any of those subjects, I thought a little knowledge and understanding might not go amiss. I made long lists of things we might need if we ever built another house. I collected magazines of house designs and visited several new houses.

"Are you thinking of building again, Jenny?" my friends questioned.

"Well, you never know. Louis is full of this retirement thing and he's mentioned building some sort of place – you know, for the dogs, the boarding kennel idea." I didn't want to discuss our differences of opinion with my friends. Some of them were unable to keep anything new to themselves. I changed the subject.

Something was missing. What about my dreams? What

had I looked forward to in retirement? I had already accomplished many of the objectives I had set for myself. I'd finished college degrees, found an interesting job, and continued enjoying my family and friends. What more did I want? I wasn't sure. Something creative? Something that would give me a greater feeling of success? Success at what? I took classes in weaving and quilting and loved the satisfaction mastering those crafts afforded.

I enjoyed organizing – people or events, whatever caught my attention and my time. With another friend, I organized the Wednesday Ski Bus group. I met more people, and made more friends with the midweek skiing. I joined Toastmasters. Louis had joined it first and I was so impressed with his skills at speech-giving, especially humorous speeches, that I wanted to try it too. I found I was good at speeches, loved the creativity, and basked in the applause when I'd done well. I became involved in the Toastmasters Organization leadership. I loved the sense of importance!

Were these enough?

I'd just have to think about it. I knew, however, that if Louis were to follow his dream, I should think about my own dream too, whatever it might be. I could join him in his, but that wasn't the same as having one of my own. I thought it would probably have to do with something creative. I had so enjoyed writing those speeches. Perhaps writing? I'd always had a dream of being a best-selling author; I'd even kept a journal now and then, and written short stories in exercise books that were filed away out of anyone's sight. I decided I'd better keep that dream on a back burner for now. I had to keep up with Louis's dream right now.

You Can't Go Back

LOUIS WAS ONCE again studying the classifieds section of the daily paper.

"There's a farm for sale up the valley. Two, actually. Let's go look at them this afternoon." He gave a tremendous scrunch to the paper as he made this announcement. I could have poured the coffee pot over him, I was so surprised! Go look at farms indeed – we'd not discussed buying a farm. Just some land…even land that could be farmed. Louis stood up, said he was going to make some phone calls, and disappeared out the door. He returned in a short while to tell me that this would be fun, that it was something we'd never done before. How right he was – we'd never looked at farms for sale before.

It was early spring, a bleak time of year, cold, breezy, and no sign of green shoots. Grey rocks half hidden by dry weeds and few stunted, bare-limbed trees were not that attractive. But the willows along the river were showing gold in the new growth, and the red twig dogwoods along the draws were a brilliant scarlet. I hadn't noticed all this color before.

"We're going to look at farmland, Jenny, where we can build your dream house and the kennel. Keep your eyes peeled for suitable sites. And we'll look at these two farms, too. They've got houses on them, but I don't expect a great deal of the houses."

He was right about the houses. They were smaller than their barns and looked as though the owners had spent some time on do-it-yourself remodeling. There were some very attractive farmhouses too, but they weren't on the "for sale" lists. The farmland wasn't much better, from Louis's point of view.

We spent several afternoons in this way: we would look at the listings in the paper in the morning, call and get directions, drive out together when I got home from work, and inspect. It was very depressing.

"Think we'd better go through a realtor?" I said, trying to be helpful. "They have the listings and even though you have to pay them for their services, it might be worth it in the long run."

Afternoons were now spent with a realtor, driving in the realtor's car around to the farms that he said were just exactly what we wanted. Louis and the realtor did the talking, sitting together in the front seat. I sat in the back seat where it was difficult to see much, so I took a book or my knitting and spent the time more profitably.

"Jenny, why don't you come out and listen to what we have to say. You're involved in this, too."

"No, I'm not. You decide what you want and it will be fine with me. It always is." I knew my voice showed my irritation. This had become a tiring and frustrating way of spending our afternoons together. Louis usually made the decisions for us both, even if he said he was doing it for me. Even if he was right, I would have liked to have been asked. Of course, here he was, asking me, and I was in no mood to offer any opinion except perhaps some very negative ones. I would do almost anything to avoid a fight. So I kept my mouth shut.

Louis opened the car door and slid in next to me. The window had become fogged up and the car smelled of stale cigarette smoke and fake pine from one of those smelly cardboard pine trees hanging from the rearview mirror.

"What's the matter? Nothing turns you on yet? Me neither. Come on out, and let's just walk around for a moment. It's going to be all right, I promise."

We kept going. I went through the classified Farms for Sale in the local newspaper and Louis looked in farming weeklies. We drove around and looked at the land and the farms for sale, either with or without the realtor. If a house was included, I became interested. A house, if it were at all what we liked, might mean we wouldn't have to build, but I always hoped there wouldn't be a house. I was beginning to get some ideas of my own about what I'd like in a house.

One cold and windy morning – a normal spring day for the area, in fact -- we drove to look at three farms, all with houses that were, according to the realtor who had the listings, just what we would like. They weren't. We had agreed it was worth waiting until we found just what we wanted, but so far we weren't even close.

Tired, ungloved hands cold from the wind, I was beginning to drag. I hadn't anticipated we'd be walking around so much farmland, and the wind was very chilly. I sat in the back seat, silent as usual, while the realtor drove and Louis looked. They were talking about bird hunting. Smoke from the realtor's cigarettes filled the car until I cracked the window next to me. Our course homeward took us along the Columbia River. An old sign on my left announced that there was a "Ranch for Sale."

"There's a ranch for sale back there – the sign said that."
We were already past it. The realtor kept driving. I spoke louder.

"Louis, there is a farm for sale back there."
He had not seen the sign, either.

"Let's go look at it." This time I said it louder and tapped
on Louis's shoulder. Hard. They could at least pretend to listen
to me.

With a loud sigh the realtor slowly turned the car around
and we drove back and up the gravel lane in search of someone to ask about the land. The sign was old, but it was still
there, so the land might be still for sale. It didn't say anything
about how much land, whether the house was included, or
exactly what was meant by "ranch," but I could see there
might be a view of the river. Otherwise, it all looked grey,
dusty, and weedy – like everywhere else. I knew it was the
time of year; another month, and things would look better.

The realtor was not impressed. This was a private sale. No
realtor was listed on what was obviously an old, home-made
sign. There was no one around to ask about the land, so we
drove home.

The next day I came home from work to find Louis unusu-
ally excited. He had been back to the "Ranch for Sale" place
and spoken to the seller. He said I should go with him at once
to have a look for myself. "Let's get going. No time to change,"
he insisted.

The place was about seven miles north of town, on the
other side of the river and with a great view of the river and
the hills in the distance. We walked around and around it
– something like one hundred thirty acres in all, and all under irrigation. It seemed to be a lot of land and a great deal
of money. But Louis was enthusiastic. This was what he was

looking for. There was enough land for him to lease to a renter, and for us to build a house, the kennel, and, most important, a barn for that tractor he couldn't do without. What was more, it met most of my requirements for a "move to the country" – no house, a great view, and not too far out of town. If there was no house, we could build one to suit us. I was relieved about that. The views were beautiful: the river in the foreground, with hills beyond, mountains in the far distance, and in the other direction the orchards and vineyards and more hills. I would be able to watch the sun rise and set, and the clouds build their castles in the sky. I would be able to have a dog of my own – a yellow Labrador, perhaps. I hadn't thought of a dog until that moment, but suddenly that was just what I wanted: a large dog that would go for walks with me, one I could talk to and that would understand me.

That day we had no idea what would grow out of that uneven rocky piece of dry, weed- covered desert where we planned to have a house, the kennel, a barn, and pastures for a couple of horses.

It was still early spring, and everything looked a dirty brown. A cold wind, fiercer than the previous day's, whipped dust into our faces as we walked around. Louis was pacing out distances, his mind already full of what could be done with the place. I retired to the car and the heater and started making lists. At the top of the list was the word "architect," because as far as I was concerned this was not going to be any do-it-yourself construction job. I'd seen enough of those in our journeying through the farmland, near and far. I had a suspicion that Louis was intending to do some of the construction job himself, with a little help from some others. He'd already said he would be the general contractor. And why else would he want a tractor, if not to do some digging? I

distinctly remembered him saying he would dig the foundations. I had no idea of building anything other than birthday
cakes and sandcastles at the beach. I wasn't sure what building experience Louis might have had growing up on a farm.
I just wanted this place to be as perfect as possible. If I were
to move to a new house, it would be my final move. I had no
intention of moving ever again – none whatsoever. Ever. A
little voice in my head said something like: "You've said that
before, Jenny."

We bought the land. I watched as Louis and the seller –
another Kansan, as it turned out – shook hands on the deal.
No lawyers, no letters and papers, just that handshake and we
were the proud owners of that "Ranch for Sale." Actually the
paper signing came later, but it was the handshake that sealed
the deal.

"You don't go back on a handshake," Louis explained. I
had never thought of what a handshake could signify. More
than a greeting or a farewell wish, a "hi, how are you" or
"see you soon" sort of thing. This handshake was a promise
made between two people, a binding commitment to something agreed upon. I knew Louis would never go back on his
promise made with that handshake.

We celebrated our land purchase a few days later with
a picnic supper and champagne. Amid the dead weeds and
the broken irrigation pipe that littered the area of what would
become the kennel and the house and the barn, I set up the
card table and covered it with a white tablecloth, silverware,
glasses, and napkins. Like those Victorian ancestors of mine
who came to New Zealand in sailing ships bringing with them
their pianos and linens, I wanted to show we still had some
standards as we watched the sun set over Rattlesnake and
drank to our future.

The Die is Cast

"YOU'RE GOING TO do what?"

The questions came in earnest. Friends and acquaintances voiced their concern and disbelief when we told them what we had done and what we planned to do next.

"What do you know about boarding dogs? Or cats?"

"Won't you miss the house? And the swimming pool?"

"Are you serious? You mean to run a business?"

"What do you know about running a business?"

"Are you going to build a kennel or buy?"

"Are you going to have some help? You'd better have some help or you'll be stuck there forever!"

"Won't the children miss the swimming pool?"

"Is this a tax write-off?"

And on and on. And on.

Yes, I'd answer, I'd miss the swimming pool and so would the family. Louis not so much – he was the one who always got stuck taking care of it. And yes, we would have some help, but probably not too much. After all, we would be retired and would and have all the time in the world to do just what we wanted!

No, we didn't want to take up golf or bridge and no, we

didn't have any plans to travel and see the world – not just yet, anyway.

We told everyone that we both had some knowledge of business management. Louis had had a successful medical practice for many years, which took some knowledge of business practices. I had been employed as a mental health counselor for years, as well as being involved in various volunteer activities, and of course had brought up four children. Did anyone think we would need more experience to run a small business? And of course, we both loved dogs and cats, and that was the most important thing – wasn't it? I mean, if you're going to care for someone else's pets, you'd better really like them.

In reality, had no idea if I loved other people's pets, let alone our own. As for our knowledge of running a business -- well, that was something I didn't care to discuss with others just yet.

Friends would nod, satisfied that they had done something helpful, planting these questions in our minds. I don't think we fooled our children, all of whom by then knew a great deal more than we did about the real world of people and how to run a business.

"We'll be moving across the river. That's where our piece of land is."

Across the river! We might have been moving to the Midwest or Alaska. But over the river? What would we do to keep in touch with our friends and all our activities? How would I get to work? I murmured something about taking an early retirement if the company offered it. We would hire some help, but running a small business probably wouldn't take up all our time. We'd have plenty of time to do other things.

I mean, taking care of pets couldn't be *that* time-consuming?

We took the family and friends out to picnic amongst the

weeds and dirt and to view the property. We did this several times during the next few weeks. This probably convinced them that we had quite lost touch with reality. The view of the river and the farmland and the hills helped, but the property back then had little to recommend it except perhaps "future potential," as a realtor might put it. The weeds appeared taller and drier, but just as dead as I remembered them when we first saw the place. There appeared to be a few more broken irrigation pipes, the ruts made by tractors driving through the mud were deeper, a hole where someone had taken some fill dirt for their own use was wider, and now in addition there was a dead bird or two. Our friends would leave, shaking their heads in dismay. Even a champagne supper sitting in the midst of all this, and my explanation that it was exactly what the pioneers had had to face, didn't do much to reassure them. It was difficult explaining that it would all look very different in a year or two. I couldn't imagine what would be different, but Louis was brimming over with confidence. He filled several yellow pads of paper with his sketches that showed the house facing this way, the kennel over there, the vegetable garden here, and the driveway and parking lot down that way.

It was hard not to be caught up in his enthusiasm, but our friends still thought we were crazy. They walked around while I set up tables and folding chairs, spread out those white lace-edged tablecloths and the good china, and laid out the food and drink that had been carefully packed in coolers. Our friends asked questions about the future of our kennel proj-ect, and I would have to say that Louis was the one to talk to because if I described anything, then it would be last week's plan and by now he would have changed things. I'd add that the whole thing was like tearing the paper off a Christmas present and I had yet to see what the wrapping held.

It was time to eat, anyway. The wind had come up and we still had no shelter out among the tumbleweeds and broken sprinkler pipe. I gathered the group together and Louis poured more champagne for a toast to our future. The sun was slipping behind the hills and a single star glinted in the pale blue sky.

"Starlight, star bright,
"First star I've seen tonight
"Wish I may, wish I might
"Get the wish I wish tonight."

I whispered the old childhood rhyme to myself as I looked at the star. What did I wish for? That the move to the country and the new house and kennel and all Louis's retirement plans would turn out well for us both. That was one wish. But I knew there was another wish -- another dream, really…one I'd only lately considered. If Louis was retiring and we were doing all this planning for him, what was I doing for my retirement? Was it a foregone conclusion that when Louis retired, I'd retire too? But from what? I could retire from my counseling job, but what would I retire to? The kennel?

I had wrestled with this dilemma recently, going back and forth in my mind. Was my future with the kennel, or was there something else I wanted to do? I had been drawn to writing my thoughts in a journal at various times in my life, and played with the idea of doing more writing. The kennel? Writing? Both?

"Starlight, star bright
"I wish to find my dream and follow it.
"Whatever it is."

I just said the words to myself in my head.

Everyone was saying goodbyes and wishing us luck with our venture. I didn't say so, but I thought we'd need all the luck we could get. We packed our picnic stuff into the back of the car and headed home to the other side of the river. Perhaps, after all, my dream was to live out here?

Research and Development

"NO MORE CHAMPAGNE parties in the desert, Jenny. We've got to get down to business," Louis announced that night after the fourth party in the weeds.

"I couldn't agree more," I said. "Shall we make a list?"

A dream is a long way from any reality. For instance, what would it take to build and run a boarding kennel for dogs and cats? We had to get down to figures and facts. What came first?

"I've got that architect coming next week – same one we've used before for landscaping -- and he'll sort out where everything should go." Louis had some ideas, but it would be good to have our old friend Glen come up with a drawing. "Then I have something to work from, or just do it my way anyway. But it'll be a start."

Glen arrived and we walked all around the land again, with Louis stepping off distances and Glen drawing lines on pieces of paper. That was when I really began to feel there was something in this for me. I'd loved the old house and would have a hard time leaving it, but what Glen was describing -- where the new house would be situated, what it would face, where the kennel would be, the barn, the vegetable garden, trees, shrubs, berms, and sunken areas – it all was beginning to catch my imagination. I could almost see it.

Glen had a way with words when describing landscape architecture.

"Landscaping is like putting the rooms of a house out-side -- you move from one room to the next, they all con-nect, Jenny. And Louis can do a wonderful job for you out here with all this space, and the view, and the river." Glen himself was carried away by the prospect of a new creation, and I was certainly hooked. We'd known him for almost thirty years, and his designs for landscaping were truly indi-vidual. Louis would change some things, but he always said he couldn't fault Glen on design.

Our eldest son had hired a local architect to design his house, and we had been impressed with the results. So we met with her and explained what we wanted...which was quite a lot, by now. A house, kennel, barn. But we already had the sketch of the landscaping with blueprints to follow.

"Which comes first, Louis?" she asked.

"The house, but really they all should be finished about the same time."

The architect raised her eyebrows, looking at us with amazement. We waited. A moment of silence followed.

"When do you want to have this business open?" was her next question.

"How about this time next year?" Louis promptly replied. I kept quiet, still not convinced that we'd be able to do all we had in mind in that time. She shrugged her shoulders and said she'd bring something to show us in a week or two. Or more, she added with a smile. I didn't think she really be-lieved us when we said next year. Even I thought it was a bit unrealistic, but I could never tell with Louis. When he gets his teeth into something, he doesn't let go.

It was time for us to take our annual fishing vacation. I guessed we'd still be talking about our retirement plans while we cast our fly rods. And we did.

Finding the Right Design for a Pet Hilton

OUR ARCHITECT HAD been at work and had plenty to offer us, though little in the way of actual design. Permits, licenses, and more permits were needed, she informed us. She also strongly recommended that we seek some guidance from those already in the kennel business.

"Have you thought of visiting some kennels, say over on the coast, perhaps California, even in the Midwest? See what's being done there. And also join whatever group there is of professional pet boarders. There's bound to be one. Jenny can look it up on the web since she's the one that knows about computers."

"I don't have a computer yet, and don't have any idea how you look up anything on the Internet." I had to point out that if Louis were to spring for a few dollars I could get one and get started. He might not have been listening but he nodded, and I took that to be his agreement to purchase a computer. He agreed that it was time to seek advice from the experts. We should visit some boarding kennels, see how they were built.

"But not the ones around here -- we've seen them all and it might not be the most political thing to let them know we're going to be competition," he said, adding, "I like the idea of finding out how other people are running their boarding businesses."

So we did. We went to the kennel experts for advice.

Our first step was to visit as many boarding kennels as we could, in Washington State, California, and Oregon to see what people in the business considered important items. I visited several in England when I paid my annual visit to my mother in Cambridge. Louis had a nephew who was a veterinarian in Los Angeles. We picked his brain and he introduced us to some kennel owners.

Each kennel we visited had some detail we liked, either in building design or kennel procedures, or safety and security features. There were also features that we didn't like, or considered unworkable in our situation, such as a swimming pool for the Labradors or television for Bulldogs.

The real test was still to come. We went to a pet boarding and grooming trade show in Los Angeles.

It was like an enormous shopping mall with aisle after aisle of booths, and salespeople standing around handing out free pens and key chains with the names of their products on them. Free samples, free literature, and free drawings for anything from a cage dryer – whatever that was – to a trip to Disneyland. I decided to have a quick look around. It might look bad, but there were bound to be some things we needed to know.

To my surprise, it wasn't bad at all. In fact it was fun, it was interesting, and the salespeople were great. Anyone involved in some way with pets would have been sucked in by the excitement and delight of the sales reps, who obviously believed in their products, as if they were the Holy Grails of the pet industry. As I walked around and paused at this booth or that to ask a question I would invariably end up telling our story – two retirees with some money and no sense who thought a boarding kennel for cats and dogs would be a great project to fill our retirement years. People loved the idea. I quickly discovered I was the new kid on the block and everyone wanted to tell me how it had been for them when they first opened a kennel business, what I must never do, what I must always do, what other kennels were doing, and if they just had enough money what they would do...and on and on. I was given business cards, free samples of dog and cat food, and told over and over in so many ways that this one product or widget would change my life – and the lives of the pets I would board – forever. I needed Louis. I needed to tell him all the wonderful ideas that were coming to me as I listened and looked. We were going to have a great deal of fun with this boarding kennel project.

We had to have a groomer, too – there was obviously big business on the grooming side of the house. All around were more people walking tall Poodles. Those dogs, if you could call them that, had fur puffed up into circles or shaved clear to the skin, and what fur was left was dyed purple or blue or pale pink. The animals were prancing elegantly around, their toenails painted to match their shiny studded collars. For a moment I wondered if there were any Poodles like that back where we came from.

I was about to ask a salesman a question about grooming clippers when I heard a familiar voice behind me.

"Jenny." It was Louis. "I want you to come and look at this special table. It's for grooming dogs. It's hydraulic and goes up and down just by standing on this switch. Wouldn't our groomer just love this?" He had given up sitting by himself and was caught up in the enthusiasm and the sales talk.

"You want a groomer, too? That's what I'm thinking!" I was so surprised to see him and hear the excitement in his voice -- not the usual tone he used when spending money might be involved. And I could see that we might have to spend a great deal of money if we were to do all that we were being advised to do. "In fact, Louis, we must have a groomer. I've been talking to this nice man here and he says grooming is a real moneymaker. I'm so glad you're looking too. And yes, why don't you order that table now? They'll deliver one next week."

"Jenny, calm down. We don't even have a kennel to put a groomer in. But we should get the literature about it. Here, put all this stuff in that bag you're carrying around, and let's go and look at cages and runs and think what would work for, say, the fifty dogs we've talked about boarding." Cages and fencing for runs. The farmer in him would know about fencing. But I should learn all about it too. I wasn't going to be left out of our retirement planning. So we looked at cages and fencing and stuff to seal the floors and a great deal more.

We split up after a while in order to cover more booths. The thrill of discovering a new world we'd never known existed had us in its grasp. I don't know about Louis, as he was always surprising me, but I had never come across things like grooming shears, "poop scoopers," kibble and "kongs," food for anxious dogs, food for fat dogs, hairball medicine for cats, and kitty litter. I decided to find some familiar ground. Computer software. That was what I needed to find out about -- software programs for kennels. That was probably going to be what I'd be involved in most, anyway. I came away with more literature about ways to keep records than I had ever dreamed I would need.

I found Louis staring at some hoses that were strung up

to some chain-link fence. His mouth was open as though he was about to say something, but instead he was listening to an enormous man explaining the importance of a "...good cleaning system in your kennel, and you need hoses for that. Here, take my card and give me a call. I'll send some one out your way." I grabbed Louis by the arm to tell him about a software program I thought would work for us, but he shook my hand loose.

"No, Jenny, look here." He was pointing to the hoses. He spoke quickly, obviously excited. "We need something like this. Don't tell me it's just a toy. This thing might work. It's like in the O.R. You don't want hoses and stuff on the floor to trip over. I'm picking up the literature on this stuff." His interest had been piqued by something that was familiar, yet new.

Panting a little from the exertion all this was taking, we split up again. If we just kept going, we should be able to cover every booth by closing time! We met at the hot dog stand. I almost asked the pimply youth selling the familiar item if these were for the two-legged or the four-legged customer... but then thought better of it. This kid was not into humor of this sort. Louis and I were both hungry and thirsty and ready to sit down. I was beyond worrying what sort of hot dogs these were, and when I explained my sense of humor to Louis, he just gave a grunt, his mind on more important things. He had spent his time talking to the people who dealt with septic systems, electrical systems, kennel and cage systems, and other important construction details. I was impressed that he knew the right questions to ask and said so.

"You forget sometimes that I grew up on a farm," he said. "That's why I know about fencing and feed and septic systems and a few other important details -- like, what you put in one end of the animal comes out the other. So as kennel owners we have to be prepared for both. Which makes me think we need another beer." He went off to get us each another beer. "So what have you learned that you didn't know before?" he asked, grinning, when he returned with our drinks. I thought he was enjoying himself in spite of the sales pitch hype.

"I learned that boarding pets is very like running a motel or hotel. Someone makes a reservation for a pet, just like I call for a hotel reservation, and there had better be space for that pet when it arrives, same as I expect the Hilton to know that I want a double room with king- sized bed and a spa tub when that's what I asked for."

I told him about something called the American Boarding Kennels Association.

"This is something you have got to come with me to see. And to meet the people there. This is one of the most important places in the whole show, I think. Almost as important as your septic things and the hoses!"

I had been impressed, but I knew Louis should see it too. Their counter was stacked with hand-out information on everything from designing and building a kennel to the importance of having a personnel policy and staff training on pet health and safety. Their annual meetings, we were told, would give us the opportunity to attend seminars on all aspects of kennel management and pet care. There, displayed on their counter, waiting for us to come by and pick it up, was all the written material, books, plans, videos and online information that answered more questions than we had thought of. This kennel business was beginning to feel more like a job and less like retirement. Were we just substituting one type of work for another?

We joined the American Boarding Kennels Association, though Louis had a few more questions, both for me and for them. Did I know anything about them? How much were the dues? Weren't there other groups like them that were into pet boarding? I reminded him that our architect back home had suggested we find some professional organization that specialized in pet boarding. Here it was, waiting for us! I left Louis at the booth to get his own answers while I wandered back to one of the software companies that had attracted my attention with the simplicity of its program. I needed to take a sample disc to share with my daughter-in-law, the accountant, who had volunteered to look into software for me. It was some time before I remembered I should be looking for Louis and perhaps some more lunch.

I found him where I'd left him: at the American Boarding Kennels Association table. He was holding a stack of what looked like handouts, and a large plastic bag stuffed with what turned out to be even more information as well as pens, pencils, and business cards. He was deep in a discussion with two men and I heard the words "septic system." His back was turned to me, so he didn't notice me until I tapped him on the shoulder to get his attention. He turned around, eyes bright with excitement.

"Hey, this is great stuff! They've got all the answers -- everything, even blueprints. You were so right to bring me here. And we have a name now. Sagemoor Kennels. Is that OK with you? Sagemoor Kennels. Sound good to you?"

If he had been the sort of man who jumps up and down when excited, he'd have been jumping up and down like one of those little Jack Russell terriers we came to know so well. Sagemoor Kennels. It sounded perfect. Our new property was at the foot of the Sagemoor Hills. Sagemoor Kennels. I said it again, just to listen to the sound of the words…almost taste them. The people at the desk were grinning. They may not have met many excited new kennel owners that day -- at least, not ones who had just christened their new venture in this manner.

The trade show lasted two days. We had collected enough information that first day to build and equip the most modern kennel we could imagine. We decided to go out to dinner and change our flight home for an earlier one.

We studied the rest of the literature during the next few days. By then, we had a better picture of what it would take to build and operate the sort of kennel we hoped to have.

"A dog and cat Hilton – or the Pasco Pet Plaza on the Tri Cities." I became somewhat ridiculous. "Bring your canine family members for a spa treatment – they may come home purple?"

After the trade show, we knew we had something to give to the architect.

Priorities - Plans and More Plans

ONCE WE MIGHT have thought that we could build a Pet Hilton, but it wasn't until we sat down in the kitchen with all that literature spread out on the table in front of us that we began to think we might be in a little over our heads. That trade show gave us the hint. From dogs and horses to snakes and mice, there was a whole industry for anything that barked, squeaked, or wriggled. We were just brushing the surface when we talked about a boarding facility for cats and dogs. We discovered that boarding kennel owners were busy developing new ideas of what would be the most efficient, safe, and secure facility for boarding pets. Safety, security and "quality care" were the words that marketed boarding facilities to the nation's pet owners. Pets and pet care were becoming the sort of business that the tycoons on Wall Street were noticing and encouraging.

In the past we had taken our pets to board at kennels that had consisted of little more than outdoor runs with a doghouse or kennel attached. We had expected the dogs and cats to be fed and kept clean, and the dogs allowed out for a run. The guinea pigs and gerbils and the fish had to survive at home with the assistance of a neighbor teenager.

Boarding kennels were usually a "mom and pop" business where a couple had enough land and a barn that could be converted. The two of them would do the work, with the help of one part-time person, usually some teenager living nearby.

Our plans were for something bigger. We were reassured by what we learned about the direction the pet care business had taken. Things had indeed changed. The kennel business was one where marketing mattered, and providing a place where pet owners were enthusiastic to return was the name of the game. Boarding kennels had become indoor facilities with spacious runs and comfortable heated dog houses. One of the advantages of the enclosed design was that any noise from barking dogs was less likely to bother the neighbors. Kennels once had been built in country settings, but now housing developments were moving into the same country setting. People who paid enormous dollar amounts for new houses didn't like to be wakened at six in the morning to the sound of hungry dogs demanding breakfast, or the hound baying at the moon and the raccoons in the middle of the night. Staff, pets, and owners as well as neighbors liked the new indoor kennel design. Some kennels had even gone as far as becoming what I called "doggy theme parks" like the one we visited in California, with swimming pools, climbing ladders, and rooms decorated as the "Cowboy Room," the "Mexican Hideaway," or the "Royalty Suite," complete with television, matching bedspreads and curtains, and designer dog bowls. Agility courses and "doggy day camps" were marketed as a way to increase sales.

Our intention had been to concentrate on a "keep it simple and safe" design. After our visits to kennels and the trade show, however, we put some meat on the bare bones of that phrase. Louis managed to stop some of my more ridiculous ideas. No longer were we at the "what if" and the "wouldn't it be nice" stage. We were now working on what had a chance for some success. No more pet plazas – just Sagemoor Kennels.

Cleanliness was of the utmost importance, up there with safety and security. We didn't want any pets escaping or getting hurt.

"Louis, you remember the smell of some of those kennels? We will have no bad smells, no urine odor about our place -- don't you agree?"

Of course he did. He wanted to get those hoses up and running and a septic system that would take care of the "poop," which would be washed down those carefully designed gutters by those hoses. I had never thought how interested I would become in "poop" and in the various methods of "scooping the poop." Now I studied catalogs looking for the sturdiest of "poop scoopers" and weighing the merits of washing it down those gutters or bagging it in plastic and letting the weekly garbage pickup truck dispose of it.

"Look, Louis – there are little garbage bags for sale to put the stuff in!"

"Poop comes in a variety of sizes and consistencies – some of it is quite loose!" had been his comment. I did not bring up the plastic poop bags again.

Each dog would have his or her own run and attached kennel. The kennel would be like a private dog "den" to which a dog could retire when things became too stressful. I had been reading up about dogs and learned that they didn't do well with change. I could relate to that! Private dens with underfloor heating sounded good. Louis didn't quite go along with all the stress-relieving schemes I had thought of, but he did agree that dogs were creatures of habit and didn't do well with change. He gave me a funny look and asked if I needed under-floor heating in the new house, too. Was I showing some signs of stress?

"We'll consult our architect about that."

Our plan was to give our boarders the best boarding experience of their lives, with good food, loving care, security, safety, personal playtime, walks, and as much fun as possible. We would personalize our care to meet the pet's preferences, based on what the owners could tell us.

"I'll bring over that old rocking chair of mine, then. It'll look good in the Cat Room next to that fish tank." My mind was running away with ideas. "And then a bird feeder outside. Entertainment, you know -- especially since you can't take cats for a walk."

I had a picture in my mind of what a Cat Room could be like. Louis had to put the brakes on me once I got my imagination going. He drew the line at little beds with bedspreads for the cats, but went along with a radio as well as the fish tank.

The design placed the Cat Room away from any noise or barking from the big dogs. There would be both cages and "condos" with several levels that could house a couple of family cats. An elaborate exhaust system would deal with any odors.

The dog boarding part of our facility would have fifty kennels and attached runs, all indoors. Outside there would be a grass exercise yard, with high chain-link fence around it, and easy access for staff to exercise the dogs. Around the whole facility were trails for walking dogs on leashes – we wanted to offer a choice for playtime for dogs.

We came up with the idea of a special room for the

"tinies," those little dogs such as Chihuahuas and Toy Poodles who needed a more homestyle facility. This was the Front Room, as it came to be called for lack of a better name. There were eighteen kennel cages in the Front Room, a radio to play National Public Radio classical music, and special soft beds for the little dogs to curl up in. Because these Front Room dogs had no run attached to their kennels, their program included five exercise breaks a day when one of us would take them all out to the exercise yard and supervise them for about ten to fifteen minutes each time.

Safety, security, and cleanliness were the words we kept repeating. We had so many ideas about how to make this the perfect kennel! As it turned out, we overdid the thinking, but on the whole we covered most of the bases. Dogs don't bark as much as we had thought they would, but they certainly "pooped" more than we had anticipated!

Items We Never Thought About

ALL NEW BUILDINGS require permits, and permits require building inspectors. We were building in the county, so we fell under the eagle-eyed surveillance of the county building inspectors. There were two of them, and we came to know them well...even on a first- name basis. They paid us weekly if not daily inspection visits before we received their signatures and stamps of approval.

The State Department of Ecology, however, was a different matter. They didn't send inspectors. They made their visits through forms sent by mail. Those folks in Olympia wanted to know what we were going to do with "all that poop," as we came to refer to their demands for information about feces disposal. Louis stared at the forms. Their questions didn't make much sense. What did anyone do with a dog's poop? What about those folks in town who had three or four dogs and just threw it over the fence, or down some drain in the yard? He answered the questions to the best of his knowledge and mailed the forms back.

It wasn't good enough. What, they asked, would be the B.O.D.s? We learned that the B.O.D.s were the Bio-Oxygen-Demands -- in plain words, how much oxygen would it take to break down the waste from the kennel? We didn't know, but we were sure some expert would know. We couldn't be the first would-be boarding kennel owners who had to come up with the right answer to satisfy the State Department of Ecology. Someone out there had been there before us. We just had to ask the right person – or persons.

It was like one of those word games or puzzles that come on Public Radio on Sunday mornings. Find the right person, and you win a chance to have the Department of Ecology leave a message on your phone answering machine! But the American Boarding Kennels didn't have the answer and neither did the scientists at our local Battelle Northwest Laboratories. We tried some of the national pet food manufacturers but again, we got no specific answer -- at least not one that the Department of Ecology would accept. We found the answer for pigs, chickens, Beagle dogs, elephants, and other zoo animals. But we were looking at the poop from a variety of dog breeds, cat breeds, mixed breeds, or completely unknown breeds, all of which would be eating all sorts of pet foods, or even home-cooked foods, not to mention the treats. And the pets weren't even the same sizes. If you're dealing with elephants you have a rough idea of size and weight. Same with Beagles, or pigs. Louis did his best, sending paperwork after paperwork. We even had a summer intern from Washington State University who was doing her thesis on septic systems. She had some ideas about the measurements requested and wrote a report, though it also failed to answer the question. In the end, the Department of Ecology gave in. Probably in desperation to get us off their backs, they issued us the permit to operate the kennel. It allowed us to use the septic tanks and drain fields to deal with the animal waste, just as we had planned. The ecologists probably just threw up their hands, amazed that someone didn't know the answer to such a simple question!

Then there was the question of staffing. We needed some help running this business adventure – and it was becoming more like an adventure into the unknown all the time. We didn't want to do all the work of running the kennel ourselves. Louis wanted to have time to train his dogs for field trials, and I wanted time to – well that was what I was going to find out. I knew, however, that I didn't want to be a receptionist kennel manager forever, and I didn't want to do the feeding and cleaning for long. We would hire someone to share in the work of cleaning and feeding, exercising, making reservations, and checking pets in and out. Louis and I planned to be fully involved right from the start so we could see if what we had planned was working the way we wanted. At the same time we knew we would need someone to work full-time, and to be there if we were away. We decided to build an apartment for the kennel staff person above the garages for the new house.

Our shopping list of plans was enormous, and kept growing. Not only did Louis and I continue to have new ideas, but there was no shortage of suggestions from family, friends, acquaintances, the veterinarians whom Louis visited, and neighboring farmers. At some point we said, "Enough -- it's time to put this thing to bed."

People were beginning to ask when the kennel would be open, and we still couldn't give them a date. In fact, we didn't have anything except a piece of land to show that we might at some time in the distant future build something out there among the weeds.

Christmas is Coming

LOUIS FINALLY RETIRED from his practice at the beginning of December 1993. Even before he had had time to close up his books, he had pulled out the blue prints for the kennel and the house.

"Let's get on with it," he announced one morning at breakfast.

I was on my way to work and didn't have time to discuss what we needed to get on with, though I was certain it had to do with retirement and the construction plans. While I could get lost in that dream world of a new house and kennel, I still had difficulty accepting the reality of the changes in direction our lives would take. Even the dry twigs and grasses of our new piece of property and the rolls of blue prints sitting on the dining room table sometimes seemed unreal. I had no trouble talking about it, but when it came to doing something about it, then my gut gave a few lurches. I had the excuse that there was still a year or two to go before I qualified for early retirement and all that Social Security might offer.

"I've got to leave now, or I'll be late to work. And there's Christmas coming, don't forget." I added that he needed to get a Christmas tree as soon as possible, too. "We should wait till January to start on the plans. There'll be more time then. And remember, Mother comes in a week and then some of the children will be here to make cookies. They planned that at Thanksgiving."

I was out the door before I heard any reply. That evening I returned to find the dining room table covered with the blueprints, and Louis was making a list of what he would need to build models of the kennels and the house. He knew what the barn would look like, and so he didn't need to build a model. The architect would be in that evening and the next morning the two of them would head for the site. He looked so happy -- I didn't have the heart to tell him to slow down. Anyway, it wouldn't have done any good if I had. Louis was off and running with his retirement plans.

Mother's Annual Visit

MOTHER HAD THIS Harris Tweed overcoat, a long overcoat of a brown and green tweed. I don't know when she first bought it -- she probably had it made by the tailor that made both my father's suits and a few of Mother's. So he probably made this particular overcoat for Mother. It was made of a typical Harris tweed of the old weave, the sort used in men's sports jackets, or the ones with leather patches at the elbows and shoulders, or the jackets and "plus fours," those trousers men used to wear, baggy and worn with Argyle patterned socks that came up to the knee.

Mother's Harris tweed overcoat was long and heavy, thick enough to keep out both the torrential rain and arctic winds. She wore it when she paid her visits to schools as School Medical Officer, when she walked to the corner shop for bread and milk if the weather warranted some protection, and she never left the country without it. She walked her corgi dog, Taffy, twice a day, wearing that coat, with a doggie treat in one of the pockets and I don't know what else. When she came to stay with us many years later, she walked our poodle, Guinness, twice a day, still in that Harris Tweed coat, and always with two dog treats in one of the pockets. Sensible shoes just right for walking -- but never tennis shoes -- a scarf round her head – it was cold out, as she always came at Christmas time – gloves, and Guinness's leash in hand.

"And don't forget, she always had a handkerchief tucked up her sleeve," one of my daughters adds when we review what Mother carried with her. There was probably an extra one in one of those deep Harris tweed coat pockets. I carry one there too. With age, one's nose tends to drip, as Mother would explain.

When I was of grade-school age at St. Hilda's I came home for lunch almost every day. We lived just around the corner from the school, on Royal Terrace. It took me all of five minutes to dawdle my way home. I remember Mother would greet me from the kitchen where she was standing at the stove, a gas one, standing in one corner of the kitchen between the window and the large wood-burning range that did everything from heating the water to burning the trash. Mother was probably stirring soup for our lunch. She had come in from work long enough to open a can of soup, dump it into a brass pan which I still have, turn on the heat, and start stirring with one hand. If my memory serves me right – and it doesn't always – she had the vacuum in her other hand and she was vacuuming the kitchen floor with this other hand before going on to do other places in need of a clean-up. But I know for sure that she was still wearing that Harris tweed overcoat while doing all this.

"Jenepher, she wasn't really doing all that at the same time. It's just a piece of family mythology about your mother," my friend Barb comments.

"Perhaps. But what about this for memory -- and I'm not making any of it up."

So I tell the story of Mother's plane traveling. There are

plenty of these tales, but this one has to do with the Harris tweed coat. Back in the late forties and fifties, the airlines set limits on how heavy one's bags could be. I think this was before the days of carry-on and everything was check-through. But Mother had her own way of doing carry-on. People back then dressed for travel in good clothes. No jeans and tennis shoes for Mother: she wore heels -- good heels -- a skirt, and a jacket over a silk blouse, or wool twinset. On top of that she wore that Harris tweed coat. In fact I remember one occasion when she wore one other coat, perhaps a lighter raincoat, under the heavy one. The Harris tweed had big pockets, and into one pocket Mother stuffed two detective books – hardcover – the print in paperbacks was too small, she explained. In the other pocket was her traveling iron, a heavy item that would have made a difference to the weight limit. I think at the last stop before her final destination, she would purchase the appropriate number of bottles of alcohol that she and Father could bring into the country. These items also disappeared into those large pockets. There was something magical about that Harris tweed coat. It consumed whatever needed to be carried, sort of like those outfits soldiers wear nowadays when heading for the hills of Afghanistan or wherever it is they need to go.

Almost the last memory I have of that coat was when Mother, now aged ninety-something, came for her annual visit, still flying from Heathrow to SeaTac for three weeks at Christmas time. We met her at the SeaTac airport, and our usual plan was to drive her back to the Tri-Cities or perhaps stay the night in Seattle.

This time we waited and waited, watching as first one group came through the door from Customs to be greeted by waiting relatives. The group of those waiting grew smaller and smaller until there was just us. At last she came, seated in a wheelchair, pushed by some airline attendant who looked around eager to locate the family member to whom this passenger belonged. Mother looked tired and ill. The warmth and protection provided by the Harris Tweed coat, wrapped tightly around her, was not enough to do the job it was meant for. She looked small and frail; her silvery grey hair was in need of a comb, her gloved hands clasping the crocodile-skin purse that my father had bought for her at some expensive London shop many years before. It just showed how quality and fine workmanship will last forever, was her comment about that purse. I have it still, though I don't use it and I wonder what to do with it. Like the Harris Tweed coat, that purse is large; it had to be to take all that went into it, such as passports, health certificates, visas, and goodness knows what else besides the travelers' checks and money and toothpaste and toothbrushes – Father's as well as hers.

She looked around, frowning, not seeing our little group at first. I think we had a banner her great-granddaughter Jenny had made that said something like "WelcomeTinyGrandmoth- erWhoGoesFlying" – that was one word coined by Jenny. So we waved it and then she saw us and raised a hand, turning to the flight attendant and saying something to her. Then she was with us and we all could see that she looked ill and tired.

No, she did not want to come back to Catherine's home in Gig Harbor for the night. She just wanted to get back to our home and her familiar bed there. Her luggage had not arrived and that was a problem that we had to reassure her would work itself out.

"We'll tell the British Airways people now and it'll be with us tomorrow. Don't you worry."

But worry was one of Mother's great skills. We all knew this, and the best thing to do was to get her into the car and head for Richland.

"No, I don't need any wheelchair now. I'm with you all and I can walk – or hold on to someone. I don't want to be a problem."

But she was a problem – how great a problem, we didn't know at that moment. She seemed to have brightened up now she was with us, and out of the wheelchair. The attendant seemed relieved to have passed this problem passenger on to the right people, with our assurances that we could take it from here.

That Harris Tweed coat seemed to have grown several sizes, or perhaps it was that she had shrunk with age. But it still served its purpose, for out of one pocket Mother pulled a bottle of gin, and one of sherry from the other.

"I thought these would be a help at Christmas time," she said as she handed me the bottles. "I finished the Margery Allingham on the plane and left it there. We can shop for another good detective story, or you might have one at home, Jenepher."

Then she dug deeper into a pocket and pulled out her Penguin copy of The Viking Portable Library Kipling – like her Harris Tweed coat, she never traveled without her Kipling. She gave the well-worn book a pat before replacing it in the pocket.

I waited for the portable traveling iron, but it didn't appear. I hadn't seen it for some time, but I remembered the times when she never traveled without it. That was back in the days when she and my father went to those elegant medical conferences. She was all alone now, had been for twenty-seven years, but at that moment she seemed more alone than ever, wrapped in that tweed coat that carried what was important, and holding on to that special purse. She took my arm and announced it was getting late.

"Jenepher, let's get going. No, thank you, I'll take my purse, it's not heavy."

We all walked slowly with her down the escalators and across the bridge to the parking lot and found our cars. I think someone had made the lost luggage report, but Mother had stopped worrying about a detail like that. She was back with family, and that was all that mattered. And she had her Kipling. We wrapped that coat firmly around her and arranged her car seat so she could lean back. She was asleep almost before we were onto I-90 and heading east, still holding her precious purse.

A Christmas Party and After

WE PLANNED A Christmas party for a few nights before Christmas. There were many old friends who wanted to see Mother, and we wanted to have one last Christmas party in the old house. I expected to feel sad, but as usual, once we were into the swing of planning I became excited about the prospect of one last Christmas party – just one big open house for friends and their families. We had a huge Christmas tree, ordered the meal from a caterer, and enjoyed having four generations of our family and our friends all together.

The caterers were old friends but they produced an unexpected surprise. One of them, Mary, asked if we needed any help at the kennels whenever we opened. She was very interested in working in a boarding kennels and was more than enthusiastic as she explained how much she loved animals. She had applied to one kennel in the area but been turned down because she had "too much experience" – whatever that meant, she added. She had plenty of work experience and knew more than we did about customer service.She sounded like someone we might want to hire. While we knew Mary, we had never considered her as a potential employee. In fact, we had done little to consider anyone a potential employee.

We were barely considering ourselves as business owners, potential or imaginary. Mary was serious about wanting to work for us.

"We're not nearly ready – in fact, we've not even broken ground, but we'd like to think we'll be ready by the fall of next year. Can you wait?" I didn't want to sound too negative. I thought Mary would be a good person to work with. "What about meeting in the New Year to talk about what our plans are? How does that sound?"

She was interested, even more interested when we explained that she would be required to live in the apartment we hoped to have for the full-time staff person.The three of us agreed to get back together to talk in more detail after the holidays.

Christmas took over after that. Kennel business and retirement plans were shelved for a while.

Cookie-making and gift-wrapping and last-minute shopping took up time, and before we knew it, Christmas was upon us. Everyone was thoughtful to include Mother in what they were doing, but she was not interested in doing much – not even her usual copper and silver cleaning orgy.

"Louis, I'm worried about Mother," I whispered to him when we were alone for a moment in the kitchen."She's not well. Catherine took her to lunch today and they had to come home early because she wasn't well. But she won't admit to feeling anything but tired.What do you think is the matter with her?" He shook his head but agreed she didn't look too well.

We managed to get through Christmas Eve, and I was relieved to see Mother eating well and enjoying all the family. There were eighteen of us for our traditional Christmas Day brunch, gift opening, and evening dinner. But Mother seemed quiet, and that night she only pecked at her food. She enjoyed the time everyone else took to sit with her. But she was looking worse as the evening continued.

This was not working out to be the perfect Christmas I had planned.

"Mom, Grammy isn't very well," my daughter Catherine told me quietly. "She's getting worse and doesn't seem to remember who we all are. Shouldn't we have her checked?" Trying to get Mother to see a doctor was one of the most difficult things to do partly because she was a doctor herself and didn't trust any of the younger generation of doctors. She trusted Louis, but even he couldn't get her to admit to feeling anything but just tired. We all spent some time studying Louis's blueprints and talking about what we could expect to be doing this time the following Christmas.

The next morning, Boxing Day, we had plans to go to brunch at one of the hotels. It was Mother's traditional treat to take us all out for this meal.But there were no sounds from her room that morning, and when I went to see how she was doing, I saw at once that she was very ill indeed.

"Freda, no arguing, but you need to be in the hospital. We're calling the ambulance now and you're going to the emergency room."Louis's words stirred her into a faint argument, but it wasn't any good. She was very weak and seemed relieved to have the decision taken by someone else.

She had pneumonia and possibly some heart problems; there was some mention of a possible stroke. It was a relief to have her in a comfortable place and under good care.

"How long will she stay in the hospital, Louis?" I asked, thinking it might be weeks before she was ready to travel home to Cambridge, England.

"Hard to say. At least a few more days, and then we'll have a better idea."

The family stayed around for a few more days and visited Mother, but she was sleeping most of the time, and seemed not to know who was who. We all sadly cleaned up and put away Christmas decorations, took boxes and torn wrapping paper to the dump, and put the turkey carcass on to simmer for the usual turkey soup that always declared Christmas to have come to an end. New Year's was quiet. The family returned to their homes. Louis had the dining room table to himself, and the blueprints appeared again. We visited Mother in the hospital. I went back to work and Louis returned to building the model of our house-to-be.

Mother was released from the hospital after about ten days. She was still not well, but her lungs were cleared and she was feeling better. She had not taken to hospital care well. The food was not to her liking.In desperation I had taken to bringing her a soft-boiled egg, toast, and marmalade every morning on my way to work. That helped.But she was glad to be back with us again in her familiar room and bed, and to have a warm fire to sit next to during the day. She could never understand why I went to work every morning – Louis was now retired, so I should be home taking care of him – and her too, I supposed. But that was an old argument we had had for many years. Mother had always believed that a woman's place was with her family first and foremost, and always said that was what she had liked to do best. A confusing view, to say the least, since she had worked professionally for so long, always coming home at lunch time to fix a meal for my father and my brother and me.I knew she meant I should be doing the same thing – staying at home and caring for family – and I had enjoyed doing that for many years when the children were young and needed me there. But not anymore.

What the New Year Brought

THE NEW YEAR, 1994, should have been full of promise and discovery. It had been our plan to put all our spare time and energy into developing our building plans and then to get on with the building and preparing for opening the kennels at the end of the year.

"Or maybe spring of the next year. It always takes longer to do this sort of thing than you think," Louis told anyone who asked. I had given up asking. My chief worry was Mother's illness and the likelihood that this would present more problems very shortly.I just wanted to be prepared for the worst.

The year started out gloomily with Mother's slow recovery. It was still too soon to make any plans for her return to England. Louis bore most of the burden of nursing her during the day. I felt guilty about this. She could be difficult, and her illness had not improved her disposition. Now she wanted me to prepare her boiled egg and toast breakfast and then she would sit in a big chair, wrapped in a shawl, by the fire in the living room. Louis was close by poring over the blueprints and building his models.

I wondered why I didn't just quit work then and there, retire, stay home and take care of Mother. Some days I drove home from work convinced that the moment I came into the house I would announce that I had decided to quit. I could almost see the delight on my mother's face, the surprise on Louis's. But I didn't do it. By the time I had reached our driveway I would remember that I needed to stay at least until the end of the year when there might be the announcement of an early retirement. I would qualify for that. I liked my paycheck and I liked the thought of full pension that would come if I stayed. Was that being selfish? One thing I knew I needed was the health insurance that was guaranteed by staying.

I was having difficulty with my hip and I would probably need hip replacement surgery in the not too distant future. Some ten years earlier I had had a serious horse riding accident when we were in the back country of Montana – fishing, of course – and the horse I was riding threw me and then rolled on me, breaking my pelvis, hip joint, and femur. It was a scary time for Louis. I had little memory of the event, except the flight in a very small plane from Bozeman to Seattle and then to Harborview Hospital where I spent five weeks and had three surgeries.

It took me a year or more to reach full recovery. I was able to ski again, but no more riding horses.In time, the hip started to bother me. I walked with a limp, then added a stick, and finally reached the point where getting in and out of a car was painful. I had not quite reached that point, however, when Mother was with us, but it was something that both Louis and I knew would have to be faced.We were too taken up with our building plans to spend much time on what looked like a small blip on the screen.

Mother took up most of my time when I might have been studying the plans and giving my thoughts for the future. I could see Louis doing the things that needed to be done –

talking to planning commissions, learning what permits were needed, all of which I was happy to have him manage. There were doctor's visits for Mother and long-distance phone calls to my brother in England and to the travel insurance company. Mother had little faith in the health care system in the States – or anywhere except in British countries. She never traveled anywhere without adequate travel insurance that covered all contingencies – lost luggage, planes delayed or cancelled, and above all complete health coverage that included, in her case, a first-class return flight home for herself and an accompanying caregiver. So she was in no hurry to leave as long as her doctors in Richland were telling her she was not ready for travel. She had come to appreciate and trust these physicians, in spite of their being American. She was comfortable, we had a friendly cat that sat on her lap and purred, her appetite was returning, and the only thing missing was her small Cambridge apartment and her circle of friends. For those she would have to leave us and return to England. She assured me that she would be perfectly fine – her words – once she was back in her familiar surroundings, and would certainly not need anyone to assist her there. I wasn't so sure about that and had assured my brother Tony that I would stay at least a week to see she was doing fairly well. My niece Vicki was going to look in on her too, and Tony promised to come and see her as often as possible. But I wished the distance between Richland and Cambridge was not a matter of four hours' driving and eight hours' flying. I felt sad at the sight of this frail little old lady sitting, eyes closed, mouth half open in sleep, fingers plucking at the wool blanket wrapped around her knees. She had been such a powerhouse of energy. I remembered the pictures of her as a student at Cambridge, rowing at stroke in the Newnham boat for two years, and later leading her two children up the hills in Wales and the Lake District of England. Dragging might be a better word in my case, but the memories were vivid. "Tiny Grammy Who Went Flying" was the name my granddaughter, another Jenny, gave her. Now we had to get her ready to fly back home again. I thought it would take some doing.

"I just don't want to be any bother, but would you get me my book?" ...or her stick, or her shawl, or whatever it was she needed. She now would wait till the last moment not to be a bother, and at that point, it usually was a bother. She meant it, I knew that now. I think all her life she had hated to think she was being a bother to anyone. Being able to do things for herself was of such importance to her that she would often put off doing something she wanted for fear of just that, causing a bother. I began to see so much I had missed about my mother all those years.

Meanwhile the new house and the kennel and all those lists I had made were put on a back burner. Louis assured me he had it all under control, the models were almost complete and already we could see where we might have to do some redesigning.

"Better now than later when it's a matter of 'change orders,' and those are costly," had been our architect's comment.

It felt as though we were in a lull, the trough between waves, that center of the hurricane when things are quiet, but you know there is more weather on the way. We had stopped counting all the steps we still had to climb to reach our goal. It seemed such a long way off.

"I don't want to be any bother." Her words came more often. There was the unspoken: "But what I want you to do will be a bother and I wish it weren't so." As she felt better she made more demands -- not big ones, and none that were any real bother, but they were always prefaced by that statement. She needed help getting to the bathroom, needed a book, needed the television louder, and was it time for a cup of tea or a glass of sherry? But she never made any "bother" about her flight back to England. We had her doctor request oxygen to be available for the flight, and we booked first-class tickets. My return one was economy – the insurance company didn't see any reason for me to travel first class if I wasn't accompanying an ill parent.

Her grandchildren and great-grandchildren came with us to the airport to see her off and wish her well. She was wonderfully responsive. But the moment we were on the plane to England, she seemed to fade away. Her eyes closed, her breathing became shallow, and I worried that she was suddenly sinking into some coma. The flight attendants were helpful, and when one of them spoke to her, asking her where she was going after the plane flight, she seemed to come to and asked for a cup of tea. Then a glass of sherry and some cheese and crackers… "If it's no bother." The rest of the flight she slept, except for when breakfast was served. I thought it must be the smell of those sausages that did it – she ate those and drank tea and began to look her old self.

"Now I don't need any help from here, Jenepher," she said. What did she mean? I explained that Tony would be meeting us and he would drive us back to Cambridge. She seemed to realize that she had been ill and still needed some assistance. How she hated being dependent in any way. I could see her lips tighten as she fought to reconcile her need for independence with her present need for help. There might be a difficult time ahead.

It was indeed difficult, but she did well. However irritated

I became with her complaints about all the arrangements I made for her care and her refusal to take advantage of the services available to help her stay in her own home, I had to admire her need to stay in control of her own life. Growing old and being ill meant losing control and the power she'd had to make her own decisions.

"I don't need that, Jenepher," she would say when I tried to persuade her to have a telephone next to her bed. "I can still get out of bed by myself and my hearing is good. Now, don't fuss. Go and make some tea for us both. Then we'll watch the news – thank goodness it's in English and I'll understand what they're saying." I tried to get her to have a television set in her bedroom, but I might have been suggesting we bring in the devil. "Never! I can listen to the news on the radio." She was a great one for the news.

She agreed to have a social services visitor come in the mornings to help with a bath – "But only every other day, I don't need a bath every day." Then she changed her mind and said she didn't need anyone.

Neighbors were helpful, but I sensed some of them thought it would be better if Mother went into the nursing home down the street. Good luck, I thought. They didn't have any more luck than Tony, Vicki or I had.

The time came for me to leave for home. It was a terrible morning. Mother had finally agreed to have a social services visitor come in every morning. This person arrived while I was still packing. She was a stout woman, with sensible flat shoes, and an apron under her heavy navy overcoat. I thought she might have some luck with Mother.

"Now don't you worry yourself about your ma. I've taken care of plenty and you've a plane to catch -- so off with you." A kind woman, I thought with relief.

But it was a miserable goodbye. All I could say was that I'd be back later in the year and we'd have a chance to do some of the things we both enjoyed doing together in the past.She closed her eyes and made no reply. I couldn't think of anything more to say. I only wished I could find a way to connect with her.

Coming Home Again

THE FLIGHT HOME gave me time to think. My mind jumped from one thing to another. I would be back at work in a day or so. I enjoyed my work. It meant something to me. I counted for something with the people I worked with. I had a salary, pension to look forward to, and that said I was a valuable person, didn't it?

Would I have to give up all that just because Louis and I had this crazy plan to go into business together? Probably. It would be difficult to do both. I'd have to make a choice, wouldn't I? Probably Louis assumed I would quit work and he was just waiting for me to get some of these other problems out of the way so I could do my share.I hadn't thought seriously about giving up my job. Some days I was for quitting, and then other times I would want to keep on with it. It was one of those things Louis and I avoided discussing at breakfast. Mother, however, had brought it up.

"You'll have to give up that job now," she said several times, never fully understanding what I did. "Louis will need you to run those kennels, won't he?"

Would he need me? Would I do it?

The plane droned on over Greenland. The flight attendant

suggested I might like to watch the movie. No, thanks. A pillow please.

I remembered there had been some discussion about Mother's remark. One of the children said something about not expecting me to change course. Whoever it was, I said a mental *Thank you, dearest.* Louis didn't add anything except that he seemed to be getting on well by himself at this point and that he didn't see that I'd have to do any changing. If I wanted to keep on working as a counselor, that would be fine with him. We could to the kennel as well, since we planned on having help. Still, I knew I shouldn't expect him to do it all. I should pull my weight too. There would be challenges with the kennel, and I had liked the challenges counseling gave me. People shared their pain and concerns with me, and doing so seemed to help. It took guts, I thought, for someone to share their personal life with a stranger. I always felt so rewarded by the trust they placed in me. I'd miss that.

At the same time, would there be rewards in taking care of other people's pets? I still wasn't sure how I would feel about taking care of pets. Past experience hadn't told me anything to indicate that I would love all pets -- other than perhaps my own. I hadn't had one that I could call my very own, just the family pets. I just hadn't had time for one of my own. Rewards from a business venture? Perhaps. It might be worth the risk. I stared out the window. We were descending and I could feel my ears popping from the change in pressure. I made the decision that I would retire at the end of the year. The plane slid through the clouds, bumping in the turbulence. Changing jobs would mean turbulence, expected and unexpected. The sign for fastening our seat belts flashed. How appropriate, I thought.

Louis met me at the airport and his embrace was a warm

welcoming one. I sobbed on his shoulder, relieved to be back with him again and relieved to have Mother safely planted again in her apartment.

"Don't count your chickens yet on your Mother's account. There's been a phone call from your brother, one from your mother, and one from Vicki, who said to tell you she had your stick safe." I'd forgotten about my stick altogether. My hip wasn't giving me any trouble on all the flights. But those other two calls might mean trouble.

The house was quiet. My brother told me Mother had fired the woman whom I had met as I was leaving. Or rather, the dear lady had given notice when she couldn't get Mother out of bed. And Mother's call was to tell me she was doing well and that the "horrible old woman" had left. Vicki called later to say she was trying to find someone else to come in to help with Mother, but she could see it was going to be difficult and that her father, my brother Tony, wanted Mother in a retirement home as soon as possible. Poor Mother. I hoped Vicki could find someone to help so Mother didn't have to move.

Now I wanted to look at the plans and see what was new with them.

"Surprise me."

Louis, reluctantly at first, but then with some well-deserved pride, showed me the models he had finished while I was away. I had never imagined we would have anything as grand as what he proudly showed me, there on the dining room table. It was all built to scale: windows, doors, roof that came off to reveal the rooms and the loft. It looked so perfect. I couldn't imagine what it had taken to build it, though I knew Louis was skilled at building such models. He'd built a model log cabin when he'd been ten years old, and we still had it sitting on his desk. It too had been the conception of a dream he still held of building a log cabin somewhere in the wilds of Alaska. I always felt guilty about my being the source of this dream not being fulfilled. How could I not follow along with the one for the move across the river and building the boarding kennel? I knew his real dream was to have the opportunity to train and run his hunting dogs. As I gazed in awe at this model of our house-to-be, I promised myself that he'd have this opportunity.

"Are we ready to start building?" I asked

"I've got the tractor out there all ready to start digging. But we've got some leveling to do first – it'll be a month or more before we can start on the foundations and we're waiting for a hearing with the County Commissioners. The neighbors could still say 'no, but it's not likely."

There aren't any neighbors, I thought. *Well, maybe a few, but they're all a distance away.*

"How's the hip doing? Must be OK if you left your cane behind with your mother."

"It's fine, but I haven't been stressing it." Well, not really, though I had to agree I wasn't walking without a limp and a lurch to one side. I was avoiding much walking if possible.

"We need to get you over to the U.W. Medical School and have it X-rayed." Louis had spoken with a friend who "did hips" and especially ones that had already had a great deal of damage, as mine had. So that was our next concern. We couldn't start any serious building until the question of my hip had been answered.

In April I had my hip fixed – a new artificial hip replaced the old one that had been giving me more and more pain. It was amazing how quickly the recovery process went. Those surgeons want you out of bed and walking around within a day, and within a week I was home and doing the cooking again. I couldn't put any weight on the leg for some weeks, but with a pair of crutches I could manage everything I needed to do except drive a car. The time off work reinforced my decision to retire as soon as possible.I wasn't going to miss work as much as I had once thought. It was only later that I realized it how long it took to say goodbye to something that had meant so much. My work had meant a great deal, but now I was caught up in the promise the new house and the kennel held for us.

No sooner was I back to work than the news came that Westinghouse Hanford was going to give early retirement to those employees who qualified. I qualified. No more worrying about my future. I would be out of there at the end of the year and able to concentrate on our building plans.

I had my new hip and was working on rehabilitation, while Louis finished rounding up all the permits we needed. That was about the high point of the year. After that we just kept our heads up and planned not to go under with the next wave.There weren't many big waves left to engulf us, or so we thought -- just the ongoing pounding of the breakers as we went from one stage to the next in the building process.

But I hadn't finished with Mother yet

Construction

IN JUNE WE broke ground. Louis and his tractor had already cleared and leveled the site. There was a great deal of rubbish and trash that had been dumped carelessly and with no thought for what some of it could do to the environment. Tires, an old toilet, wooden pallets, and junk that made us wonder what it might have been in a previous life. It was enough to make several large piles the size of a small truck or SUV. Louis announced that he would set fire to the piles, adding, "You can come and watch if you like. It'll be a real Fourth of July blaze."

He must have had some firebug blood in him, because he always liked large bonfires...he preferred them about the same size as these piles of rubbish. I came out to watch. While I am scared to death of fires, I would rather keep an eye on one to see it doesn't get out of control. What I'd do if one did, I didn't know. But I wanted to be there if the fire department showed up to arrest Louis for burning illegally. I tended to be a little suspicious of some things he did, and lighting large fires was one of them. The fires went off without any problems, though how no one noticed the tall plumes of black smoke, I don't know. I hoped it had been a legal burn day in the county.

Now it was time for the foundations to be dug for the house. As he had always planned, Louis would measure the land and dig the foundations, and he would be the general contractor for the house, the barn, and the kennel. He would be in charge of hiring the subcontractors who did the work, and he and the architect would supervise the work. Framers, electricians, plumbers, drywallers, painters, carpenters, finishers...I lost track of all the people involved in the construction. I knew very little about building anything, having never constructed anything more complicated than a quilt, and the closest I had come to reading a blueprint was following a knitting pattern. Surveying land, following blueprints, marking out and digging foundations were all beyond me. Louis appeared to understand all that.

"Where did you learn to survey?" I asked.

"In the Army. Learned a lot in the Army." Louis had served in Korea between the wars, but never spoke much about it. He had a fund of stories about his experiences running an enlisted men's club in Yong Dung Po, South Korea.

"I kept a baseball bat behind the bar in case of fights."

He impressed our children with the stories of how he could always tell when a fight was about to break out, and he'd come out from behind the bar with that baseball bat swinging.

My assignments in the house and kennel construction had more to do with office and organization details, such as deciding what fixtures we would need in bathrooms, kitchens, and the kennels. This was all new territory for me. No one wanted to talk to me about their dreams, their abusive spouses or demanding bosses.

"Always get three bids and ask for references. Take the lowest bid unless there are very good reasons not to." Louis's words ran through my head as I talked to printing and marketing people about a brochure and design for a logo. The American Boarding Kennels Association once again was a great resource for help with drafting policies and procedures, designing forms for reservations, boarding agreements, and record-keeping. I wondered how these would work in practice, but it was a start.

I looked for flooring; I chose colors and design of tiles, countertops, and office chairs. What I liked usually cost more than our budget. Actually, we didn't have a budget – just this "three bids and take the lowest one if possible" rule. I was amazed at what it takes to set up a business.

I took some classes on running a small business, accounting for a small business, and one called "Entrepreneurial Success" that guaranteed to teach all one could possibly need to run a business. Everyone else in the classes had businesses that manufactured things, built things like roads, had budgets in the millions, and no one had a business that was planning on taking care – special care, mind you – of pets. Everyone had computer skills and knew how to use the Internet for their research. We were to do research for a feasibility study for our planned business. I looked in the Yellow Pages of the phone book to count how many boarding kennels were in the area and then called one or two, asking if they had space for a dog for Christmas. When I learned all kennels were full, I knew we had plenty of reason to build our own. It may not have been as detailed a feasibility study as some were, but I had the information I needed.

Meanwhile, back at the site, Louis was busy with his old Bronco, his newly purchased and not so old tractor, and his own very personal method of record-keeping. I don't know what year the Bronco came off the Ford assembly line, but it had manual transmission, no air-conditioning, a tendency to weave at certain speeds, and a pronounced smell of wet dog and dead bird. The Bronco would continue to play a part in the development and ongoing life of Sagemoor Kennels, from driving out to turn on the irrigation system on the far side of the farm, to taking sick dogs or cats to the veterinarian, or pulling the trailer full of prunings to the burn pile or taking trash to the dump.

During the construction phase the Bronco was Louis's field office. Every morning he would drive out to the site in it, armed with a telephone book, a cell phone, and some pads of "yellow stickies," those two and a half inch square pads of yellow paper that can be attached to things to remind you of something. Those yellow stickies were the basis for Louis's records system. Louis entered names, dates, numbers, quotes on bids, ideas -- each on its own yellow sticky, and plastered them all over the front seat of the Bronco, on the steering wheel, the brake handle, the dashboard, and the shelf up by the windshield that things always fall off when you stop too quickly. He assured me he knew where each one was, and I wasn't to move even one!

I bought the cell phone as a birthday present for Louis because sometimes I was desperate to find him when he was out at the site and there was no phone available. He was re-sistant to this new technology, frequently refusing to turn it on unless he was expecting a call. In the end he admitted that it was a great help.

His back-up office was the kitchen table. That table also held yellow stickies, a phone book and blueprints, catalogs and numerous lists, and other documents too precious to be moved elsewhere. I tried paperweights and filing boxes, dreading what a light breeze might do to the piles, but Louis preferred to take the risk of having to sort through them again rather than lose sight of them, hidden away in some box, drawer, or filing cabinet.

While Louis was driving his tractor and digging the foundation ditches and I was taking classes, we both had our minds full of other details. I had my book of lists, and one was the list of what I thought we would need for running the kennel. At the top of that list was the computer. If Louis had his tractor, I would have my computer, as well as printer, copier, file cabinets, desk, and fax machine. Our children found us to be a great repository for their old office equipment. We inherited from them a fax machine, a printer, a monitor, a desk, and even the computer. They were wonderful at researching what software we needed. They were able to put me in touch with the best people to help design a brochure, logo, and letterhead, and to do printing at a reasonable cost. They saved me a great deal of time instead of walking my fingers through the Yellow Pages of the phone book. My daughter-in-law Sandy – also our tax accountant -- made sure I had the accounts set up properly. I think she didn't want to have to rescue me from some tax mess.

We were like a couple of terriers, always on the move, never where you think you can find them, jumping from one thing to another. The person who kept us from going crazy was our architect, who would meet with us weekly to see how the building was coming. We were concentrating on the house first, while the barn and the kennel progressed at a slower rate. The house was the most important, as we needed to have somewhere to live when we sold our old house.

The New Emerges from the Weeds

WE CONTRACTED WITH a timber frame building company in Port Townsend for the design and construction of our house. The timbers for the posts and beams were constructed of recycled Douglas fir that had come from an old warehouse somewhere near the mouth of the Columbia River. They were over one hundred years old and had weathered to a rich gold color, their age showing in the cracks that ran through them. By the end of summer these timbers and the walls they framed were ready to be put in place in our new house. Were we ready for them?

Louis had the foundations dug and ready for the massive posts to be placed, bolted, and held in place by metal hurricane straps. The walls attached to these posts were of plywood, with six inches of Styrofoam for insulation, and backed on the inside with drywall. The timber frame company had everything loaded and ready to roll in early September. The date was set and we were all ready: Louis, the architect, friends, and others. I was assigned the responsibility of cutting some evergreen branches from the old house for the final ceremony of the house raising. Timber frame houses and barns have been built for centuries all over Europe and there are rituals associated with the moment when the posts and beams are raised into place.

The house raising day was cold but clear. The prepared foundations were surrounded by dirt and rocks, and beyond, sagebrush and weeds rattled in the breeze that came up from the river below. Across the river lay the Hanford highway, along which I drove daily out to work. This day when I drove back from work to the house raising I looked across the river, but there had been no sign of any timber frame construction breaking the flatness of the ridge. When I arrived, our friends and the lunch were already there, waiting to cheer the raising of the timbers. And cheer we did, as we watched the crane haul into position those massive posts and beams. In the past, the posts and beams would have been pulled into place by teams of horses or men. We had no team of horses, or men to pull the posts and beams, and instead had one of the large Lampson cranes to do the job. The traditional celebratory champagne lunch followed. Then both Louis and I climbed up a long ladder to place the evergreen boughs from out old house on the ridge pole, where they would eventually be covered over by the roof shingles. We drank the health and good fortune of all who constructed the house and all who would live in it. I hoped the gods of the forest and the hearth were pleased.

There it stood. Our house. The timber frame craftsmen were securing the beams, joists, and posts with wooden pegs – not a nail in it. Louis and I walked around the outside and around the inside. No floors or windows yet, no electricity or plumbing, but there it was. Its posts stretched upward like the trees from which they had been hewn; the clouds could be seen moving slowly high above the long ridge pole. It was sturdy, built to last more than just our lifetimes. Louis and

I entered on tiptoe. It was quiet and dark after the sunlight outside, but the posts and beams glowed golden in the light that came through the window spaces framing the view of the river and distant hills. There was that smell of newly sawn wood that made me think of the first timber frame house we'd seen back in Montana. Voices outside called to us.

"Can we come in? Can we have a tour?"

"I want to whisper in here, Louis. It's lovely, isn't it?"

He nodded. I knew we would enjoy living in it.

"Come on in," I called out, and with great pride we showed our friends around our new house.

It took the craftsmen another few days to finish securing the beams and posts and placing the walls securely, but I knew I would never forget that moment when we saw it standing there on the piece of barren weed patch that would never be the same again. A house was now there, ready to become our home.

It would be several more months before the house was finished and ready for us to move in.

Every day Louis was over at the site digging foundations for the barn and the kennel as well as supervising the subcontractors who were working on the house: framers, electricians, plumbers, drywallers, painters, cabinetmakers, finishers, and many others. I lost track of who was doing what at any one time.

I was still driving daily out to the Hanford site where I was in the final stages of my job as Employee Assistance Counselor for Westinghouse Hanford. I had enjoyed the twelve years I'd held that position, working with employees, managers, engineers, and scientists -- anyone seeking some confidential help for some problem, personal or work-related. But now, as I caught sight of our newly raised timber frame across the

Columbia River from where I drove, I found myself more and more excited about the prospect of the new challenges the kennel might offer me. I would be stepping into a new world, though one I found hard to envisage at that time. I pictured myself balancing on a rock on one side of a stream and ready to leap across, all the time looking for a safe spot on which to land. It had felt safe standing where I had been for so many years, but now I felt unbalanced and as though my feet were about to leave a comfortable place. Any moment now, I would be in mid-air. Where would I land?

July 1995

"I CAN'T REMEMBER what came first. It all seemed to be happening at once."

I still couldn't believe we had done it. We'd moved into the new house and were ready to complete the kennel. Cabinets had arrived, counters and desks, washer and dryer, grooming equipment – though we still didn't have a groomer – a computer and software that I had no idea how to work, light fixtures, hoses -- you name it, things were coming together. I even had some forms and advertising designed. Brochures with logo arrived one day and the next day the Department of Labor and Industries sent me more forms and posters with instructions as to what I should do with them.

Louis and I sat with our drinks looking over the river, some green shoots showing where there would be lawn, and a scattering of shrubs -- small, but still alive. I knew there were still boxes left to unpack – or would I just take them unopened to Goodwill and never know what I was going to do without?

It was the hottest day of the year and we still had no air conditioning but we'd moved.

I wasn't sure I knew anything about taking care of other people's pets and I was fairly sure I knew little about running a business. We had our first employee hired and living in the apartment. We had our first boarder booked. We were ready to open.

We never set a date for opening. It just happened, Someone called and made a reservation and we declared ourselves open for business.

What Every Successful Business Needs

I HELD MY breath a great deal during those first few weeks. The phone kept ringing and the reservation requests kept coming. More pets arrived and left each week. The numbers grew in a satisfying manner. Louis, Mary, and I all worked at feeding, cleaning, and exercising the dogs and playing with the cats. We checked them in and out and answered the phone. Owners smiled as they wrote checks for their pets' boarding.

But were we doing all we could to ensure a successful business? I had read that most new businesses fail in the first two years. Or was it the first five years? Whichever it was, I wanted to make sure we weren't in either group. I read all I could find about the boarding kennels industry, about dogs and cats, and everything the American Boarding Kennels Association published about the industry. I went to classes on small business ownership whenever I saw one advertised.

We listened carefully to our clients and tried to cover all their needs. From the questions we were asked, I soon realized we needed a brochure that provided specific answers. People wanted to know not only about our hours and our fees, but also about grooming and exercise. Did we require any vaccinations, and could they bring toys and treats? When could they come and visit? "And a map – please add a map," someone said after spending more than a couple of hours trying to find us.

I designed forms to cover more situations than I had ever imagined we would meet. There was a reservation form, in which some information was entered when a reservation was made. Then when the pet arrived more was added – such as the pet's food needs, if the owner wanted playtime for the pet, and whom to contact in the case of an emergency. Finally the owner had to sign a boarding agreement that included not holding the kennel responsible for any damage the pet might do, or any harm that might come to the pet while boarding. I was becoming obsessed with all the advice those boarding kennel and business experts gave. If they said to have forms, then we would have all the forms they suggested. Some in fact even gave examples I was happy to plagiarize. Louis complained about the amount of paperwork generated. I would point out that some things a computer could keep for us, but there was other "stuff" we needed to keep ourselves -- such as owners' signatures on the boarding agreement!

Pets came with luggage. Beds, bedding, favorite toys, treats, food, and sometimes a bag to keep it all in. We made notes about all the luggage, stored it carefully if it was not appropriate to be given to the pet, and labeled it, afraid of what might happen if we lost some item. Of course we did lose things, and I spent some afternoons returning a chewed up toy or piece of blanket or a sack of dog food.

Pets came with medications – anything from vitamin pills to antibiotics. More often than not the owner had no idea for what condition the medication was prescribed. Often the labels on the medication bottles were not for the pills contained, and just as often, the directions were out of date. I became familiar with the veterinarians when I called for information as to what might be current on the medications.

Pets came with vaccination records. Or they were supposed to. We found that many times these records were out of date, which required more phoning veterinarians for updated vaccination records. They were very helpful and appreciated our concern that only pets with up- to-date vaccination records would be accepted for boarding. But many of the owners were not so understanding.

"My dog's never been sick -- why should I bother with those?" was a comment I heard frequently in those first few months.

"It's for your pet's protection that those vaccinations are needed," I'd reply.

I was becoming increasingly authoritarian by the day. I was also becoming more and more aware that I knew less and less about running a business and taking care of pets, but there wasn't time to take a careful look at gaps in my knowledge. Mary and I studied the software computer system to see if we could understand how it all worked.

Louis had as much interest in learning how to work the computer as I did in running the tractor. I asked him if he wouldn't just learn some basic computer skills, such as turning the machine on. He said he'd learn just as soon as I learned how to clean the septic system filters. No contest there.

As Mary and I started to enter information into the computer, we began to feel more comfortable with it. We could do the billing and enter the reservations. We both felt we were accomplishing a great deal when we could do that much. But there were some things the program failed to tell us. For instance, it didn't tell us how many kennels were filled and how many were empty and when they would be filled again.

We weren't worried. After all, if we had more dogs in, then we were doing a good job. Just how important that piece of information was, we didn't learn till it was almost too late.

At home the laundry was piling up, home bills weren't getting paid, and my life was getting more and more disorganized. I hadn't yet unpacked all the boxes Louis had so carefully packed and labeled and moved over from the old house. His suggestion of sending them all to Goodwill or even to the dump sounded more attractive every time I looked at them, carefully labeled and piled in a spare room! If I kept the door shut, then I didn't have to think about them.

I found the kennel work was taking more of my time than I had anticipated. While Mary and Louis did the feeding and cleaning, I took over the job of receptionist and bookkeeper. I checked pets in, answered the phone, made reservations, did the billing, and developed a "lost luggage" box to save my having to drive around three towns returning articles left behind at checkout. The three of us walked dogs, threw Frisbees or balls on the exercise yard, or played with a cat. Mary took over from me in the afternoon until she left for her evening job at five o'clock. We were lucky to have someone like Mary. She had all the experience with customers and pets that Louis and I lacked. She was quiet, energetic and, in our eyes, the perfect employee. Louis and I anticipated a long business relationship with Mary.

People told us they had heard good things about our kennel. We must be doing something right. I wondered how long this could last. It was all going so smoothly, it was almost too good to be true. But it was taking more and more time to keep the increasing number of clients happy. Was I doing the things I had hoped to do for myself? Such as what? Scooping poop and washing soiled bedding wasn't on my agenda for retirement.

It was just a matter of time and things would get easier, I told myself. We were learners, and of course we didn't know all that there was to know. We were probably trying to do too much. It was bound to get easier.

The year-end holidays were coming, and I realized I'd better find time to write some cards and do some cooking. Family was coming. My head spun as my mind went in different directions.

Perfectionism had me in its grasp. It would be a while before I would be able to loosen its grip. I was worrying what could go wrong, but people were telling us what a great job we were doing – how crazy was I?

Lessons Learned from
Our First Holiday Season

ABOUT TEN DAYS before Thanksgiving, I looked at the number of pet reservations for that holiday and at the chart I had devised for assigning kennels. To my horror I realized I had not been keeping count and more pets were signed up to board than there were places to put them. And new customers were calling to make reservations for their pets.

"Help, Louis! How do we stop this? People keep calling wanting to get their pet boarded and we've nowhere to put them." He must have heard the panic in my voice. It was as though I had forgotten someone's gift at Christmas and now must do something to make up for my oversight!

"Just tell them we're sorry, but we're full. We can't take care of every pet in the Tri-Cities. They'll understand." He made it sound so reasonable. Of course people would understand.

"I'm so sorry, but we're full for those days. I can take your name and put you on a waiting list and let you know if there is a cancellation."

I tried to be positive, but Louis was wrong. People did

not understand. This one had plane reservations, that one already had a full house and the grandparents didn't like dogs. Another had to find a place for the cat because someone had allergies to cat dander. I listened to all the reasons and kept repeating the words about being full and we could put them on a waiting list.

Fortunately there were a few cancellations, but only enough to take care of the overbookings. I had to have a better system so that I could always know how much space we had available.

Did our computer software have some magic system for reservations? I studied the software manual but found that the system would tell me only when we reached the total number of kennels and had no more room. There was nothing to tell me in advance what space was still available. I designed another chart to give me some answers. Better. But I was not the best at designing charts on my computer. There should have been a class on chart-making back a year or so ago. I declared there was no more I could do. They weren't all going to show up anyway – were they?

They did! Opening time was nine o'clock. Cars were driving in at eight-thirty the day before Thanksgiving.

We were full for that first Thanksgiving. Not a spare kennel or cage anywhere. It would be a real test with so many, but were we worried? I was. But Louis asked what could go possibly go wrong? We'd have to work a bit harder, but that was what we wanted when we had planned this project, wasn't it?

We didn't realize that we might need the sort of plan that emergency preparedness folks have for dealing with hurricanes and similar disasters. It was like the first day in school, grade school, middle school, high school – the same rush. The same feeling of being in the wrong place and not knowing where to go. Instead of looking for my locker or classroom, I was desperately trying to find which run or house we had assigned to which dog or cat. Things were bound to go wrong, and they did.

Our expectation, based on the past experience of only a few weeks, was that the owners would bring their pets in, do the paperwork, and be on their way, leaving us to feed, exercise, and clean the pets according to owner's instructions. When the owners returned, we would be ready to greet them with the bill and their pet.

How could it be a problem now that we were going to have more animals to care for than we had had before? Feeding, cleaning, and exercising this number might take a little more time, but in addition to Louis, Mary, and myself, we had our family home for the holiday. We were sure some of them would love to help with the exercise and feeding. Grandchildren would enjoy taking the "tinies" out to the exercise yard and playing with them. It all sounded so simple.

At nine o'clock the morning before Thanksgiving, however, I was dismayed to see rows of cars, trucks, and SUVs, lined up in the parking lot.

The morning's feeding and cleaning had been done, and Mary and Louis were about to start exercising those dogs already boarding while I checked in the new arrivals. Even though we expected a greater number than usual, I thought they would arrive one, maybe two at a time, and at intervals during the day. Instead they arrived in two mobs: one before nine in the morning, and the other after five o'clock in the afternoon. It rained hard that day and at five o'clock, not only was there a heavy downpour, but it was dark and we had frantic phone calls from people who couldn't find us.

When I saw that line of vehicles waiting that morning, with rain just starting to fall, I summoned Louis and Mary to stop whatever they were doing and come and help me. I felt panic grab me! It takes time to check in a pet, and make a record of its luggage, exercise, feeding, and medication requirements.

Time was one luxury we didn't have at that point.

Owners were waiting, dogs, and a few cats, were waiting, and I was waiting for the first fight to erupt. It didn't, but that was because Louis and Mary were quick to take pets back to their assigned kennels or houses. I, however, was still trying to deal with everyone at once, so busy that I was forgetting clients' names, or calling them by the wrong names. The phone rang. I picked it up and asked the caller to hold for a moment, while at the same time I tried to answer a question from an elderly woman with two Labradors whose leashes were becoming wrapped around a table leg. Luggage piled up. I remembered to see who was still "holding" on the phone. They had given up. I wrote names of owners and their pets on yellow stickies and stuck them on food, bedding, and toys as they were dropped on the counter together with verbal instructions. I hoped I was getting them right. The yellow stickies ran out and I tore off sheets of copy paper, wrote names, and stuck them on with Scotch tape. I saw out of the corner of my eye that some of the stickies had fallen off. Just who was Jackson, and did he eat Pedigree or Alpo? And who belonged to this sheepskin bed with the Orvis label? There was no time to sort it out then. The next owner was coming in with two spaniels in tow – did I remember making a reservation for two spaniels? Owners asked questions and I wasn't sure if I was making any sense with my answers.

"Do you give insulin shots? Because my cat needs an insulin shot twice a day – she's diabetic."

"Of course we can," I replied, thinking that Louis must have given shots at some point in his medical career. I took the insulin and the syringes and instructions and looked for a safe place to put them. They wound up in my purse in the filing cabinet.

"Can you give my Benji his special treats? I cooked them last night." Of course we could do that. Seemed simple. She handed me a plastic bag with what looked like chicken wings in it. There were some feathers still on them.

"I killed the chicken yesterday. Benji will love the taste."

An owner explained that her Akita couldn't "go" on concrete, and so would have to be taken out to the yard twice a day. I wrote this down on the kennel card. I was just wondering if an Akita was a small dog when I glanced up to be met by the eyes of a very large dog gazing at me across the counter. Not a small dog. Louis removed the Akita. Next was the cat that had to have some ear drops and would scratch the moment she saw the tube of ear medicine. One wouldn't eat unless someone sat with her, and another had to have some vitamins sprinkled on her food in the evening. I tried to write it all down, but I was forgetting some important items.

About midday, there came a lull in the traffic. I sorted out the luggage, saw the right pets were in the right places, and started feeding again. I even got some of the exercising done.

We found dogs like to do their business as soon as they hear the latch click on the kennel gate. We needed to do a second round of clean-up.

"Breathe Jenny, breathe," I told myself. I had found the bag with the insulin and syringes. Louis agreed he could do insulin shots. The three of us were ready in the afternoon for the next arrivals.

After that Thanksgiving experience, we agreed we needed to work out a more systematic approach for checking in so many pets at one time before we faced the Christmas and New Year's holiday rush. Some things we hadn't expected. For instance, we soon found out that boarding is a stressful experience for pets, and that nervous dogs have stomachs that upset easily. We were faced with a great many dogs with diarrhea. Every time one of us walked through the dog kennels we found runny stools waiting to get hosed down. We thought we would never get through all the hosing and cleaning and laundry this sort of operation demanded. And then there was the feeding, Many of the dogs, and cats as well, had their own food with instructions on how to feed and when to feed. I said a silent prayer that the right food was given to the right dog. Or cat.

That was inside the kennels. Outside, our family had pitched in to walk dogs in cold, windy, and wet weather. The dogs didn't seem to mind, and I found raincoats and parkas for the walkers. But when the dogs and walkers came back inside, both tracked in mud. Mud clung to the dogs' paws and legs, and dogs low to the ground had mud on their tummies. I hadn't given much thought to what happens when fur, paws, and mud mix. We laid down newspapers and then toweled the muddy fur tummies and paws. Then more hosing. Then more laundry for the muddy towels.

There were two Shih Tzus boarding that holiday – Charlie and Teddy. I had never met Shih Tzus before. They have long flowing fur and faces that ask to be kissed – if you're into kissing dogs, as I am. Louis isn't, but he loved those two for their energy and disregard for dirt and wet weather. Those two dogs were down for exercise every day. They are a small breed and normally we would have put them in the Homestyle Room, but the owner asked that they be together and have plenty of room. So we put them in the main kennels, sharing a house and attached run. Between the hosing down of their run inside and the mud and rain that they met on their walk outside, these two looked a terrible mess. Those long flowing feathers brushing the ground were now like muddy mops that spread more dirt. But they were so happy. They grinned from one dirty ear to the other and jumped up and down, eager to put their feet on anyone who came near. We gave them both a bath and brush and left them in a clean cage in the grooming room on the day their owners were scheduled to pick them up, not wanting to risk muddy paws on a back seat.

"What did you think about how we managed Thanksgiving?" I asked Louis, for reassurance that it hadn't been a complete flop.

"I guess the good thing was that we were full – both dogs and cats. And we didn't lose anything. Or any pets." Louis answered.

We were sitting next to the fire in the living room, watching the lights blinking across the river. This had been not only our first kennel Thanksgiving, but the first Thanksgiving in our new house. The family appeared to approve of the house and of their parents' new business venture. Now, just the two of us, we snuggled together on the sofa, ready to pick each other's brains about our new venture.

Louis had given up on his business suits and sports jackets in favor of khaki work pants, Penney's shirts, and lace-up work boots. That evening he had his boots off and his feet up on the coffee table. He had a tendency to keep his thoughts to himself so I had to dig to get his opinions out in the open. But he was ready to talk about that holiday experience.

"Mary was wonderful," Louis continued. "She knows how

to deal with those anxious clients who always seem to have anxious pets. Of course, she also knows how to handle the owners who are anxious about the bill." He rolled his eyes.

"Thank goodness the family was home and stepped in to do some of the exercising." I was still feeling overwhelmed by the whole event. "What was the worst part, Louis?"

"The poop – all that poop. They were painters…some of those big labs painted the stuff all over the floor and sides of their run. It's still there, I swear it is!"

"What about that big white Poodle that came for the week?" I had my own story to offer. "I forget her name now, but I let her out the gate when her owner came to pick her up. He said just let her out and she'd run to his car. Well, she didn't; she just kept running along the ditch beside the field, getting covered in mud. And guess what he said? Why did I do that? I was polite and kept quiet. Anyway, the door was open and it was only a little while before she was back. And in she popped onto the front seat, mud all over the place. I was kind and brought him a towel, and said he could keep it."

"Do we see the dog again?"

"Oh, yes. They've made a reservation for Christmas." A thought came to me. "What about all those dogs that went home still muddy and wet from their walks and from our hosing their runs? Shouldn't we at least wash and brush them out?"

"You mean those two long-haired ones, Teddy and Charlie? They certainly looked a mess." Louis shook his head as he spoke. "Great fellows, love the water, just try hosing out their run -- they're right in the way of the hose!"

I broke the silence that followed with something that had been weighing on my mind.

"I was blown away by all the special food people brought

for their pets. Hot dogs and salami and liverwurst. And the written instructions about when and what to feed. We're going to have to limit some of that – meal time is first thing in the morning, and then late afternoon. I'm not having my life ruled by a pooch!" Little did I know what was in store.

"You know, Louis, cats are no trouble to board." I made it sound like I'd discovered some scientific secret. "No diarrhea, no anxiety, at least none that shows. The rocking chair for the Cat Room is a winner. Just let me have a moment or two of quiet, holding a kitty and rocking, and I'll get my sense of humor back in no time. Cats can be so stress- relieving. And they don't bark. It's peaceful in there. We should take Cat Room breaks. You should try it sometime."

That idea just got a grunt. Taking breaks was a sticky subject.

"Have you called your mother, Jenny? Tell her how it's going, wish her Merry Christmas and Happy Birthday?"

Yes, I should. I felt sad and guilty that she wouldn't be with us for the holidays, but that would have been impossible and anyway, she had said how much she was looking forward to spending them with my brother and his family. I'd miss her, but on the other hand it was easier without her, too. I thought of the Christmas when she became sick and what happened afterward. Hence the guilt.

"You could plan a visit to her soon," Louis added.

"You trying to get me out of the way? Then you can get things organized the way you want?"

"No, I need you here to keep things going, and I just need you here anyway!" He smiled as he added, "But I think you're going to need a bigger break than rocking cats can give you. Just keep it short!"

What a long way we'd come in the three years since Louis

had declared himself retired from his medical practice and I had told myself that I wouldn't move out of our old house. We'd retired, we'd moved – twice – and we'd built a house, a barn, a kennel, and a business. The business was still in its early construction stage and there were bound to be many changes as we found what worked and what didn't.

I'd never thought of myself as a country girl; I probably still wasn't one, but it was peaceful out here, away from the traffic and the everlasting shopping list. If I didn't need it, then it could wait, unless it was gas for the car. And no gas in the car was a great excuse to stay home. All I needed was a gas station – and one that sold milk. I made that pronouncement frequently and was reminded of my words later as more than a gas station that sold milk came closer and closer.

I stood later that night after we'd given the little Front Room dogs their last chance for a run in the yard, and looked over the river at the lights on the other shore. It was dark and cold. If I went in to the warmth of the fire in the living room, I could share a drink with Louis. Here I was, a city girl from Down Under, where the summer sun would be shining, and I was now becoming part of the American farming scene – and the business scene, too. People would bring me – us, really – their pets to care for, and they might never guess what my life had been like up to that point. They might assume I was American. Until they heard me speak.

"Where are you from?" someone would ask. I was tempted to say "Pasco," but they would just laugh.

"No, really, where are you from?"

"New Zealand."

"Oh, I'd love to go there. Hear it's a beautiful place."

I would agree that it is a beautiful place.

"So how come you live in Pasco now?"

And I filled them in with some of my history.

"And how did you meet your husband?"

More story. Then they would want to know how come we had a boarding kennel and how did we like living out in the country. Some of them remembered Louis as an orthopedic surgeon.

"He fixed my back." Or leg, or knee, or mother's knee, and how wonderful he'd been.

"And now he's taking care of dogs and cats. Bet he's enjoying it."

I'd agree. In fact we were both enjoying it, living out here in the country.

Sometimes I'd be asked how I liked living in the States. "Great," I'd say. "It's home now." Sort of, because I felt I had a foot in two worlds and had to hop back and forth from one foot to the other to keep my balance.

My mother had moved from one country to another – and she had always said England was Home with a capital "H." I could understand her need to return there, though I couldn't see myself returning to New Zealand to live. Not permanently, anyway. I had family here and most of the time I felt I belonged here. But this having a business and owning land in the country, as we now did, gave me a different view of myself. I could almost feel the roots growing out of my feet. I thought of Mother and wished she could see what we were doing. Would she understand? I should phone her, but I would wait until tomorrow -- it was too late tonight. There were times when, like tonight, the vast dark canopy of sky studded with stars so bright seemed to hover just above my head, while below me the river shimmered like a wide band of silver asking to be touched. I threw my arms out to test the space; it was so wide I couldn't touch the sides, and no neighbors could hear me if I wanted to yell and sing out loud. I thought I'd better go in and get that drink, before I started to think of more problems.

Settling in and Settling Down

THE RUSH WAS over. We survived those first important few months. We could call ourselves business owners. January came and went, and the number of pets boarded dropped so dramatically that Louis was sure someone was putting out a "whisper campaign." The slower pace gave us a chance to catch our collective breath and see what we wanted to do differently. I had the opportunity to go into recovery from my holiday and business obsessions.

I called my mother frequently to give her an update on our progress as business owners. I could visualize her shaking her head, mouth held tight with disapproval. She would change the subject quickly to ask how the children and grandchildren were doing. She had settled in to the Residence and seemed reconciled to being there. I couldn't allow myself to think of a time when she might not be there when I called, ready with her questions. I reported my progress with the kennel and what we did to care for the pets. She always had some advice to offer. Something about using our common sense was her usual contribution. I knew she meant well, and if I goaded her too much she would remind me that I had a "good brain."

I could not leave the kennel organization alone. I decided

we needed a manual of policies and procedures. My daughters who worked for large organizations assured me that such a manual was essential, and gave me a short course in putting one together. I started with procedures such as feeding, exercising, and cleaning, only to find that by the time I had composed it, we had found new and better ways. I gave that up, saying I'd take up the policies and procedure manual later on when we could all agree what they should be.

Next I studied the manual that came with the computer software, one that was written by some pediatrician in California who also ran boarding kennels and liked to write software. It was not the easiest manual to understand. I set it aside. When the computer gave a problem, I would study it again then.

I considered more ways to bring in business besides advertising. I wrote a newsletter to send to clients. The newsletter was popular because it was a good reminder of some of our practices, as well as snippets of information about pet care and quotes from various authors about their dogs or cats. The only drawback to the newsletter was the astronomical cost of postage.

My next move was to hire a groomer. She would bring in more dogs for boarding, as well as some income. We were about to put an advertisement in the paper, but someone must have let the word get out because Charmaine showed up one afternoon and announced that she would like to work for us if we were looking for a groomer. She liked the grooming rooms we had designed with both special dryers and a deep tub for bathing dogs. She started work the next day. In addition to her skill as a groomer, Charmaine was a breeder and professional handler, which meant that she spent many Saturdays at dog shows and brought some of her retrievers to the kennel to show to potential buyers. I was encouraged by the favorable reports we were getting from her customers. She didn't always dress as professionally as I had hoped. But when I encouraged her to wear a smock while working, saying that it looked more professional than the stained t-shirt she usually wore, she replied, "But it's a dirty job, Jenny, and this I can just throw in the wash and put on another one." She must have washed at least three shirts a day and changed into a clean one each time. I didn't have an answer for that.

She was always willing to talk about dogs and cats and her vast knowledge of breeds and pet health was intimidating to me, since I knew little. She liked to groom purebred dogs and was not happy that we boarded so many "rescued" dogs and cats, and those whose parentage was somewhat uncertain. But she had a following of loyal clients who kept her busy. I was afraid to ask the questions at first, but I needed some answers. Such as what is the right clip for a Shih Tzu? And what is a Shih Tzu, anyway? She had the answers to my pet questions. What was this breed, and what was that? Shih Tzus, Doberman Pinschers, something called a PBGV, Bostons and Boxers, Tibetan Spaniels that weren't spaniels at all, and then the cats – I knew what a Manx cat was, the one with no tail, but I'd not met the beautiful Himalayans before. She was more than happy to keep me informed. While Charmaine was an excellent groomer, there were some deficits in her performance, and the one that stood out for me was that she never cleaned the grooming rooms, leaving the floor covered in fur and wet towels. Her answer was that we should hire someone to do the cleaning, and that person could also do some of the bathing. "You don't pay bathers," she added. But we never got a chance to find out.

Between learning more about the computer, thinking

about that policy and procedure manual, writing the newsletter, studying up on the dog breeds, and working in the kennels several hours a day, I was keeping busy. .

There were no blips on the horizon...at least, none that we anticipated, and I didn't look very hard.

Two Erratics Come Together at Last

THE PHONE CALL came in April. My brother's voice. I knew it would not be good news. Mother wasn't doing very well; she seemed "poorly," and the nursing staff at the Residence suggested that I might want to consider a visit as soon as possible. That was about all I could get out of him, though the head nurse was more helpful and told me that Mother "could go any time, but at present she is awake and able to recognize us." That sounded terminal to me, so I was on a plane a day later and in her room the next.

I was surprised but delighted to find Mother sitting up in bed.

"How good of you to come -- but of course now you're retired, you have more time for travel. Did you bring Louis?" She looked over my shoulder as though expecting to see him walk in behind me. I replied that he had had to stay behind to run the kennel. She launched into a long list of complaints about some medical procedures she didn't regard as necessary, but which the doctor had requested. I decided to stay two weeks, perhaps longer, just to make sure and have some time with her in case she suddenly decided to "pop off," as my brother described it.

She and I spent the mornings and evenings together. I came in time for coffee and then read the newspapers to her. Her eyesight was bad now. It had been poor for years, but she insisted on using my long-dead father's glasses – "Dr. Rutherford told me they would be good enough for me too." She had never been one to spend money on something if there was an alternative just sitting waiting for her. But the most she could see was the headlines, so I enjoyed reading to her about English politics, and book and theater reviews. Then I put her in a wheelchair and pushed her around the grounds of the Residence. It was spring and the daffodils, bluebells, and white thorn were in bloom, their perfume filling the air.

"Women lose their sense of smell as they age; I've lost mine," she told me, not for the first time. I sniffed hard, afraid I might be losing mine already. She didn't want to go for a drive, preferring to sit and sleep, look out the big windows of her room, or go for wheelchair walks. She fell asleep easily and then would suddenly wake up to ask what the time was and if Walden – my father -- was coming soon. I found it hard to bring her back to the present day. We talked about times when my brother and I were little, of the war years when we spent time together, picnicking in the hills, riding bikes, reading together.

She wasn't interested in what Louis and I were doing with our kennel business. She had never asked a question about my work as a mental health professional. When I started to talk about my work, she would nod her head and close her eyes and fall asleep. Why did I continue to seek her approval, or at least her interest? Perhaps I didn't really need her approval, but I couldn't let it go.

I took advantage of some afternoons to visit local boarding kennels and see how the English did the boarding business.

I had visited kennels on previous visits to get some ideas on how they were designed here, but now with personal experience behind me, I could ask knowledgeable questions, and see things from a professional point of view. It was fun to talk to others in the dog and cat business and to find that things didn't look much different here from the way we did things back in the States, with one significant difference. In England, boarding kennels for pets are licensed by a health group that can close a kennel down if certain standards are not met. I was vaguely aware of these regulations but was surprised at the reception one kennel owner gave me.

"May I see your identification, madam?" The tall woman was not smiling as she continued her questions. "And you are with what agency? We had an inspection only last month, so I don't think you need to spend any time here! We passed with flying colors!"

I asked if my passport would do for identification, as that was all I had. I explained I was just visiting and had a kennel back in the States, and had thought to drop in. I tried to make it sound as friendly as possible, but I felt intimidated by the direction this visit was taking. It took some explaining, but after a while the woman softened and explained the situation when kennels were subject to unannounced visits from the licensing authority. I met some other kennel owners who, like this one, were not sure that I wasn't a representative of such an organization. Until I protested my ignorance of such a group, several were hesitant to talk with me, let alone show me around. What would we do if we had such a regulatory organization in our state? I'm not one to welcome regulations and restrictions. Sometimes they can present a standard for quality, but they can also hinder new and creative ideas.

Many kennels in England board only pets with health

insurance. This meant there would be no discussion as to who was responsible for any veterinarian bills incurred while boarding. We had a statement in our boarding agreement that a client signed, indicating that we would not be held responsible in such cases. Pet health insurance is available in the States, but few owners have it. I wondered if it had anything to do with the high regard the English have for dogs! After all, the Royal Society for Prevention of Cruelty to Animals was founded some years before the Royal Society for Prevention of Cruelty to Children. I found that all kennels gave the boarded dogs a daily walk – and at no extra charge. Some of the places those dogs were taken were through beautiful woods and along quiet country lanes, always accompanied by a kennel worker.

After such explorations I returned to Mother in time for afternoon tea. I never missed a meal at that place. We would share afternoon tea, scones and jam, sandwiches, and cakes -- all homemade. Then it was time to watch some television, particularly the evening news. We had a glass of sherry with the evening news -- a ritual that went back as long as I could remember. I remembered when my father came home from his medical practice, he and Mother would discuss the day's happenings over a glass of sherry before dinner. Now it was a pleasant way to feel a connection between us and the past. We ate dinner in her room; then we watched the shadows lengthen and dusk fall. Every evening across the fields from the Residence, we saw the farmer's cows walking in line toward their barn.

"I see them in the morning doing the same thing, going to be milked, I expect. And then I see them going in the opposite direction to spend the day in the field. I like the cows, very peaceful animals." Mother commented on the cows most evenings. I found myself missing the dogs and cats at the kennel when I watched those cows.

All too soon, it was time to leave for home. I felt a tremendous pull to stay with this small white-haired woman who wanted so desperately to continue her independence but would miss me when I left. A strong streak of independence ran through her. She was proud to say it was due to those northern ancestors of hers. Taking care of her children was still her job, and I saw she ached to do so.

"When you get to Heathrow, remember to go to the Terminal for Overseas. The taxi drivers always want to take me to the one for Europe for some reason. And don't tip him too much." She still gave me directions on what to do, where to go, and particularly what I should avoid.

"Oh, you shouldn't try driving. Too much traffic. I gave it up years ago."

The truth was she couldn't pass her driver's test at eighty years of age, but she would never admit to that.

We said goodbye without the tears I felt were ready to spill. She didn't want me to leave, and at the same time, she wanted to get this painful parting over. I felt the same.

"You'd better get going and get to bed. You've got an early start in the morning."

"Yes, Mother."

Would we see each other again? So much was left unsaid, could not be said, and all I could say was that I loved her. So few words to say so much. Her last few words were the important ones, and even then I didn't understand what she was saying.

"You've always done so well, Jenepher. I'm proud of you."

I'm proud of you too, Mother.

Home in the Columbia Basin

I WAS HOME. Back to Louis and the Columbia Basin, home to so many of us "erratics." It felt good to be back in my niche on the banks of the Columbia River with Louis and the kennels and all those dogs and cats that belonged to those people who thought so highly of us. I hoped there had been no disasters to change anyone's mind. I'd been away almost three weeks, longer than originally planned, but I was glad to have had the time with Mother.

The boxes in the spare room that would one day become the library were still waiting to be unpacked and still had the labels such as "kitchen stuff, jam jars, plastic containers and biscuit tins" or "winter clothes and children's jackets, small." That one should go to Goodwill – we didn't have any children around, and we'd been through one winter without the benefit of whatever clothes were still boxed.

On the other hand, Louis asked me if I had noticed any changes. His question told me that I had better notice them quickly and make favorable comments on what I saw.

"We've got lawn!" I shouted at the sight of the green velvet all around the house and out toward the lane and the kennel.

Louis had spent the time I was away completing the irrigation system, and it looked as though the kennel had run itself without me. What should I be doing? I needed a purpose. Everyone had a purpose around the place, even the pets. Everyone had a job and everyone was busy.

I decided it was time for me to get a dog of my own.

"I'd like to look for a puppy!" I announced one breakfast, after studying the Pets column of the classified section in the newspaper. I'd been thinking about a puppy for some time. Not anything special -- a yellow Labrador, perhaps. People seemed to think they were wonderful. They appeared in advertisements for everything from cars to shoes and women's clothes, the expensive sort. I hadn't put much thought into this idea. My not having had a dog previously had to do with my feeling that it wasn't fair to a pet to keep it penned up at home while its owner spent the day at work. Now that we had the kennel, I thought I should become acquainted with what it was like to have a pet. I'd get a better idea of what our clients' pet experiences were like; I could be of more help that way. Louis said that sort of thinking had to have come from being a mental health counselor, and was not a good enough reason to get a pet. Did I have any idea of what was involved in owning a dog? No, not really. But I could learn, I replied. We'd had Louis's hunting dogs as family pets, though I personally had had little to do with them.

I had a list of yellow Lab puppies and Louis and I went to look at several. I had no idea how to choose a puppy; however I now had several months of boarding kennel experience. We had boarded several yellow Labs -- not puppies, but fully grown yellow giants. Gentle they might be, but they all were full of energy, bounce, and the ability to clear off a coffee table with one swipe of the tail.

Labradors. That took me back in time. A long, long way back in time. I had a quick picture of a wet black nose poking through the slats of a wooden crate on a deserted railway platform. I was six when my father left for the Middle East and World War II. He had enlisted almost as soon as war was declared in 1939. He sent us a puppy, a black Labrador puppy. I remembered going to the railway station to collect the puppy. The platform was empty except for a crate at the far end, and a porter standing next to it. He kept turning his head from side to side as though looking for something – or someone. He let out a shout when he saw us and we hurried toward him.

"You looking for this dog, missus?" He addressed Mother.

"Probably -- I mean yes, we've come to collect a puppy."

"Well, you'd better get him something to drink soon. He'll have had nothing since Oamaru and that would be more than an hour ago and it's a hot place in that guard's van. Guard's been keeping an eye on him, but didn't want to let him out. He'd be gone in a moment."

That wet black nose appeared between the wooden slats of the crate, followed by two black paws, the sounds of claws scratching, and a pathetic yelping. We put the crate in the back of our old Ford and drove home. It might have been wiser to let the puppy out sooner. We opened the car windows, Mother muttering something about the crate needing to go on Mr. Ramsey's burn pile as soon as possible. When we arrived home we hurried the puppy through to the laundry tub, where Mother gave him a thorough washing. Even then, he smelled for days like a public lavatory and lavender soap.

His name was Victor Walden. Victor because of the war, and Walden after my father. He was Vic for short. He had a kennel and fenced run outside in the back yard. For the first few nights while he got used to us he slept in the back kitchen and the sound of his yelping and whining kept us all awake. Mother relented and let us take him and his basket into the hall outside our bedrooms.

He ate his basket and bedding. Vic ate shoes and anything that smelled good – and especially things that didn't smell so good, such as the manure from Mr. Ramsey's horse over the fence. He could reach anything on the kitchen table and frequently pulled the tablecloth so that more stuff came within his reach. He chewed on the legs of tables and chairs until our butcher took pity on us and gave us bones for him to chew. Then he dug up the garden to bury these treasures. Tony and I did our best to teach him some basic commands, but we didnt know what they were. Vic was certainly good at coming for food. He pulled hard in all directions when we took him for walks on a leash.

Vic was a bomb just waiting to explode. He barked at anything that moved, and at plenty that didn't. He went everywhere with us, through the bush, all around the streets and parks near home, mostly on a leash until we reached some field or open space where we could let him run. He chased sticks thrown for him, he chased cats and tennis balls, and he chased motorcycles. We loved him dearly. He was our friend and companion.

Mother saw him as a menace, out to destroy her peaceful life, as she told us many times.

"I don't know what your father was thinking of when he sent Vic to us." But then she would sit on the front steps with an arm around his neck and stroke his soft black ears. We knew she loved him too, until the next time he jumped up and grabbed at food on the table.

It never seemed to matter that he wasn't well-trained, since there were few cars on the road and our neighbors became used to Vic tearing through their shrubbery chasing a cat. He could be counted on to be sitting in the kitchen, mouth open, tongue hanging out, tail beating a tattoo on the floor as he waited for his meals. He was always friendly and never bit anyone.

From Mother's point of view, however, Vic was large, unruly, and had muddy feet and a tail that could do damage to furniture and clothes. He jumped up on people in his enthusiasm to be a friend. Most of the time he was just plain bad news, as far as Mother was concerned.

The day came, however, when Vic's behavior caused a major problem. All he did was bark at another dog. Tony and I were sure he never meant to upset the dog. Vic barked at dogs all the time and usually they just barked back. But this time was different.

Every afternoon an elderly lady and her little fluffy white dog walked past our house, though on the other side of the road. Vic had taken a dislike to this intruder in his space and would bark furiously at it. This afternoon Vic not only barked, but ran out of our open gate, across the road, and stood squarely in front of the little dog, barking and barking. As each bark grew louder, the little animal cowered down, and seemed to quiver in place. Mother called Vic home, but the damage was done. The little white dog now lay on the pavement, dead. The lady assured Mother that Vic had done nothing more than bark at her precious dog, but that had been enough. The poor little dog had died of fright.

Mother had had enough of Vic.

"I don't know what your father was thinking of," she said again, adding the fateful words, "Vic needs a good home in the country."

We kept a careful eye and a tight leash on Vic from then on. It was now too late. Mother announced one day that she had found someone who would take Vic to his brother's farm out on the Taieri plain.

"He'll have a good home there. Bob says his brother will use him to retrieve the ducks he shoots, and there'll be plenty of room for him to run. We'll drop him off next time I get the car filled with petrol."

Bob ran the petrol station we went to once a week for petrol. In spite of petrol rationing, Mother was allowed a certain amount because she was a medical doctor. Mother announced that Bob would take Vic off our hands. Tony looked very seriously at me as he said, "You know what that means, Jenny? A good home in the country? It means that Vic's going to be put to sleep."

No! Mother wouldn't do that. Or would she? She had had enough trouble ever since Vic had grown to full size. And now him killing the little white dog. What would he do next? I was too afraid to ask her where Vic was going. Even Bob's words when we arrived at the petrol station did little to reassure me.

"Mrs. Fitzgerald, my brother is looking forward to having this lovely dog. Here, come on, Vic -- come to Uncle Bob, he's got a treat for you."

Vic would do anything for a treat; it was one of the few words he understood. Vic pulled lose from me and bounded over to Bob, who grabbed hold of the leash and held it tight.

"Best be on your way, Mrs. Fitz, and I'll let you know how he does with the ducks," Bob shouted over Vic's barking. Vic could see his car and his family slowly moving away and he barked furiously, but to no effect. Mother was not turning around; her mind was not changing. I couldn't say anything.

I just watched while Vic gave up and sat down next to Bob and we drove around the corner and out of sight. I felt like a traitor.

It was several years later when I learned what had happened to Vic. Soon after Father returned home, we stopped at Bob's petrol station. I sat in the back seat, still remembering Vic's fate. I heard my father talking to Bob.

"So he turned out to be a good retriever? I'm glad to hear that. Freda found him more than she could handle. Always appreciated you taking him on." Who was Father talking about? It couldn't be? Vic?

"Your kids were real broke up about losing their mate. I asked your wife if she'd bring them out to the farm to see the dog, but she didn't think that a great idea. Probably right about that. That all you want today, Doc?" I was out of the car before Father could say anything more and drive off. Bob had disappeared.

"Dad, who were you talking about?"

"That puppy I sent to you when I left for Egypt. The one who caused your mum all that trouble. Bob's turned him into a fine retriever now. He's got a good home there." Father got into the car and we headed for home. "Want to see him sometime?" he asked.

"Perhaps," I answered. But we never did. I was just glad to hear Vic was alive and doing well. I always felt I should have done more for Vic. I didn't know what, though.

Probably my need for a yellow Lab had something to do with my memory of that wet black nose and the loud insistent barking from Vic so many years ago. But Labs hadn't changed much over the years, and my experience now with them at the kennel convinced me that I should look for a smaller dog. A Jack Russell terrier would be ideal: small, bright, intelligent.

But they seemed to come in pairs. And they had teeth, and ways of escaping by nipping at my ankles when I brought them food or fresh water. So no Jack Russells.

My mother had had a Welsh Corgi when I was a teenager. I had been away at boarding school at the time, and then at university, so I didn't get to know Taffy well. He had been a cheerful small dog who could walk miles and traveled everywhere in the car with Mother when she went to schools and clinics as school medical officer. His nose marks covered the windows of the car. I didn't remember any problems with Taffy – he was just a nice friendly little companion. I would look for a Welsh Corgi.

"He used to go for my ankles whenever I came to see you, Jenny," Louis reminded me. Did my mother put Taffy up to that?

I found Lucy, a Pembrokeshire Welsh Corgi. I fell in love with her small, bright dark eyes with black rings around them, her black fur saddle, red neck and white fur ruff, and white feet that she licked clean anytime she stepped in mud. I fell in love with her ornery disposition, her attitude of "I'll do it because I want to and not because you tell me to." She was a character and a dear companion, who taught me why people have pets and why they find it so difficult to leave these companions at a boarding kennels.

Lucy was joined by Buddy, and much later by Benji. The "Three Little Piggies," my granddaughters called them. More like Hobbits, I thought. Their backsides bounced as they ran after soccer balls, Frisbees or the cat, mouths open in a continual grin and seeming to listen to every word I'd say to them. They were obedient to a point, but after that they seemed to delight in finding a new way to do whatever they were instructed to do. Corgis have attitude. Opinionated, loving, and highly intelligent, these three were constantly waiting around my feet for me to trip over them. I found they were good listeners -- but did they understand what I said? Did it matter if they didn't? Their thick coats were forever shedding, and did that matter? They were each individuals with their own personalities, tastes, and preferences.

Lucy was the Queen Bee of the threesome. She was fed first, received the first treat, and had her leash put on first before going for a walk. She had an acute sense of time and at six o'clock in the evening she would push her wet nose against my knee and look up with those dark-ringed eyes. It was obvious what her sharp bark meant: "It's my dinner time." She was obsessive about playing with a soccer ball, pushing it along the grass with her nose, her feet flying under her. She was fussy about her appearance, licking her white feet clean even if they didn't appear dirty.

Buddy arrived later. He was supposed to be called Gus, but Louis took one look at him and announced that this dog should be called "Bud" – pronounced "Buurrd" -- and he should have a can of Budweiser in paw to complete the picture. Bud soon learned that he was next in line after Lucy when it came to food and the soccer ball. But both could chase the cat together.

Benji arrived much later. He was no longer a puppy when he came to live with me. His insecurities showed at once and he would stay close to me, afraid of losing the one he had bonded to so strongly. Puppies need to leave their litter home at a certain age if they are to feel confident about being on their own, and Benji had been left a few months too long before I met him. But he was the champion of Frisbee catchers. The other two couldn't touch him for a skillful leap and catch followed by the return to me, carrying his prize.

Corgis are chubby dogs with no tail and very short legs. They are a herding dog from the Welsh hills, where their speed and short legs made them very effective for herding cattle and sheep by nipping at the heels of the animals and staying out of the way of the kicking hooves. There is the Welsh fairy story that tells how the fairies chose Corgis to ride – hence the saddle markings on the backs of Corgis. I would look at Lucy and her black saddle and visualize the fairy queen riding her Corgi over the green Welsh hills. They have an acute sense of hearing and will round up anything that moves – soccer balls, children, cats, cars, other dogs, as well as the more traditional herds of sheep, goats, cows, and ducks. These three would bark at anyone who came to the door, then immediately fall over each other to welcome friend or stranger with wet tongues and noses.

Different Strokes for Different Dogs

IF ONLY WE had some control over our lives! But change happens, and we have to find ways to cope. Change always presents opportunities to learn. Rusty came to board soon after we opened. He presented us with plenty of challenges and opportunities to change some of our ideas about how to provide quality boarding care.

Rusty was a "rescued" dog.

"Rescued" dogs have not had the best of experiences from the past changes life has given them, so when they board they appear to remember those experiences that have been thrust upon them. This makes them very nervous about any new situation, and they may respond with growls and retreats into their kennel. Some will even threaten a kennel worker with bared teeth and every appearance of attacking if that individual moves in closer. The first of these canine refugees to come our way was Rusty.

Rusty was a victim of change early in his life, and even though he had found a wonderful home, he was forever haunted by the nightmare of his early years. We never knew what he might have experienced, but whenever we boarded him we could see that the experience for him was reliving some of those early losses. Rusty's owners were devoted to giving him all the care and reassurance possible, but they also had commitments that took them away. On those occasions they needed to leave Rusty with someone who would do the things they considered important for Rusty's emotional health. They didn't want to come home to find Rusty hostile, angry, and dangerous. Rusty was a large dark-furred German Shepherd, and their fear that he might become dangerous when anxious was real. Rusty had a large set of teeth, a low growl, and a way of looking at you that clearly said "stay away."

Rusty came for trial visits, an hour at a time, in preparation for much longer stays. Each time Rusty came to stay, his owners brought the same set of instructions about his care. Each time was a learning experience for us as we saw the importance to him of the familiar routines we followed each time.

We were all grieved when we heard of Rusty's death. I wrote him a letter in the Kennels Newsletter. If I talk to dogs, I could certainly write Rusty a letter. Here it is.

"Rusty, this one's for you. You were one of our first boarders. Ten and a half years ago Shirley brought you to us for a trial board. She was armed with hot dogs, carrot chunks and pieces of cheese. You just stared at us, a slight growl coming from your barely curled lips. I'm not sure who was the most terrified - you, Shirley or us. There were just three of us running the kennel then - and we were all still learning the business. Rusty, you taught us so much, and we are forever grateful for those lessons.

"We had several trial boards with you – about half an hour each time to begin with – and we would go past your run, give you one of those special treats, call your name, and say something about what a good dog you were. We each did that so that you would get used to seeing us. At first we would put the treat in your bowl, but there came the day when you took a piece of cheese from my hand! When you came for a full boarding stay we continued that practice – after all, it was part of what you expected. You always allowed us to come into your run and wash it out, but we learned never to look you in the eye. You didn't want a choke chain put over your head and around your neck, so taking you for a walk was out of the question. But one day you came out of your run and followed me down the aisle to the outside door. Only then did you allow me to put that choke chain around your neck. Then we went for a walk together.

"For ten and a half years, Rusty, you were our guest and we loved and respected you, watching you grow from an anxious teenager to a dignified old man. You were always a great walker and appreciated those treats and a comfy bed. Above all, you taught us the real meaning of caring for a pet, especially one with memories of bad times. We have cared for other dogs, and cats too, who have been abandoned and mistreated. They all learned how hard it is to trust us humans. I think it is the same for all the pets who stay with us, for however long their owners are away. They are not in their familiar surroundings and we must remember to treat them with respect and allow them the dignity to be themselves.

"We will miss you, Rusty -- thanks for the memories and for all you taught us about what it's like to be rescued."

Why Would Anyone Board Their Pets?

"HELLO, SAGEMOOR KENNELS. How can I help you?"
"You board dogs?"
"Yes, we board dogs and cats. How can I help you?" I anticipated that the caller wanted to make a boarding reservation, and I wondered what sort of dog this one would be.

"How much does it cost to board a dog? He's not large, a small Lab. Very sweet, real friendly."

I explained our fee schedule. There was a pause. The small Lab weighed something over a hundred pounds. Our potential client did a quick addition sum.

"That includes feeding?"

That included feeding, but not exercising, and not giving medications.

The potential client asked if there was space for his dog and gave the dates.

There was room, and I explained about our hours. I knew he wouldn't remember them, no one did, and I asked him if he wanted to come by and see our place. I'd mail him a brochure to give him more information.

"And don't forget to bring your vaccination records with you too. We need to see them."

The dog's name was "Bongo" and Bongo got his name because he used to jump up and down "just like a bongo drum."

Bongo came to board a week later – with his new shot records and his blanket, as I suggested. Bongo's owner explained that Bongo had never been boarded before and "... maybe he'll be a little shy – you know, sort of nervous – he may not eat at first, so I bought him a bone to chew on tonight."

I loved clients like this. Guess who was nervous? But this owner really cared about his dog, and just in case he became a little nervous, Bongo was going to have the joy of an enormous beef bone. I wondered what his owner would have for his anxiety? But I knew Bongo would be just fine, as I assured his owner, who was trying not to leave – not just yet.

"It's like leaving your child at daycare for the first time, or kindergarten. It's really hard to leave, but just give him a pat and tell him you'll be back soon." I personally thought it was worse than leaving a child in kindergarten. Parents heard all the gory details of that first day in school later from the child, but that beloved dog or cat can't say what it was like at the kennel.

At last that owner was out the door and away – one of many owners who found it painful to leave their best friend and companion in someone else's care. This was a story that we saw repeated many times, with minor variations.

Some people said outright that they would never, ever, board their pets.

"It would be too hard on him, or her, or them," they would say, adding that they would never be able to trust that the boarding kennels would do what they said they would do.

I knew just what they meant. Those deep brown eyes looked up at you as you gave a farewell pat, assuring them that you would be back in no time – a flat-out lie, and you knew they knew it too. But even if your pet has never shown any sign of anxiety when you leave, all the same, halfway down the road you wonder if he or she will be all right. What if they were sick? Would the kennel's staff know what to do? Had you left a phone number where you could be reached? The veterinarian's phone number? A cell phone number? And the nagging question – will he or she miss me?

I'd been there too, leaving my three companions behind at the kennel – and even if the kennel staff were our own, and I knew how painful it was to leave those companions whose language I didn't always understand. I would go over details in my mind. Favorite blankets, treats, a toy for each, Benji's Frisbee and Lucy's soccer ball -- had I put them in with their luggage? Because I would miss them probably more than they would miss me.

These experiences of our own enabled Louis and me to help first-time boarding clients to feel less anxious about leaving their pets behind and still take care of whatever business was taking them away. A tour of the kennel facility, a free afternoon trial board, reviewing what we did if a pet became hurt or ill while boarding and -- my favorite -- making a list. The list would have two sections. One list would have items for the pet to take to the kennel, such as a blanket, the owner's unwashed sweatshirt, toys, treats, and phone numbers where the kennel might reach the owner in case of an emergency. The second list was for the owner to take away, and it would have the phone number of the kennel, and what I called "tranquilizers" – and I didn't mean anything medicinal. I meant items to reduce anxiety, such as a book, a magazine, a planned anxiety-reducing activity – mine was frequently a list of places to shop.

I included my own list of what not to send with your pet, such as treats, food, or toys that were unfamiliar and would perhaps add to any anxiety the pet might be having about the new surroundings, or would be likely to induce stomach problems.

Some people had to leave their pets at a kennel because they didn't have anyone at home to take care of the pets once their own children grew up and had lives of their own. Same with the neighbors, who had grown tired of taking care of somebody else's pets. But either it was a vacation that beckoned and the pets couldn't go, or it was business travel or an assignment that didn't include bringing a pet along. Bob from Bechtel had two Schnauzers, but he couldn't take them with him on his Baghdad assignments. I told him not to go when the news of the place was so bad – I'd just worry, though I didn't think the Schnauzers would notice! He went of course, but there was the time when the Baghdad airport was closed and he couldn't get out of the place for a week and couldn't get word out for several days. I certainly worried and listened to the news with an anxious ear. But Bob returned and collected his dogs -- to their relief, his, and ours.

Then there were family illnesses, someone having surgery, and no one to keep an eye on the family. Weddings, births, graduations, anniversaries, funerals, and all the other family occasions at which pets never seem welcome are times to find a good caring boarding kennels at which to leave the cat or the dog. One young couple had a baby born too early – it weighed a little over a pound and was kept on life support in an incubator. Mother and baby were in Spokane and Dad commuted between the Tri-Cities and Spokane, leaving two small dogs with us while he went to join the rest of his family.

New fences to be built, carpets to be cleaned, remodeling to be done, fire damage to be fixed, workmen on the property, and so it went on -- all good reasons for pet owners to find someone to care for the pets. Sometimes owners had time to plan for boarding, but often an emergency would arise and the pet needed a place immediately. Louis and I felt it important to be able to open the kennel at any hour for such emergencies – we knew so well that we don't always have the control over our lives that we would like. Boarding kennels provide people a valuable resource for their pets at those times. We opened for such situations many times during off hours – even at two in the morning one time when a baby was arriving at an unplanned hour.

I wrote in a Kennels Newsletter about my personal experience of leaving my dogs behind while I flew off on vacation. I wrote:

"It's hard to leave your pet in someone else's care when you have to be away from home. After all, he or she is part of the family. I think it's harder on you, the owner, than it is on your pet. And you can't always understand what they are saying to you – though you can make a good guess. Certainly they will miss you – probably for the first twenty-four hours, perhaps longer, depending on how often they have been to the boarding kennels and how well they have been treated there. You will miss them – and every time you see another dog or cat you will think of your family member and you may even go up to this stranger dog or cat and give it a pat, stroke its ears, say something to the owner about how you have one 'just like this one' – only you had to leave it behind. Sound familiar?

"This January Louis and I went out to New Zealand – my roots – for four weeks. I left Lucy, Buddy and Benji behind in

WATCH WHERE YOU STEP

the care of our wonderful kennel staff. I was just like you – I felt bad about leaving them, I missed them every day, and whenever I saw another dog I would pat it, stroke its ears and tell the owner how I had three Welsh Corgis and then I'd add something about their names and their ages. If by some chance it was a Welsh Corgi that I was meeting then it was worse! Louis says two Welsh Corgi owners can take several hours discussing how wonderful their dogs are – and how much fur they shed and how they round up cars and more and more details.

"It doesn't matter what breed your dog or cat may be, purebred or mixed, it's just the same. As pet owners, we will spend time talking about these family members when we are separated from them. We all understand the pain at leaving and the joy when reunited. As the plane flies into Pasco it usually comes over the kennel and I send a little message down to the dogs –'I'm coming home, I'm coming home!'

"Don't tell me that you don't do this too!"

What They Bring with Them

CHILDREN LIKE TO bring a favorite toy when they spend a night away from home. Often it's a blanket, well-worn and stained, but it's their comfort blanket. The way it feels, the way it smells, its whole look, mean security to the child, separated for however short a time it may be, from its parents and all its familiar surroundings.

Dogs and cats are the same. Whenever a new client made a reservation, we suggested that they bring some of the pet's bedding, a favorite toy, something familiar. We added that what really makes a difference to the pet is if its owner includes an article of his or her clothing – an old t-shirt or sweatshirt for instance, unwashed, because the owner's smell is what would be most reassuring to the pet.

"Don't worry if it gets torn up," we told them, "your pet isn't trying to chew you up for leaving. But have you ever seen a little child suck on the corner of that beloved blanket when it's nervous? Same thing!"

Louis learned the importance of an old hunting jacket from one of his English Setters. He had been out looking for quail but when it was time to return to his truck, Cloud, his Setter was nowhere to be seen, would not answer his whistle, and didn't come back to his truck. Louis waited and waited until it was dark, but still no dog. He decided to leave Cloud's crate that he used for transporting her, and his hunting jacket in it with the crate door open, in case she came back. He placed the crate next to where his truck had been parked, and then headed for home. He phoned some of the farmers in the area to alert them to Cloud being lost, but nobody had seen her. He was afraid she had been caught in a coyote trap, or even by a hungry coyote. Next morning, as soon as it was beginning to get light, Louis set off for the place where he had left the crate. There was Cloud, lying on the jacket and delighted to see her owner again. Louis had similar experiences with other dogs that wouldn't come back to the car. We decided it must be Louis's smell on the jacket that told the dog Louis would be back. Certainly the jacket was important enough to the dog that he or she stayed with it until Louis returned.

New clients would frequently ask what they could do to make the boarding stay as easy as possible for their dog or their cat. I told them the story of Louis and Cloud and the jacket. As a result we saw plenty of t-shirts and sweatshirts, some nightgowns, socks, sweaters, slippers, and old jackets. A few were chewed up, but most could be seen somewhere close to the sleeping pet.

Dogs brought their beds, sometimes their crates, bedding, and blankets -- even pillows. Once a kind owner brought a feather pillow for his dog, and, without thinking of possible consequences, we put it in the kennel with the dog, who spent the night chewing it up – and we spent the next day chasing feathers. Some dogs are chewers when they board, and on many occasions we had to return, in a plastic bag, the remains of a comforter, blanket, or bed.

Many owners brought treats for their pets. Dog and cat

treats, special food – it was often something that the pet had never had before, but the owner thought something was needed to make up for being left at a kennel. Owner's guilt often brought out all the things a pet had not had before and might do better without! When I heard that little Suzie was being put in "jail" for a while, I knew the owner was feeling guilty. If the treat was something that the pet had never had before, the chances for an upset stomach were high.

Labradors, Chesapeakes and other retrieving breeds usually brought a "bumper" with them for play time. Bumpers are dog training toys used to teach good retrieving skills. They are about eight inches long and two inches round with a hole at one end for a piece of rope to go through We would be expected to throw the dog's bumper for him or her to retrieve during exercise time. Sometimes if we were not careful, the bumper would land on the kennel roof and we would have to get a ladder to retrieve it ourselves. Hunting owners believed their hunting buddies should have their bumpers in their kennels with them – sort of to remind them of the hunting season. Bumpers came in red plastic with sharp knobs on them that could cut when the dog pushed its retrieved "game" into your hands, or in canvas, which was softer. The canvas ones usually came in camouflage or white, well-ingrained with mud. These would be chewed to pieces if the dog preferred to take his prize and keep it away from the person throwing it. They would be certainly be chewed to shreds if taken to bed. Hunting dogs, such as Labradors, also came with huge camouflage-colored beds redolent with wet-dog dead-bird smell and often too big to fit in the doghouse. Their luggage always had the dog's name on it, as well as that of a prominent sporting goods store.

The favorite piece of luggage for many German Shepherds

was a ball. These came in all sizes and colors. Tennis balls were not a welcome item at the kennel, because they rolled under the kennel run chain-link doors and down the gutter to plop into the drain, from where they would disappear into the septic system, or have to be retrieved by one of us. Not a pleasant chore! We explained this to owners and offered an option of putting the ball away to be brought out at play time only in the yard where there was no chance of it getting into the septic system.

The tiny dogs that go in the front room brought small toys, usually ones with a squeaker in them. The noise of that squeaker could set the whole room of small dogs to barking. The canine owner of the squeaking toy would spend a great deal of time digging out the squeaker and chewing it up. Dachshunds brought special beds to dig and hide in. They burrowed into blankets or comforters, leaving their heads sticking out to watch for passing prey. In winter, small dogs brought a variety of sweaters and raincoats to keep them warm and dry when going outside. After shrinking some wool dog sweaters in the laundry, we decided to provide our own.

Cats brought mice – toy mice, but some of them looked so much like the real thing that on more than one occasion I was ready to scream for help. Two cats came in sunglasses, and several came wearing jackets, with hats to match. Photos and mirrors were often brought for very "special" cats. I don't every remember seeing a cat look at either.

More than once owners arrived and insisted on placing photos of themselves, framed, in a prominent position in the kennel so that their dog could see them and be reminded of whom they were missing. At least, that was the best reason for the photo that we could come up with. Two brought CD players to go in the doghouse, so their dogs could go to sleep listening to music. I thought that rather a good idea, but there was the danger of the pet, if a dog, eating the item. I put the CD players away until the dogs went home. But I agreed with the concept that dogs liked to listen to music. What we needed was to have some music playing in the kennels, especially at night. I thought about it, but couldn't think of a way to do it without it costing an arm and a leg. We had a radio in the Front Room and in the Cat Room, but the main kennels should have something. That was just another of my ideas that had to go on a back burner for a while.

I often wonder what, if given a choice, a pet would want to bring for boarding? Their familiar blanket or bedding and something that has their owner's smell. Perhaps some familiar treats so they can have their usual treat after a walk or at bedtime. Maybe a favorite toy. But definitely no new food and no new toy that needs to be chewed up – or just shoved in a corner of the kennel, since it's still got that new shop smell.

Cats

WE HADN'T PLANNED on boarding many cats. We had space for no more than twelve cats in our special Cat Room. We couldn't bring ourselves to call it the Cat House, and another name didn't come up. But we had put a great deal of thought into the Cat Room, with its system of six adjoining cages and five tall "condos" that could accommodate two or three cats if all were from the same family. There was the fish tank with its brightly colored tropical fish, and the windows gave a view not only of the bird bath and feeder, but also of people coming and going along the path to the house, or working in the vegetable garden. Some cats appeared to watch whatever was going on, and others just curled up and waited for someone to bring them their food. Most were let out while their litter boxes were being changed, though not to play with each other. Some were friendly, but others were not beyond a well-aimed swat with open claws at the hand that put the food in and poured the water into the water bowl. The cats were much easier to board than the dogs. They appeared less demanding of attention, and they usually didn't make the messes that the dogs were prone to make! But the biggest difference was the noise level in the Cat Room. Cats may meow and they may purr and occasionally hiss, but they do not bark and they do not jump up and down and they don't try to escape from their living quarters. Dogs bark, jump, and generally try to escape. The Cat Room was therefore a quiet, meditative place. I could visualize the boarders there all in some contemplative state, or waiting patiently for whatever life event was coming. They never seemed to be in any rush. In fact, the cats encouraged me to slow down and take a moment to sit in the old rocking chair and wait for any storm to pass.

Calvin was a memorable cat. He had enormous stripes and glowing eyes. He would close those eyes and stretch his mouth wide to reveal a great set of sharp teeth. Calvin was diabetic but always calm about getting his insulin shot, and not above a swat with claws out when it was over.

Christine came only once, though it was for a long stay. She was not a happy cat, though we wondered if that had something to do with her owners. She had white fur and arrived dressed in a blue jacket and matching eye shade and blue-rimmed dark glasses. Her owner insisted on making sure that Christine's condo was arranged to her liking – the owner's, that is – Christine made her wishes known later. The owner – two of them, husband and wife – wore the same blue- rimmed dark glasses and sun shades, though not matching jackets. They carried Christine into the Cat Room in a white crate decorated with flowers and brought her food and toys in a matching bag.

"Christine doesn't like to be touched by strangers, so you will be considerate, won't you?" was the owner's only request. They had left a long list of instructions for us and phone numbers for us to call in case of emergency. I assured them that we would all see that Christine was well cared for, and that the time they had spent with her would help her adjust to her new surroundings.

It was later when we saw how they had arranged Christine's condo.

"They've feng shuid it!" I exclaimed when I saw the result. Her crate was on one level facing toward a window, and on another level sat a mirror next to her water bowl – I was sure it was crystal -- and on the top level they had placed a blanket backed by framed photos of themselves. Toys were scattered around in an artistic manner.

Christine was sitting in her crate with her back to us. Her blue jacket was pushed to the back of the crate, but we never knew where it had been put originally. Christine had strong views on her owners' decorative ideas. By the end of the day she had removed the sun shade and glasses and pushed them down the ramp that led to her kitty litter box on the bottom floor of the condo. The glass water bowl followed, ending its life in several pieces. What excuse could we make for its demise? We probably overlooked it. But we retrieved the mirror and photos before they went the same way. At least we didn't have to clean up any more broken glass.

Once she had rearranged her furniture to her liking, Christine showed herself to be a regular cat who would sit and watch whatever was happening, ate her meals, and purred when she had her neck rubbed. She never showed her claws and it was only later that we discovered she had been declawed. I wondered what had led to that painful and, in my opinion, completely unnecessary operation.

Cats are different from dogs. They don't bark, whine, jump up and down, grab at you with their teeth – well, some do – and they don't grab at the hose when a run is being washed down and make you send the spray over yourself instead of over them – or the floor. They don't grab for a treat and they don't pour their kibble all over the floor and then upset their water bowl so you are standing in kibble porridge. And they don't push past you at the gate and run up and down the aisles setting all the dogs off in chorus.

Cats are peaceful. I enjoyed the Cat Room and its guests. But I am not a "cat person" and while I have a cat of my own, I don't have to have Nicholas around in the same way that I want my dogs around me. Cats may calm me, but dogs certainly energize me. I get ideas with a dog around, but not with my cat – it's just not the same.

I admire cats for their independence, their dignity, and their capacity to fend for themselves. Rudyard Kipling knew his dogs and his cats when in his "The Cat that Walked by Himself" he wrote "that when the moon gets up and night comes, he is the Cat that walks by himself and all places are alike to him." Even so, the Dog had the last word because "all proper Dogs will chase him up a tree." (Rudyard Kipling *Just So Stories*, MacMillan and Co, 1936) I remember the story's illustration where the Cat is walking down the road edged with tall trees and he is waving his tail in just the way all cats do. Nicholas, my large grey cat, will walk away from me in that way, tail high and waving slightly from side to side. There's a message in that tail. A "see you around" message. He's not too interested in hunting, leaving the dogs to do the chasing and catching of mice and small birds.

We once had a cat called Tammy. Tammy belonged to my daughter Catherine who, as we found out later, was allergic to cats. Tammy had many litters of kittens before we were able to catch her at the right time and have her spayed. One day we couldn't find Tammy anywhere. Several days passed before we heard pathetic little meows coming from somewhere. But where? We looked and looked, and then after another day or so passed and the meows grew louder, we saw her at the top of the telephone pole outside our back fence. But she wouldn't come down. We put food down for her and called, and still no Tammy. We didn't want her to jump for fear of breaking her legs, and she wasn't coming down the way she had climbed up. I called the Humane Society and the Fire Department and the telephone people. No one had any suggestions or offers of practical help. Then we saw a telephone ladder truck drive past the house. I ran out to signal that we needed its help, and explained the situation. Sure, they'd see what they could do with their ladder. They drove to the bottom of the pole and extended the ladder. The children and I and several neighbors all clustered around, heads raised, to see the man take hold of the poor little cat.

Tammy had different ideas; a true Kipling's cat that walked by herself, she wasn't having any man grab hold of her. She jumped. We all watched open-mouthed, gasping in horror. Tammy landed and bounced at least twice – depends on who is telling the story – and disappeared. We were all sure we would find her pathetic little body somewhere in the grass and sagebrush that surrounded the pole. The telephone truck men were very apologetic about not being able to save the animal. And then as we were all disbanding our search group, Tammy walked over toward us, tail raised with a slight curve to it as she waved a greeting, very slowly. Truly, she was a cat that walked by herself and all places were the same to her – the top of a telephone pole, or wherever she had been.

Someone at the Humane Society or the Fire Department told us not to bother trying to get a cat down from a tree or a pole. They will come down when they are ready. And if they get help getting down, they will just go right back up again. And that is what Tammy did. She had a few good meals, put a little weight back on, and there she was again – at the top of the telephone pole. We left her there. Ten days later, now very thin, she was back, walking her lonesome way in through the front door. She never went up that pole again. Which only proves what Kipling was saying about Cat, that went out into the "Wet Wild Woods, or up the Wet Wild Trees, or on the Wet Wild Roofs, waving his wild tail and walking by his wild lone."

Boarding kennels are not used for boarding cats as much as they are used for boarding dogs. Most people seem to find it easier to leave food and water out for their cat and have a neighbor check on the cat from time to time. The cat will do well left to his lonesome like this. There may be a little show of "attitude" when the owner returns, but that also happens when the cat owner picks up the pet from boarding. Cats will express their displeasure at being taken for granted and not included in whatever the owner was doing. We hear tales of a cat marking his territory or tearing up a bedspread, or even disappearing for a few days. "I'll show you." That's the message I'd get when I left Nicholas behind and he would stalk away from me, tail raised in that question mark way.

Changes in the Wind

SOME PEOPLE MANAGE change well and some even welcome it with open arms. I was like that once, but after the many changes presented by the kennel, instead of becoming more resilient, I was becoming less so. I labeled those changes as stressful events and over-reacted to even the smallest ones.

Dogs, I learned, are no different from humans when it comes to changes in their lives – and they certainly do not like anything new and unusual, whether it be food, where they sleep, or a new puppy moving into the family.

The change that topped all others, I believed, was coming to stay at a boarding kennel. Dogs reacted very negatively to this change. For some it was just a simple case of diarrhea for a few days when they arrived, and for others they might lose their appetite, act aggressively, and then, after a few more days, the diarrhea would strike. When we first opened we had so many dogs that had never been boarded before and never with us that we were on a constant clean-up brigade. But after a while and after more dogs were familiar with us and the place, the diarrhea occurred less and less.

Sometimes it's the little things that set us off. If Lucy's

water bowl was not where she wanted it, she would nose it around, spilling water as she went, until it was back where she considered it should be. I could understand this about Lucy. I too liked the water bowls in my life placed where I could see them. I didn't want to be surprised by any sudden changes in position.

Changes in our kennel life that could be labeled stressful events came about in any number of ways. There were major disasters, staff problems and problem staff, dissatisfied customers, and our personal health problems.

There had been many remarks about our kennel being so wonderful, so well-run, and how great a job we were doing that I was quite taken in. I believed them all.

Until this couple. They had been married five years. No children, just this dog. It was her dog. He'd never wanted a dog, and didn't like this one. It was a rescued dog and it probably didn't like men. It had peed on the husband's foot early on in the relationship. So the feelings were mutual. The couple went on many trips but he refused to take the dog – "I mean, it's a Doberman and we've just bought a new BMW." I could see his point. She wanted to leave it with the people "who give such great 'peace of mind care'." That was us – in our Yellow Pages ad. Each time she brought the dog for boarding, she said she expected the best because "everyone says so." But we cost money. He didn't like to part with a penny on "that damned dog of yours." She knew that, and we knew that too, because she told us. She always asked in advance what the boarding fees would be so she could write the check and hand it quietly to us when they picked up the dog. That way, her husband would never see the bill. This was a most important consideration, as it turned out, and one I should have remembered. But one Sunday evening, when the front office was full of owners, without thinking I handed her the bill, at the same time announcing the charges. Her husband stood next to her and when he heard the cost, he walked out to his car, not waiting for her, or for the dog. You could tell he was upset, even furious, and I knew trouble was waiting for someone. My first alert that something had come up was a phone call later that evening. From her. Irate was too mild a term for the tone of voice in which she accused me of charging too much, and of sending her dog home smelling of urine and with filthy bedding. None of this was true. But she was upset and had probably had a difficult time explaining to her husband the boarding fees, let alone the need to board.

Another couple had three retrievers. They were the husband's dogs. The wife had a little Dachshund, a plump little fellow, but always game to play chase with the other three. If she made the reservation, then all four dogs were to get exercise time together. If he made the reservation then only his three dogs would be signed up for exercise time. Problems arose when the dogs were picked up and the bill was presented. If she came and saw that her dog had not had exercise, then we were to blame. If he came and saw that the little Dachshund had had exercise with his three, then it was our fault for charging for something he had not requested, even though his wife had made the reservation and the exercise request. I decided that the only way not to get caught in these marital tussles was for the responsible owner to sign for whatever they were willing to pay for.

A sick pet was always a major concern. Sometimes a pet was so sick that we considered it serious enough to take it to its veterinarian. We knew that taking a pet to the veterinarian without consulting the owners could get us in trouble. On the other hand, there was the occasion when we did not take a pet to the vet, and not consulting the owners landed us in small claims court. That was a most unpleasant experience, and one I never wanted to go through again. I felt like a felon who had joined the ranks of those who had their names in the paper for misdemeanors and felonious acts. This pet owner accused us of ill-treating his dog, because we did not take it to the vet for a cut on its ear. When he took it to the vet and had to pay the vet bill, he decided we were the ones that should pay, and he took us to court to do it. The judge considered it a case where both sides had some responsibility for the situation and his decision was to "split the baby." In other words, we were both to share in the costs equally.

I was mortified by the whole business and decided we needed to have something in the boarding agreement stating that the owner would pay vet bills for any injury sustained while boarding with us. I went to our lawyer to make sure we had the wording right.

Louis thought I was over-reacting. I thought it was good sense. Our lawyer agreed with me and came up with the appropriate wording to add to our boarding agreement.

Boarding agreements and lawyers had no control over those events labeled natural disasters or "the worst winter in years," and weather could cause more stressful events than we had ever thought about, as we were shortly to find out.

The New Year's Eve Great Flood

ANOTHER HOLIDAY SEASON came and was rapidly going. We congratulated ourselves on managing this one so much better than some in the past. The weather had been worse than ever: colder, more snow than usual and no thaw forecast, but who could trust the weather prophets? In spite of that, we reached New Year's Eve without too much trouble.

That New Year's Eve became known as the Eve of the Great Flood.

During that day, a Chinook blew in with warm winds. It hit middle of the afternoon, and since we were closed all day and not expecting anyone to come to pick up a pet, we didn't worry too much. We listened to the drip, drip of the melting snow and dried off little wet feet of the dogs that had to go outside. There were several Home Style small dogs in the Front Room, but we had been able to exercise all the larger boarders in the morning when the snow was still solid underfoot.

The last time the little Home Stylers went out was about nine o'clock at night, and we could still hear the drip, drip, drip. The sidewalks were now almost clear of snow. It promised to be an easier day in the morning.

I woke up about midnight to the sound of rushing water. This was not a usual middle-of- the-night sound. This sound made me think of movies where the canoe is approaching rapids and the ninety-foot waterfall is just around the next bend. I thought I must have been having a nightmare, but the sound continued. I woke Louis. Had a pipe broken under the house?

"Louis, I can hear water running fast, or else there's a flood coming from somewhere." I was out of bed and staring out through the window, thinking I would see some wall of water approaching at full speed. But there were just the bare trees bending in the wind, and clouds scudding fast overhead. Louis joined me and we stood still, listening.

We put on boots and jackets and trod gingerly through soggy lawn out to the edge of the property that overlooked the lane.

There was no lane. Instead there was a torrent of water pouring off the alfalfa field behind the kennel and rushing down what had once been the lane, taking great chunks of dirt and rock with it. As we watched, we saw a side of the hill collapse into the waters and dissolve into thick muddy paste. It was dark and the wind rattled the elm tree next to us. It was a warm Chinook wind that would thaw the snow and send it down the lane. Somewhere there was a moon, obscured at that hour by the clouds. But its light was enough for us to see the damage that had been done.

"Louis, we're stuck. How long do you think this flood's going to last?"

"Until the snow is all melted. Trouble is, the ground beneath is frozen solid and it's going to take a lot more warm wind to unfreeze it. This should be finished washing down by morning. Then we can see the damage."

"Where's it all gone to?" I had a sudden horrible suspicion where all this water and mud and rock might have ended, since it had to have gone somewhere. Our lane ended at Columbia River Road. which was a heavily used road connecting the Columbia Basin with Pasco, Richland, and Kennewick. But on the other side of Columbia River Road from our lane was another road that went to a new housing development with some large expensive houses sitting on the bank of the Columbia River.

"Probably it's blocking Columbia River Road," Louis said. "It may have traveled across some of the yards of those new houses below the road, the ones overlooking the Columbia. In fact, it's probably traveled all the way into the river. Some folks may be pretty upset about all this."

"Well, I'm a little upset myself now," I said. "This is scary." We heard a sound like a groan, and the crash as more rocks hurtled down the hillside. My boots were leaking and my feet were wet and cold.

"It's going to take a hell of a lot of work getting that lane put right again," Louis said.

"And we have people coming in tomorrow evening to pick up pets. How will we get them in with the lane like that?" I asked. What was it going to take to get all those pets out, I wondered? Depressed and worried, we went back to bed. I couldn't sleep.

"You want an early breakfast? Or a drink, or something to eat?" I asked.

"Got any bacon and eggs? Coffee? Let's see, it's almost five o'clock; we should be getting up soon anyway. No use expecting the paper to be delivered – the box has probably been washed away."

Over breakfast we listened to the radio but there was no

news of floods in north Pasco. *We're just not that important,* I thought.

In the daylight the next morning, the lane looked worse than we had imagined. An eight- foot-deep canyon now replaced the neat gravel lane, once lined with juniper and sagebrush. We stood together and looked at it again. Muddy water still moved down but at a slower rate; the worst had already happened. An occasional rock tumbled down the steep sides of the newly formed canyon.

We shared the lane with our neighbor, Wanda. Louis and Wanda spent time reviewing what could be done now and what would have to wait, who could help us, and since this was a holiday time, was there anyone willing to come out and work? They contacted someone with a heavy-duty backhoe to level the lane and someone else with a dump truck to bring in loads of gravel. The county road folks were great. Of course the mud had slid across their Columbia River Road, cutting off access for a great many people, so they put up notices stopping people from using that route. By now the radio had spread the news too, but as it turned out, not everyone listened to the news or read notices.

It would take time to fix the lane – more time than just the next few hours. It would be many days, if not weeks, before it could be used. A twenty-four-inch drainpipe would be installed, and a bulkhead constructed to direct water into the drainpipe. In the meantime, while that muddy water continued an alarming trickle, Louis and Wanda were negotiating for the necessary twenty dump-truckloads of gravel and heavy-duty backhoe to do the grading and leveling.

The kennel still had to function. The holiday season had left us with a large number of boarders, so Mary and I concentrated on feeding and cleaning and exercising.

There remained the problem of getting people in and out with their pets that Sunday evening. Since it was a Sunday we were closed during the day for customers, and open only in the evening for people picking up their pets. But it was the day after a long holiday period, so there were more than the usual number of owners coming to pick up their pets. I phoned all the owners due to come in that evening, and explained the situation. We had a back lane behind the kennel, used mostly by farm machinery. It led out to the main road. But it was little more than a track, deep in mud, and only trucks and SUVs would make it through to the kennel that way. However it was the only way out now we had no lane.

"Do you have a truck or an SUV?" was my question to expected owners.

"No," was the usual answer.

"Then Louis will meet you with your pet at the corner of Columbia River Road and Helm Road. Wait for him there, and he will collect payment at the same time." I gave the clients the total charges for their pet's boarding stay and hoped I had called everyone who would come out that evening. It would be dark. I warned people that they should look out for the signs saying Columbia River Road was closed, and how to look for our back farm track. I was sure there would be someone who would not see the turnoff, and there were those whom I had not been able to reach. It promised to be a difficult day and a worse evening.

There was George, anxious to get to his spaniel puppy. George hadn't noticed the barricades and signs the county had posted, nor the barricade Louis put across the lane's entrance. George swung the wheel of his SUV to the right and ploughed straight into the wall of dirt, and he was stuck fast.

The first we knew of George's plight was when we heard

the sound of a man's voice coming from across the lawn. The swear words used told us this was not a happy customer. Then a dark figure appeared at the door and muddy hands reached for the door handle. The swearing continued as the door was flung open and a man we recognized as George, owner of a spaniel puppy, stood looking at the three of us.

"I want my dog and I'm not going back down into that canyon again. Someone's going to have to drive me home." There were a few more swear words to describe his experience. We understood he had climbed out of his SUV to sink up to his knees in soft dirt liberally laced with rock and gravel that had been washed down by the flood waters. From there he could see that it would be no use attempting to struggle up the lane, sinking in knee-deep at each step. He decided to take to the side hill and climb up. The hill was steep, with little to grab hold of except the occasional sagebrush and rabbit brush, and the footholds were slippery and threatened to give way at each step. But he made it to the top and staggered over soggy lawns to the kennels.

"I just got off a plane from California after a wedding, and these were my good clothes. Just look at me now. Bubbles won't recognize me!"

Bubbles was his spaniel, and my guess was that Bubbles would recognize her owner under any circumstances.

"Believe me, you folks might be the best pet care in town, but I'm damned if we're coming out here again." And there were more words from George emphasizing his feelings about us and our services.

We were at a loss as to how best to be of help. Louis found the best approach. He suggested that George use the bathroom to clean up and that in the meantime, Louis would take his Bronco around to where George was stuck and retrieve a suitcase so he could change into some clean clothes. The swearing lessened, and George handed Louis his car keys.

"Don't know why I locked it, but there's a suitcase in the back. Appreciate it."

George recovered considerably once he had cleaned himself up. I gave him hot chocolate but wished I'd had something a little stronger. I must have said something about this, because the next thing I knew, George was waving a bottle of brandy before my eyes.

"Never travel without a little something to warm an evening, but I didn't expect I'd need it as much as I do tonight. It was in my suitcase that your husband so kindly delivered to me. So, skol or slante or here's mud in your eye!" And he poured some into his cup and into mine. Louis was out delivering a dog to someone waiting out on the main road. Most people were understanding and helpful, appreciating the way we helped avoid the possibility of their getting stuck in the back lane by Louis coming with his truck to meet them.

Later, warmed by a second cup of hot chocolate and brandy, George was telling people how lucky they were not to have run into a wall of mud – as he had. The details of his story became more and more like the script for a horror movie – mud and ice falling all around him, rocks about to roll on top of him, the hillside a mountain threatening to collapse. I felt we should be asking the governor for emergency relief funds after a while. George took over the job of making coffee and hot chocolate while he waited for Louis to help with his car.

We still faced the next morning, and the mornings after that. Louis and his Bronco ferried pets and owners back and forth along the back farm track where the ruts were becoming deeper and the mud stickier. Several times Louis had to pull a car out when its driver had not taken our warning seriously when we said only SUVs and four-wheel drive vehicles could make it. Some loads of gravel were spread, and that helped.

The damage to the lane took longer to fix. And the worst was still to come. A thick cover of ice still lay over the alfalfa field. It had to melt sometime. We hoped it would melt slowly. It didn't. A few days later, it rained. Once again we woke to the sound of water rushing somewhere. The melting ice washed the lane out again. All those dump-truckloads of gravel went down and across Columbia River Road and over someone's new yard before it reached the Columbia River. We were back to where we had been on New Year's Day, several thousand dollars poorer.

A couple of days after that second flood we were once again gazing down at the eight- foot deep and twenty-foot wide grand canyon of Sagemoor Kennels. The repair work had not started but the flooding was over. There was no wind and in the stillness we heard a voice coming from somewhere far below. A man was standing there. All we could see was a balding head several feet below the top of the canyon wall. He looked up at us and asked in a demanding sort of way if we knew who was responsible for all this devastation, and in particular for the damage it had caused to his yard. We gazed up at the sky without saying anything. We might have been waiting for a word from on high. Then one of us muttered something about the lane being a natural drainage system for more years than we cared to say. And we walked away. We never heard anything more from whoever it was down in the canyon. But I expected a summons for another court appearance any day. That man had sounded very upset. But nothing happened.

The problem had been that the bulkhead built to prevent

the water going around the 24- inch plastic drain pipe had not been able to deal with the large quantity of water coming from the rain and the melting ice. The water simply went around the bulkhead and once again rushed down the lane, taking all the gravel with it.

This time it took many more dump-truckloads of gravel, a wider metal drain pipe, a larger culvert, and a better-engineered system to deal with any excessive water. We've had heavy rains, melting snow and ice since, but never again has the lane been washed out. Once was enough, but twice was just too much. There is only so much a business can do to make sure the weather is under control.

This time it got us down but not washed out with the rocks and mud that eventually must have reached the Columbia River. Our facility was climate controlled, there was good heating and air-conditioning, and the only thing that might interfere with those was a power failure. Sure enough, we had one that must have lasted overnight and longer. It was enough that Louis decided we needed an auxiliary generator to produce whatever power was needed to keep the pump working, the heaters pushing heat into the kennels and the computer puttering along. It was a business saver on more than one occasion.

While we thought we had all the elements under control, there was one source of power over which we had no control, and just as we thought we had all the answers, something would come up to show we'd not thought of everything. And that was the staff.

Staff Changes

THE DOOR SLAMMED behind her and with some angry accusatory words, Charmaine, our groomer, left. We didn't do things the way she wanted and she flew into a tirade of name-calling and called it quits with us. That was the first staff change. While I worried that we might lose boarding clients, her resignation had no effect that we could see. The event was like water off a duck's back to Louis.

"We'll hire someone else," Louis said simply.

I felt a heavy blanket of gloom and doom descending on my shoulders.

We had failed to negotiate some accommodation with the groomer, and from what she said, she held me responsible. We decided to wait a while before looking for another groomer. "Temperamental" was the word someone used for groomers, and this one had been more than a little that way. Bu her leaving didn't seem to have any effect on our clients.

So we waited.

The next change came when Mary, our full-time kennel worker, announced she was getting married. It was not unexpected news, but we had made no plans for what action to take when she said she would be leaving in a short while. "But I'll wait till you find someone," she assured us.

The first concern was the need to hire someone to take Mary's place while she was still with us and could do some training of the new person. We put an ad in the paper in the Classified Help Wanted section. We hadn't done this before and so we put in our phone number for applicants to call. Big mistake. The phone never stopped ringing, and most of those interested in the job were unsuitable. Louis decided I was too kind-hearted, that I would give the job to anyone who said they loved animals.

"No, Jenny, no ferret lovers allowed."

"She said she loved cats too, but just wasn't sure about dogs," I answered.

"They have to be sure about dogs. So let me take the phone calls."

I was delighted to get rid of that duty.

We asked for resumés from the ones that sounded as though they might do the job. The resumés showed up the gaps in experience for several possible applicants. "Red flags," we called them. Someone who had held six jobs in the past year wasn't going to make it with us either. Children were another red flag, since the apartment wasn't big enough for a family. "No driver's license but still driving" told us something about a person's value system. "On disability but able to work" didn't cut it either. At least "Need a place to live" was being honest, but he had no work experience except delivering pizzas. We were impressed by the ones that wrote they had volunteered at the Humane Society. I thought that spoke well of them, especially as they were all teenagers or young adults. It was only later, and after we had hired and fired several, that we learned this meant they were doing their community service for some offense.

We narrowed our list of possible employees down to a young woman who had had experience at a veterinarian's office and who was attending the local community college. She said she was "obsessive" about cleaning. Cleaning kennels and walking dogs were just what she liked best. She also had computer skills. Just what we wanted. We hired her. But we had taken longer to find someone than we had planned, and Mary had only a few days to do any training. We weren't worried. I was happy to continue training for the front desk and reservations, and Louis would show her all she needed to know about cleaning, sanitizing kennels, and exercising dogs. I brought out my unfinished Policies and Procedures Manual and added some more items to it. She would do all right if she just followed the manual and Louis's instructions about cleaning and exercising dogs.

Heather moved into the apartment. Her family helped her. I thought that a good sign – family support was important. I was confident that while we'd miss Mary, this young woman would fit in well with us. She was a quick learner, met the public well, and obviously loved the pets.

Another Thanksgiving came and went and if I wasn't entirely happy when Heather announced that she would need Thanksgiving afternoon and evening off because her mother wanted her to be home with the family, I agreed that this was a family occasion and we'd feed pets earlier in the afternoon. Louis and I would give her a hand as we'd agreed, and then we would all have more time for the evening. We had family home too, and so everyone helped with the afternoon feeding and exercising.

Christmas was coming up and I was going to have time to do cards and some baking, for the first time in two or more years. Even the weather was calm and warm, and no snow or

WATCH WHERE YOU STEP

freezing temperatures were forecast. The lawn was up and the few trees still had some leaves; the maples had about six red leaves between them.

Heather was an almost perfect employee – or so we thought. But there was always some small thing happening that took her away from working at the kennel. One week it was a test to study for, another it was a paper that had to be written and handed in that afternoon. Or her mother had declared some emergency at home for which Heather was the only person she could trust to help. Other times it was things that Heather expected from us. One weekend there might be too many dogs for her to walk; another time she wanted our help sanitizing kennels, which she should have done – but she had to study for an exam! Sometimes I wondered how long our relationship would last. I was getting rather frustrated. But we survived almost another year. Then Louis and I took a trip to Kansas to see his family and friends.

We were gone about a ten days. It was a slow time for the kennel – early November and before the Thanksgiving rush. It had been planned for some time, and we left Heather well prepared for all emergencies. I promised to call her daily if she wanted me to. No, she thought she could manage things "just fine" by herself. Louis and his brothers and friends were spending time together – that male bonding experience – hunting quail and pheasant. I phoned frequently and it was always the same, some unexpected problem had arisen, but Heather assured me that she had coped "just fine."

When we returned, Heather told us we had been away too long and she had had to work extra hard to keep up with all the work! I think she might have been expecting a bonus. I had anticipated the need for some reward and had brought her some items I knew she would like. We were back on good terms, and ready for the holidays again.

But on Christmas Day, Heather got even. Before she had fed any dogs or cats, she announced to Louis that she was quitting. The work was too hard. She wasn't getting enough time with her family. Her mother was upset that we had left her alone while we went to Kansas. Small but significant problems that had come up before now had taken on more weight.

We persuaded her to stay until the New Year, and we went through the advertising process again. At least she had given me an excuse for not sending Christmas cards out again.

As Louis said, "You have to grin like a jackass eating briars and get on with it."

We found a new kennel worker with little trouble, though once again we failed to see the red flags that were there. In addition to one full-time employee who lived onsite, we also hired another two part-time employees. Business was up and it was taking more time to provide the sort of pet care we wanted. Our reputation was growing. The faces of pets and their owners were familiar, as we greeted returning clients. We heard stories of dogs barking with excitement as their owners drove up the lane, and one especially beloved Siberian Malamute would sing from the back of his truck as he was driven into the parking lot.

We found another groomer who also introduced more potential boarding clients to the kennel. While finding staff, interviewing and checking references, was time-consuming, it was nothing to the time and effort spent on training them. The first time we went through the hiring experience we learned a great deal, but we had to go through it many times and become much more hard-nosed about it. I should say "Louis," not "we," as he was much better at the hiring and training process. But we were slowly becoming a working team, sharing in the business of management, and we were learning a great deal about the habits of our boarders as well as those who liked to work with them.

Escape Artists and Gate Crashers

DOGS ARE NOT unlike humans, but we learned a great deal about dogs and cats that showed us they do not behave exactly as humans do. Of course humans aren't put into confinement unless they have broken the law, but pets don't have a great deal to say about being put in a boarding kennel while their owners are away somewhere, leaving only a toy and a blanket to remind the pet that things might get better someday.

Some dogs have strong feelings about being boarded and put in a kennel, however big the attached run may be, and they may make it their goal to get out of the run by whatever means necessary.

Cisco was just such a dog. He was a large Rottweiler, about one hundred and fifty pounds of muscle, charm, and a great fondness for being with people at all times. He probably thought of himself as being no different from the humans who let him use their cave and threw him his bones – his owners and us at the kennel. He was an escape artist par excellence, a Houdini of the canine world.

The first time Cisco escaped was in the winter. We woke one morning, early, not much light in the sky yet, and were surprised to hear a sudden bark outside. The "I need to come in" sort of bark. We opened the front door and there was a large dark shape sitting on the porch, wide mouth spread in a delighted grin, tongue hanging out with a tendency to drool at its tip. We knew it was Cisco, though we had no idea why he was sitting on our front porch. Our immediate thought was to find a leash and take him back to the kennel where he belonged. Had someone come to work early and left a door open – several doors in fact – or had someone left some open the night before? And just how long had Cisco been running free? He followed us into the kitchen as though he lived with us – he might as well have lived with us, we were to learn. He was agreeable to being leashed and to having a dog treat or two, before being led back to his kennel. The gate to his run stood open. That was the answer. Someone had failed to close the dog-proof latch fully, and Cisco had been able to push in open. But that didn't quite answer the question as to how he had managed to open three doors, all of which he would have had to open by pushing down on the handle and then pulling the door toward him. No one had the answer to that. We didn't worry – somehow they must have been unlocked, and perhaps the wind had blown the outside door open. But the next day he was at the house again, with that grin and drool that endeared him to us all. We put him back in his kennel – and added a clip to the dog-proof latch that would prevent another escape.

It didn't. This time we decided that he had climbed the six-foot chain-link fence around his run and escaped that way. So we built a roof to the run. He again greeted me the next day at the front door when I went out to get the paper. His grin told me he knew I was coming. He always was happy to be escorted back to the kennels, where he knew his breakfast would not be long in coming.

There remained two other possible avenues of exit for us to close. In order to get out of the kennel and over to the house, Cisco had to have opened the main front door. At all the other kennel exits he would have run into the seven-foot-high fence topped by more fence leaning inwards to discourage climbers. The front door would need a deadbolt. The deadbolt put an end to the early-morning meetings at our house. Poor Cisco was trapped, but not in his kennel. He could still open his kennel by pushing up on the lid. The fasteners to these lids were easy for a dog of Cisco's size and strength to push open; then he could lift the lid, and wriggle his way out. Easy! All we had to do was put something heavy on the lid so that Cisco couldn't lift it. We tried one forty-pound sack of dog food, then two forty-pound sacks, then some lead weights. Cisco used it all for weight training. In the end we had to admit defeat, and Louis measured a two-by- four to stretch across the lid, drilled holes, and bolted that heavy piece of wood across. That put an end to Cisco's breaks for freedom. It wasn't freedom that Cisco wanted so much as a place at that caveman's fire and a bone to gnaw on. He wanted to be with people. During the day there was plenty of activity to satisfy him, but at night as it grew quieter, he must have thought it was time to find some action somewhere. I always thought it was that old instinct telling him it was time to find his caveman family.

Cisco's owners were fully aware of Cisco's behavior. We all agreed that this was one clever dog: intelligent, a problem-solver, and definitely a people dog. But each time a reservation for Cisco was made, Louis reached for the drill and the two-by-four, and bolted the doghouse lid shut.

Cisco wasn't the only one to make a break for freedom. Jesse was a Border Collie. Border Collies, like most of the herding breeds, do not take well to being kenneled. They are always on the lookout for the danger lurking in the distance, the signal from their shepherd to move the flock of sheep this way or that. The presence of other dogs makes them uncomfortable, so above all, they need to be free to go where their keen intelligence tells them they are needed. If kenneled, dogs like Jesse will either mope in the back of their doghouse, or plan an escape. Jesse could see the escape route, and it was over the top of the six-foot chain-link fence that surrounded her run. We put a partial roof around the top of the chain-link. That suited her very well. It was an ideal perch for her to sit on and watch the action below before she jumped down into the walkway and made her way to the door. She would place her paws on the handle, pull it down and toward her and slip out. She never could open the doors to the outside, or she would have been off and away. But she found the doors to the storage rooms where the pet food was kept. We would find her helping herself to some snacks. We added a full roof to the run and that became Jesse's run whenever she was with us. She learned how to open the so-called dog-proof latch to her run – and we added a snap to the latch. That was the end of Jesse's attempts to gain her freedom.

Nor all escape artists let us know by barking outside the front door. One gave me a real scare.

It was a dark night, no moon, but still some light. I was fast asleep. Louis was away at a field trial. The sound of the security alarm woke me. It pealed its warning twice. Then another two peals. That meant that one of the kennel doors to the outside had opened and shut. Twice. I sat up in bed, my heart beating fast. I tiptoed through the house and peered out to see if I could see any sign of someone over at the kennel. The security alarm sounded again, twice. Someone was certainly moving over there. Perhaps they were taking animals out. Who knew what was going on?

I phoned 911 and after explaining who I was, where I lived, and what was the problem, I was told a sheriff's deputy was on his way. Not to worry. I waited, and a few more warning sounds rang out. But no sheriff. Twenty minutes passed. I thought I caught a glimpse of someone or something moving out on the exercise yard. I was by now convinced that someone was out there and they were letting our boarders out before driving off with them to some unknown destination. I called the sheriff again and was assured he would be there shortly.

I decided I could wait no longer for some help. I called Henry and Sandy, my son and daughter-in-law, who lived a couple of miles away. They were over in two minutes and assured me there were no strange cars of trucks parked anywhere close, and no lights on in the kennel. Henry went out to the kennel to see what might be going on, and came back to say the only problem was one large German Shorthair Pointer who was having a great time by herself dancing all over the exercise yard, but now was ready to go back to her run in the kennels.

"Where do you want me to put her?" he asked.

We escorted Daisy – for that was her name, and she was a new boarder -- back to her run. The gate was open, and she had obviously been one of those who knew how to open the latch – she earned a special clip on her gate and the notice in her chart that this was a "gate opener."

I called the sheriff's department to say that it was too late now and that we had caught the culprit. They were a little surprised to hear what had happened.

Opening doors and gates were not the only means of

escape, and other escape artists used other methods of dealing with their need to be out and away. Some had special talents for escape.

Gate crashers give no warning about their strategy for escape. Gate crashers come in all sizes, from large Labradors to Bulldogs, small Schnauzers and Jack Russell Terriers who look at you with head cocked to one side as though to say, "I'm doing my best to understand you." You'd think butter wouldn't melt in their mouths.

The expert gate crasher will sit quietly and wait for a staff person to come along to clean the run, fill the water bowl, or put out food. Sheba was such a gate crasher. Her head up, tail wagging a welcome, she was one large, possibly overweight, German Shepherd who looked as though she just wanted me to come in and give her a pat as I put her food bowl down. Her mouth was wide with that grin that seemed to say: "There's no hurry, Jenepher, take your time." And every time, I believed that smooth routine. I'd unlatch the gate and, food bowl in hand, would take that first step inside, gate open behind me.

Timing is everything. Before I knew it, Sheba slid past me, her nose first; then I felt her shoulders push past me and through the gate. I turned to grab her collar, to try to pull her back inside the run. She took that for a sign that I wanted to play, and in a moment she would be jumping up and down, then her feet landed on my chest, the bowl flew out of my hand, and kibble was scattered all over the walkway. She rushed up and down the walkway, back and forth, while I leaned over to pick up the bowl and scrape in some of the kibble. Then she gave me a push and this time I lost my balance and fell onto the wet floor. Water and the food turned into a porridge-like mixture that quickly spread all over the walkway.

I would be up again and wondering if there was a leash or something to throw around her neck. But Sheba knew well how to avoid any of our attempts to capture her. She received a great deal of encouragement from all the other dogs who were barking, howling, and looking for ways to join their lucky mate. There was a leash hanging on the hook, as it should be, next to the main door out from the kennels. I reached for it. Sheba saw me do this and decided to lend a hand -- or rather, a paw -- and she too reached up, pulled the leash out of my hand, and let it drop into the gutter where all the dirt goes. It too was now wet and covered in something I would rather not know about. But I was beyond any such concerns. I just wanted to corner this renegade and put her back in her run. I did it at last, and Sheba acted delighted when at last I was successful. She walked sedately into her run – with me beside her. Now we were once again both inside the run with the door latched and I had to get out – without letting the gate crasher out. Sheba knew the opportunity this moment presented and she planted herself between me and the gate. I told myself not to be fooled by the quiet demeanor Sheba presented. The moment I tried to open the gate and slide past her would be the moment she would dive through that narrow opening. As I thought about it, I could see she had the instinct to dive for the prey the moment it moved and, once again, we would both be outside of the run, and round two of the game started. There might be rounds three and four to go through before either help arrived, or Sheba became bored or thirsty and retreated to the run for a quick drink. I learned that the best solution was to keep some treats handy in a pocket. But I had to learn that from experience.

Small dogs were just as capable as large ones of being gate crashers. They had the advantage of fooling the unsuspecting kennel worker who might think that size matters, that the smaller dog would be at a disadvantage when the gate was opened and that a quick handler would be able to slide out without letting the dog out too. For example, a small Jack Russell with sharp teeth could nip ankles and hands, while Bulldogs had weight on their side and would use it like a tank pushing its way through jungle. The teeth of a Jack Russell would put off the bravest kennel worker from trying to loop a leash round the squirming little body, and a Bulldog didn't have any neck for a leash to grab onto.

Bulldogs were the real challenge of all gate crashers, and Bentley was the Gold Medal winner in that category. He re-minded me of Winston Churchill with the background of the Union Jack, his cigars, and those famous words about fighting on the beaches and never surrendering. Bentley believed in never surrendering to the situation in which he found him-self behind chain-link at the kennels. There was nothing mean about Bentley, just determination. The first time Bentley came to stay with us, a kennel worker led this large, but meek-look-ing Bulldog back to his run. He walked slowly, sadly, head down, his huge jowls shaking from side to side, a choke chain hanging loosely against his heavy chest. He stood quietly as the gate to the run was opened. Then it happened. Sandy, the kennel worker was not sure what happened first, but before she knew it, she was on the inside of the gate and there went Bentley, trotting off down the aisle, his mouth open in a wide grin, stopping at one gate to lift a leg. Sandy stood, also open-mouthed, still holding the leash, an empty choke chain at its end. She went to retrieve Bentley, thinking that somehow she must have let him go and all she had to do was put the choke chain back around his neck and lead this gentle tank of a dog back to his run.

"But what neck?" Sandy later said. "I didn't realize that Bulldogs don't have necks – not the sort that will hold a choke chain or a collar. Bentley's built like a football player – the sort with no neck -- and when I thought I had slipped the choke chain over his head, I didn't see that all he had to do was pull his head back and there was the choke chain lying on the ground."

We still had to get Bentley back into his run. We resorted to food. Remembering my experiences with Sheba, we thought of a treat. Treats usually worked with most dogs. Someone should go into the run with the treat, and someone else should give the dog a gentle shove through the gate. Bentley trotted in happily and took his treat carefully, his lower jaw acting like a bowl into which the treat could be dropped. Then he turned with remarkable speed and headed for the gate. I was on the outside and shut the gate, never thinking that I was also shutting Sandy in with Bentley. Somehow, we had to get Sandy out. She approached the gate. So did Bentley. She put her well-booted feet against the gate. Bentley slid his feet on top of her boots and fitted his body between her legs and the gate.

"I swear my boots bent under his weight – I could feel my toes squashed flat!" Sandy told the story of Bentley again and again, each time he seemed to grow bigger, and Sandy smaller. We wanted to come up with a plan for dealing with large tanks like Bentley.

Bentley loved his food and he loved his walks, but this problem with his neck that wouldn't hold a choke chain, and his freedom-seeking tendencies, were giving us a few headaches. We found that if one person diverted Bentley's attention with a treat, or just talked to him, another could, if quick, put his food bowl in his run before the noticed the

WATCH WHERE YOU STEP

gate opening. But he was scheduled for exercise as well, and we were not about to risk Bentley running off with one shake of that huge head to rid himself of that bothersome choke chain and leash. So we tried just taking him out to the exercise yard on two choke chains, with two leashes and two attendants. I think he felt that this was his due, as he always behaved with decorum while he led the way outside. But the return trip could be difficult. I'm sure he liked to keep us guessing as to whether he would try to run for it, or to just walk in with never a pull on the leash. Bentley was a Churchill at those times, reminding us of what he could do if things got too bad. At other times, when he put his weight and strength into crashing through the half-shut gate, spilling food, upsetting water bowls, and reducing staff to shivering wrecks, he probably saw himself as leader of a revolutionary mob. He wasn't a barker, but he certainly set all the other dogs barking a chorus.

"Go for it, Bentley -- we're all behind you; we'll follow you to the barricades!" The only problem for them was that they weren't skilled gate crashers like Bentley.

Another variety of escape artist was the one that knew what was in store before the car had even stopped in the parking lot. He or she might be sitting quietly in the car or maybe not quiet at all, but barking and jumping up and down, nose marks on all the windows. But he or she was waiting for the precise moment when the owner opened the car door and reached to attach leash to collar. I had seen those thrill-seekers, poised ready to jump. Maybe it was like the bungee jumper, tensed for that leap into space. But I saw many of these "leash escapees" or "car jumpers" whose owners never recognized what danger-seeking urges resided in their four-footed companions!

However, as kennel owners, Louis and I needed to take some steps to restrain these dogs, and train their owners.

It became apparent the first year the kennel was open that there was potential for a wild mix-up of animals and owners, rather like what happens at a rock concert or international soccer finals. Dogs meeting other dogs, owners carrying their pets' luggage, some pets on leashes and some not, leashes and bedding getting tied up, and pet food being spilled all over the parking lot...and that was before pets and owners were more than a few steps out of their vehicles. There never was the big free-for-all that I imagined happening, but there were some minor fracases and as a result Louis put up a sign at the parking lot, in full view of all who came, saying "Please Leash Your Dogs." Just in case that notice wasn't read, there was another at the front door, and still another inside on the counter. Three notices should have done it.

But notices were not always read, and there was the occasions of the four Bulldogs and then there were the three English Setters, and there were a few more. It seemed the problem came when owners were unable, or unwilling, to put a leash on their dogs while the dog was still in the car, or truck, or SUV. Our notice said to "Leash Your Dogs," but it didn't say when the owner should do this. We just assumed it would happen before the owner took their pet out of the car, but there were several occasions when we were quite wrong. Usually it happened when an owner was bringing in more than one dog for boarding and perhaps had only one leash or when two or more dogs, bored with sitting in the car, were ready to jump at the earliest opportunity to escape. I think the dogs always knew when the opportune moment arose for a mass exodus.

One escape artist in particular was a small Jack Russell

terrier named Bobby Jo. Little Bobby Jo knew the certain moment when her owner would not have the snap on the leash
ready to attach to the collar. That was the moment to push forward and slide quickly under Mrs. Rose's outstretched hands,
which now were trying desperately to grab hold of Bobby Jo's
smooth fur without meeting those needle-sharp teeth, and at
the same time to find the metal loop on the collar on which to
snap the leash. But Mrs. Rose had lost hold of the leash and
its snap and the dog, and there went Bobby Jo, running wildly,
dust flying behind her, down the lane and out to the furthest
corner of the potato field.

One thing Bobby Jo hadn't reckoned on was the center
pivot irrigation system, whose extension arm was watering
the corner of the field and Bobby Jo was headed straight into
all that water. She didn't like water coming out of hoses, or
irrigation systems or the cleaning hose at the kennel, and
she turned quickly around, only to run into the arms of her
owner who, panting and soaked with irrigation water, was in
no mood to be gentle with what she called "You little miserable mutt, I've a good mind to send you back to the Pound!"
Mrs. Rose wouldn't do any such thing. She had been caught
by Bobby Jo in this way before and she muttered something
about "How come I can't learn to put that leash on sooner
while we're both still in the car?"

I watched and brought out some towels, not for Bobby Jo
but for her bedraggled owner. I told her about the four Bulldogs that did the same thing to their owner.

"Four Bulldogs! That's too many altogether. Whatever did
she do?"

I explained that the owner, a professional man, wearing good office suit and tie, had been given the job by his
wife, another professional, to bring out their four Bulldogs

for boarding. The dogs had been here several times. His wife told him clearly that he should put a leash on the dogs before bringing them into the kennel. He must have listened carefully, because that was what he had in his hand when he opened the door and got out of the car – one leash. He went to open the back door of the car, planning to put that leash on one dog and then go back for the next. A scientist by training, he was going to do this leash business in a scientific manner, one leash, one dog, one at a time. He had underestimated the intelligence of a Bulldog.

If there is a way to escape, a Bulldog is on to it at once. So here was their opportunity. I always suspected that those four had been planning this moment for days -- weeks, even. When their owner opened the back door to his very smart sports car, leash in hand, all four dogs erupted out and swept past him. They had spied Nicholas the house cat meandering past the house, and those four were going to nail that feline if it was the last thing they did. At full cry they tore across the lawn, around the side of the house, through the roses, and onto another lawn where they were seen by the Corgi crew sitting quietly inside the house. The Corgis would have liked to join in the cat hunt, but no one was letting them out of the house. They barked and ran back and forth along the windows that ran almost the length of the house, leaving a trail of nose smudge marks. The Bulldogs now stopped hunting cats and stood at the windows, Bulldog nose to Corgi nose, all dogs at full bark. Bad language was exchanged among dogs and myself, now concentrating on keeping all the dogs separate.

Meanwhile, who should appear, hot and flustered and still carrying one leash, but the owner, who now leashed one Bulldog and retreated to the kennels. He returned minutes later with three more leashes. The dogs had now found the front door and were setting up a Corgi – Bulldog chant, nose to window. They were cornered and an orderly retreat was managed by all. The cat had disappeared under the front porch. Nicholas would do anything to start a chase.

We've been lucky. None of those escape artists and gate crashers in our care has been mean. They are just doing what their instincts tell them to do. It's all part of the game! I could certainly appreciate their need to get out of the place and back to what was familiar. It was always a relief to get back to my own bed after a vacation.

Sickness in the Family - the Pets' and Ours

"IT'S JUST SOMETHING that's going around. We'll keep an eye on it."

"Or it could be serious – perhaps it's kennel cough?"

I had not given more than a very passing thought to the health of our boarders when we had first discussed our small business venture, the boarding kennel. If a pet got sick, we'd call their veterinarian. Simple. All the literature we'd read about boarding pets told us that we should always contact the veterinarian if a pet was sick. And we were very careful to record the name of a pet's veterinarian. It was, however, a new concern for me as a boarding kennel owner that the pets we boarded might have health problems. Just like people have health problems.

There were dogs and cats with diabetes, needing scheduled insulin shots; pets with ear infections needing ear drops; eye infections requiring eye drops, or other problems for which antibiotics were prescribed; and pets that had seizures, epileptic or otherwise. Pets came with their boxes, bottles, pill containers for each day of the week, and lists of medications and when they should get them. If we had any questions, we asked the owners or called their veterinarians.

But it was those minor things, the coughs and runny noses, diarrhea and "upset tummies" that reminded me of what it had been like with small children. Always something, and then those words, "Mommy, I don't feel good, my tummy hurts." Or the head, or the throat. And then they stayed home from school.

These pets were no different, except they couldn't tell us in so many words about the pain, and we had to learn from observation. And they couldn't stay home from school. We would watch them if there was a cough, examine a foot that was being favored on a walk, cut back on food if there was diarrhea, sponge eyes that were full of dirt. Louis was often called in for a consultation and if a run to a veterinarian was called for, then he was the one to take the pet, sit with it, and wait for the vet's decision as well as making sure the owners were notified.

That first Christmas season, a Labrador boarded with us. He had just had surgery for a broken leg. We put him in a grooming room kennel, which was large enough but did not allow for walking around. Then Louis had the job of taking him out to do his "doings."

When it came to Rocky, a large Airedale, we were thankful that Louis was around. He and I had read something about "bloat" – an often fatal problem that shows up with very subtle symptoms. Rocky was a young dog, very active, bouncy, who loved his exercise time as well as his food. But one morning when he returned to his kennel after an exercise time he seemed less active. He hung his head and just stood in one place. That was unusual behavior for Rocky. The kennel worker called me to say Rocky seemed sick. It was only about five minutes after Rocky had returned to his kennel, but when Louis and I saw him it was obvious that something was wrong. He was still just standing there, head down, and he was shaking his head and retching as though he wanted to vomit but couldn't.

"Jenny, call the emergency vet and Rocky's owners, and I'm going to get him to the vet now." It was Saturday and the Emergency Pet Services were the only ones available. "It could be bloat, and that means we can't waste time."

Louis was off with Rocky in the back of the Bronco, and I called the emergency vet to tell them to expect Louis and Rocky. Then I tried to locate the owners. This was more of a problem. They had given a relative as an emergency back up, but she was in Chicago and the owners were in New York, or it may have been Europe. But I couldn't get hold of anyone to pass on the word that Rocky had had to go to the vet. Louis phoned to tell me that Rocky had indeed had an attack of bloat, where the intestines twist, forming a pocket in which gas can build up. The only treatment is surgery, and if this is not undertaken promptly, the dog will die. Rocky was one of the lucky ones – he survived the surgery and was back to his usual bouncing self. Our kennel worker had been quick to notice the unusual and Louis was prompt to put Rocky in the car and get him to the vet, no questions asked, no permission given by the owners, but with bloat one just can't wait. The owners were very happy indeed with what we had done for their special family member.

We dealt with the health problems of our boarders, but we also had our own. I had become used to one surgery after another to correct the wear and tear of joints and the damage caused by my horse-riding accident. But Louis was another case. As I saw it, like many doctors, he refused to accept his own illnesses. He'd broken his leg skiing not just once but twice, and was back on the slopes, cast off, before he'd ever have recommended such an action to a patient. So I was a little surprised when he one day climbed off that tractor announcing that his knee was bad and he'd have to see a doctor about it. A trip to Seattle and a day in hospital for laparoscopic surgery on the offending joint, and he was back to his usual action-oriented self. His only complaint was that he'd been given too much anesthetic. His recovery from the knee surgery seemed easy. So I was not sure what to expect when he agreed to undergo open heart surgery for a heart valve repair, or possible replacement.

It was in January when we drove to Spokane for consultations with a variety of cardiologists and cardiac surgeons, all of whom were firm in their diagnosis and recommendation that Louis have surgery to repair the valve in his heart. Before making a decision, he went to the medical library and reviewed all the articles about the condition and the need for surgery. He was nothing if not thorough. This convinced me that this was not just a simple knee repair. This was the Big Event. Having one's heart opened up was not something to be taken lightly.

Louis agreed to the surgery and we made arrangements to be away from the kennel for at least a couple of weeks. I stayed in a motel close by the hospital so I could spend as much time with Louis as I could. January was a slow month for boarding after the holiday rush. It was that time when people were more interested in income tax and skiing.

It was cold and snowy in Spokane, with icy roads and grey clouds just waiting to let loose the next load of snow. It was a depressing outlook, and not the best for positive thinking.

While Louis was in surgery I sat in the waiting room with all the other families who had someone near and dear in cardiac surgery. Every now and then someone, possibly a surgeon, would come in and speak quietly to one family group or another. It was always in a low murmur, but I thought I saw everyone incline their heads a little closer to hear what was being said. I tried hard to hear too, but those green-gowned surgeons had a practiced low murmur that made it difficult, and after a time I gave up and went to find some coffee.

When I came back to the room, nothing had changed: the same family groups and the same medical murmuring. Now and then the tension was broken by the sound of a cell phone. In spite of the notices plastered to the walls requiring cell phones to be turned off since they interfered with the electrical equipment, some of the folks had left theirs on, unable to cut those cords connecting them with others who were not lucky enough to join the waiting room scene.

"No, nothing yet." A rather large woman spoke quickly, pulling an arm away from a teenager who was leaning heavily against her. The teenager had pink hair and I had a fleeting thought that if I came out of open heart surgery I might not want to see pink hair looming over me.

"Doc said she'd be out of surgery within the hour, but that was ages ago." This was from a young man who promptly passed the phone to someone who looked like his father, but who just grunted something into the phone and passed it back.

"We'll call you when we know," the son said before snapping the instrument shut.

I was getting claustrophobic as well as hard of hearing and decided I needed to go for a walk. I managed to get lost. One corridor led to another and then there would be the sign saying something about hospital personnel only beyond this point. It took a long time and several questions before I was back in the waiting room.

"What do you mean, you have to wait till tomorrow for the surgery?" A heavy man, dressed in overalls and a thick jacket that had some oil stains on the sleeves was speaking. He had not been there earlier and was now engaged in a loud and angry conversation with a well- dressed man in suit and tie.

"Like I said, the anesthesiologist wants to wait. It's standard in these circumstances." The well-dressed man spoke softly, but that just seemed to make the other speak louder. He wanted to know who was going to pay for his motel room and for another day's work lost. What about the medical insurance? Would they cover another day in the hospital? All eyes in the room were fixed on the pair. This was much more interesting than waiting for an illicit cell phone to ring. I didn't hear the end of the debate because a nurse called my name from the door.

Louis was out of surgery and I could go and see him, though only for a short visit because he wasn't really awake yet.

"He'll not be looking his best, either -- just so you don't get too much of a shock."

Louis looked awful. The nurse was quite right – "not looking his best" was an understatement. I didn't want to leave this grey-faced man I loved, even for a moment. Tubes seemed to run from everywhere and there were monitors above his head clicking and sending signals to outer space, for all I knew. Nurses came in and out to study screens that had patterns running up and down, or to check on the many tubes. I wondered how long it would be until I had my regular Louis back again. How soon before he would be doing what he liked to do best – out and about with his dogs, roaming the hills above the Snake River? But the surgery had been a success and the prognosis was good. I think that was what I learned from the doctors and nurses who came to check on him.

He was up and out of that bed as soon as he could be,

holding onto a walker, his cart with the tubes rolling along behind him, and his hospital gown open down the back. I had
a hurried visit to Nordstrom to buy pajamas, dressing gown,
and slippers so he could go on his walks in a more respect-
able style. And walk we did, along those corridors, which
were sometimes quiet but more often bustling with activity as
nurses went to their patients, food technicians delivered meals,
and cleaning ladies moved the dust around from one room to
another. Louis had often said that the one person who really
knows what is going on for a patient is the cleaning lady. They
were usually chatty and no one took much notice of their comings and goings, so they picked up the gossip, passing it on to
whoever took time to talk to them.

Louis was not feeling like doing much talking, so I talked
to whoever came into the room. During my own hospital stays,
I had been labeled a "bad patient," which meant that I asked
a great many questions and made demands that some nurses
consider unreasonable – one nurse even suggested I needed a
"psychiatric evaluation," but she didn't get far with that one. I
believed, however, that the patient who was interested in his or
her recovery, who asked questions and who might even refuse
some treatment offered, had a far better chance for early recovery. Louis may not have been able to ask the questions, since he
was doing a great deal of sleeping and was still suffering from
the effects of the surgery and the anesthetic. I was prepared to
ask those questions on his behalf, becoming a "bad spouse,"
even if it irritated him at times. On one occasion however,
my interference prevented him from undergoing a procedure
which was not called for, at least not at that time. Large hospitals, I thought, do not always have the best of communication
patterns, and in this case it seemed that some departments
didn't speak to others. I wanted Louis home and I wanted him

well again. I was prepared to be an interfering spouse if that was what it took.

Meanwhile, I kept in touch by phone with the kennel. January was a slow month, and so no problems came up. We had a full-time manager now and a team of part-time kennel workers who worked well together. Once again, the manager was living in the little apartment above the garage and kept an eye on my dogs, brought in the mail, fed the cat, and kept the place warm. It was a big relief to have her there.

Our children came to visit and eventually the big day came to bring Louis home. We had a convoy of vehicles and arrived home to find large signs everywhere saying "Welcome Home Dad, Granddad, Louis."

It took a while for Louis to get back to his old self. That sort of surgery left a person "sort of goofy" as he put it. That was something he hadn't been prepared for, the way his mind took longer to recover than his heart.

There were still some bad moments. He fainted one morning and had to be readmitted to the hospital, this time in Richland, just across the river. He had episodes of fibrillation and learned that caffeine and alcohol might have something to do with this. So he took up decaf coffee and non-alcoholic beer. I learned slowly not to ask him how he was doing.

"How do you think I'm doing?" he always replied. "I can't drink alcohol and I can't have a decent cup of coffee – what's left?"

He was back to his old self with his dogs in no time, complaining that they had forgotten all their training while he'd been away. We were back to running the kennels, not anticipating any more interruptions.

How Do You Say Goodbye?

THE PHONE CALL came in late November. Mother had died peacefully in her sleep. It was not unexpected. But even so, when that call came, I was not ready for the news. She and I had so much in common and so much yet to share.

Louis and I made the trip to England and spent time with my brother and the few remaining relatives there, but I came home wishing I had had the opportunity over the years to ask Mother questions only she could answer. Why had she never returned to England to live? Was Father unwilling to move? Why did she not stay on in New Zealand after Father died? She had friends and his family there, and she had been there almost fifty years. Now it was too late to ask her. I thought of her as an "erratic" -- one of those rocks or boulders that are swept up in a flood, pulled and pushed along by strong currents until at last they find a niche into which they wedge themselves, digging deep into the soft dirt that feels most like home.

Mother held not only the smooth polished side of an erratic rock, but also the scars and gouging picked up from the rough tumbling and rolling of travel from one place to another. She could criticize and comment with a cruelty and lack of feeling that I could find no words to stop. When I was a child, my friends were never good enough, and even my New Zealand relatives never met her standards. She never changed, later criticizing some of my children and friends with stiletto-like cuts. Why did she do this? More to the point, why did I not tell her that such comments left lasting wounds? It had become obvious that I had spent my life trying to make myself into what Mother wanted me to be. That smooth side of my own "erratic" self covered some deep wounds with falsehoods and denials.

Yet, didn't Mother deserve some love and support? She had done a good job of bringing two children up without their father during the war years. She never stopped loving her husband, and he had loved her deeply, even knowing how critical she could be. She never hesitated to tackle problems and to try new experiences. I didn't have the answers. I needed something to bring my mother's "erratic" soul home. I decided to have a wooden bench with a plaque built and to place it where it overlooked the river and the distant Horse Heaven Hills. Junipers and sumac surrounded the spot, and birds could be heard settling themselves in for the night. We could enjoy it, and I thought she and Father would have enjoyed it too. Louis built the bench from teak wood and added the plaque commemorating both my parents.

Unlike Mother, who always wanted to return to England, I had reached a point where I knew I would never return to New Zealand except for visits. Those visits were like a return to my past, but that was not what I wanted for my life now. Returning home to the Columbia River after Mother's funeral, I was convinced that this was where I wanted to make my niche. The bench would be an anchor for me while also connecting me to my past. It was a small symbol, but significant, and I loved that bench.

Now I could focus on the kennel again, and this time the dogs grabbed my attention. There were so many, and what amazed me was how like us humans they were. I'd always heard owners come to look like their dogs, or chose dogs that look like them. Dogs indeed have much in their makeup that is similar to humans, and what I discovered for myself was that I could discuss problems with them, and they seemed to have the answers!

Not always, but sometimes a small furry mutt could give very reassuring answers.

Take Eddie, for instance.

By no stretch of the imagination could Eddie be called beautiful. Striking-looking, perhaps. One would definitely take a second look at this small ball of fur that resembled a large "dust bunny" – those things that lie under beds or sofas just out of reach of the mop. His rough dun-colored coat stuck out in all directions, and his overbite with its three remaining teeth was guaranteed to make any canine dental surgeon reach for his instruments. But his eyes were bright – at least one of them, the one not dimmed by an advanced cataract. Even so, Eddie was well aware of what was going on around him and who might be within biting range. With only three teeth, Eddie wanted to make every tooth count.

He was a terrier of mixed ancestry. Perhaps a bit of Cairn, a bit of Yorkshire mixed in with some Norfolk and some Border -- several historic British dogs had donated Eddie his stamina, his temperament, his longevity and his independent spirit. Something of Shakespeare's Henry V lay in that low throaty growl that challenged the troops to rally "once more into the breach dear friends, once more," whenever a stranger might invade his territory uninvited. We all had a healthy regard for those three remaining teeth. They were razor-sharp and could nail whatever came between them.

Eddie was no longer a young dog when we first met him. He was "rescued" from the Pound by a family who could not resist his looks.

"No one wanted him and he looked so lost and lonely, he needed saving," one of his owners told us early in our relationship with Eddie. The Pound had failed to tell Eddie's new owners that it had been his attitude, not his look of neglect that had kept people from saying, "That's the one for me." Eddie was for no one. He agreed to go with the Mitchells, as he had agreed to stay at Sagemoor when the Mitchells went on vacation trips. "Sometimes you just have to take what comes and deal with it," his grin seemed to say. He'd have agreed with Louis about grinning like a jackass eating briars and just getting on with life.

Eddie stayed at Sagemoor many times. In spite of his fifteen years, he managed well. He was the leader of the Home Stylers, or the Front Room Gang, as they came to be called. The Front Room Gang were taken outside to the exercise yard to do their "doings" and have a run five or six times a day. Whenever Eddie was boarding, he would challenge his "band of brothers" with throaty yap to follow him out to the yard at full charge, agreeing to come back inside only when he was ready. He liked it outside and was the last one to do his "doings." We were sure he waited on purpose to give his Gang as long as possible outside, before returning to "lockup."

There came the day when Eddie moved more slowly, and his appetite for his home- cooked meals, lovingly prepared by Mrs. Mitchell, faded and then disappeared. He still led the gang out to the exercise yard, but at a slower pace, and was eager to return to the comfort of his bed. The Mitchells left on a cruise to the Greek Isles, confident that if anything happened to Eddie, we would let them know.

Eddie's health declined rapidly. He was no longer eating, and frequently refused to go outside. We would throw a blanket over him, not trusting those three teeth, and carry him out. But he wanted back in as soon as possible. We tried to contact the Mitchells. But even the most luxurious of cruise sailing ships make contact difficult. We called all the emergency numbers we had been given. But all had the same response from the cruise company – they could take a message and would forward it when the ship next made radio contact. His veterinarian diagnosed old age and heart problems for Eddie.

"He's failing. His folks know. It's just a matter of time. Nothing to do but keep him rested."

The morning came when we found Eddie curled up in the corner of his kennel, his blanket around him. He was stiff, cold, and dead. He looked peaceful, but those three teeth still held the hint of a grin that suggested there was some bite left in the old boy.

We had not heard from the Mitchells and dreaded telling them of Eddie's death. We left phone messages with their emergency numbers, asking that we be contacted. It was two o'clock in the morning when the call came. We woke at the sound of the phone and guessed at once who it might be. Louis handed me the phone. It was, of course, the Mitchells and by the end of the conversation we were all in tears. They asked that we take Eddie to the veterinarian, who would arrange for Eddie's cremation.

In the morning I placed Eddie in a box, his blanket carefully tucked around him, and his two toys next to him. The

Mitchells had asked that I keep his collar for them, but I was loath to do so. He looked so vulnerable without it, so I put it back on. I would tell the veterinarian to take it off and keep it for the Mitchells.

Some dogs grab your heart, and Eddie grabbed ours at Sagemoor.

"He was one tough cookie," I said as I closed the lid on the box and put it on the front seat of my car.

"A born leader of the pack – he always got them that extra five minutes outside, sometimes even fifteen," was a staff comment. The Front Room Gang was much loved by all, but Eddie was special. Someone would give him an extra brushing and wash his backside, which was none too clean those last few days. He'd lick our hands before planting his teeth in theone closest. Now our faces were wet with tears for this little mobster.

As I drove I talked to Eddie, there in that box on the seat next to me. I told him that he was one of the great con artists of the dog world.

"Eddie, it is safe to say that your ugly little face with that one working eye and your mean disposition to match has made all the staff love you. They will never forget you. They will remember you with affection every time they notice one of the scars your teeth left in their hands."

We drove slowly.

"Eddie, I hope you know we love you. That the Mitchells love you, too." I had my hand on the box, and I patted the lid.

"Eddie, I wish you'd known my mother. You two would have gotten along well. She was a most remarkable woman, you know, Eddie. Just like you've been a most remarkable dog. You've moved around and not always liked where you were moved to, I think." I tried to watch where I was going, but I had to pull over to the side of the road to finish my conversation with this little traveler.

"Eddie, you've had to make sure your bed was where you wanted it and that people paid you proper respect. My mother had to do that too, Eddie. Eddie, if you run into her ever, tell her Jenepher loves her and is proud of her." I remembered her parting words to me when I'd seen her last. Words I had so longed to hear, that she was proud of me. Had I ever told her I was proud of her? I hoped she would hear me – somehow.

I patted the lid of the box again with my hand. It was safe to pat now. As I started the car, I noticed I too had a scar on the back of my hand – it had to be from Eddie. I thought how those we love the most may leave the deepest scars.

Eddie was not our first loss, though he was one of very few to die while boarding with us. While Eddie was memorable, Sara Grace was lovable.

Sara Grace was small and skinny, with large soft eyes and an attitude. She was mostly Dachshund, but looked as if there might have been a Chihuahua for a grandpa. She was a Front Room dog like Eddie, and loved to go outside with the rest of the Front Room Gang. Her owner warned us that perhaps we should take Sara Grace out more often, but we washed her bed and made sure she was warm and dry, and then she would snuggle down into the corner of her bed with delight. Sometimes Louis would carry Sara Grace outside, and sometimes she would just run ahead with the rest of the pack. But she always insisted on walking back to her house on her own. If her house was on the second floor then she would stand in front, nose pointing to the spot where she knew she belonged. Louis loved to see Sara Grace run back to her house when he took her out last thing at night.

"Her tail's waving like a flag, her legs are trotting, but you can hear her toenails clicking on the tiles as she runs."

Sara Grace's owner introduced a young Pomeranian as a friend for Sara Grace, and the two came to stay for a few days. No one noticed anything different about Sara Grace, but this time her owner said something about Sara Grace being very fragile and that if anything happened we were to call her at once.

"After all, she is sixteen years old, and she has slowed down some."

One night Louis called me from the kennel about nine-thirty to say that he had found Sara Grace dead, and that he was about to call the owner. Did I know anything else about Sara Grace – had any staff written any notes about her?

No, all we had were the notes we'd written about what her owner had said about calling her if anything happened to Sara Grace. She must have had some premonition about her long-time companion.

Louis called the owner. She wanted us to keep Sara Grace, and told us that she would be able to pick Sara Grace up the next evening.

The weather was warm and even though the kennels were air-conditioned and cool, we needed to do something with Sara Grace for the next almost twenty-four hours. When we built the kennel, such an occurrence had not been overlooked and we had invested in a refrigerator large enough to hold most sizes of dog if the need arose. There was even a freezer section that might hold a smallish-sized Labrador.

I left it up to Louis to do what he thought necessary with Sara Grace.

The next morning, early, there was a phone call from Sara Grace's owner. I took the call, knowing that she was already aware of what had happened to Sara Grace. She wanted me to know she would definitely be there that evening to pick up Sara and the other dog, Max. She said something about wanting Sara Grace to be just as we had found her, "still soft to touch" was what I thought she had said. "And her blanket with her too, so she's warm."

"Louis, Sara Grace's owner called. She's coming tonight and wants Sara Grace, warm and soft to touch – that's what she said. And she wants her wrapped in her blanket to keep her warm."

"We'll get her out of the fridge, then, and you can wrap her up. It'll take a little while for her to warm up, but she should be fine by tonight."

I wondered what the owner might think of us putting her dog in the fridge, but then I thought that she might well have guessed, given what she had said to me on the phone. But what else could we have done?

It is a strange feeling knowing that one of the boarders, someone we've cared for and loved, is dead. And in the fridge. I couldn't get over to the kennel quickly enough the next morning to take care of this little dog's body. I found a large box, clean and with a lid, and I put Sara Grace's bed and blanket in it and laid her on it. She fitted in well. I put one of our small sheepskin blankets over her and closed the lid. Then I put the box on the table in the office. It was Sunday. There would be no clients coming until late in the evening, so no one was going to bother Sara Grace. I checked on her several times during the day. She looked peaceful. That little bouncing body was still for once. I hoped she hadn't been in any pain, that it had just been a matter of her heart wearing out and finally stopping. She had been still bouncing, though slowly, the day before. Sara Grace had looked at life with her nose in the air, as if to say to us: "I know something you don't!" I often wished I could know what those dogs were saying to me.

Outside the front door of the kennels the roses were looking spectacular: deep colors, small buds about to burst open, and the full-blown blooms heavy with perfume. I snipped one bud that was about to open, its petals showing a pale pink. I placed it in Sara Grace's box. Later in the day I picked another blossom, darker red this time, and then a third, this one pale yellow. Sara Grace would have had a full bouquet if there had been time for more rose-gathering. I thought three buds would be plenty for this small sixteen-year-old who had been such a good friend and companion. Later, when her owner picked her up, I explained about the rosebuds and how I thought Sara Grace tipped her nose in the air to tell us she knew more than we did.

"I always thought she was telling me she would do it her way – guess that's a good piece of advice for us both."

Her owner agreed and we both cried together.

Sunday Night Check-Out - End of the Day-Go-Round

THE MAIN WORK of the kennel, the feeding, cleaning, exercising, petting, and record- keeping, was done by our staff team, though Louis and I frequently pitched in. We had a full- time manager who lived offsite with her own family. This worked much better than when we had someone living onsite and for whom the free apartment had been the main attraction for taking the position in the first place. We had a great deal of learning to do about hiring employees. I had left that part of kennel management up to Louis. This new full-time manager had had more supervisory experience than some we'd hired. She managed the reservations and staff scheduling. She also proved to be a great buffer between us and the other staff.

But Louis and I continued to keep an active involvement with the kennel, the pets, and their owners, as well as the staff. It was our business and we wanted to see it run the way we had planned. While Louis would manage anything to do with septic systems and maintenance, I had my computer and did payroll and paid the bills. I wrote the newsletter and handled general correspondence.

Sunday night check-out was one occasion in which we kept our involvement with both clients and their pets. I enjoyed the excitement of seeing owners and pets reunited after only a couple of days or a couple of months. It was hard to say who was more excited – pet or owner. The dogs in particular were so delighted to be back with their "dads" or "moms" again. Jumping up, tugging at the leash, kissing everyone on sight, peeing on the floor – or on their owner, just thrilled to be back with that special person. Cats were never quite so given to showing their feelings, though I remember one cat who purred and purred – and it was no soft purr, but something like a motorbike roar – from the moment his owner stepped into the Cat Room to retrieve his companion.

Sunday night check-out might start at five o'clock in the evening and last two hours, but preparation for check-out started much earlier. The bills had to be prepared, records checked for additional charges, bedding had to be clean, luggage checked, medications and leftover food had to be put out. There were the regular chores of feeding, cleaning, and exercising to be done before everything was ready to go. Louis and one staff person would collect pets and bedding and take them to the waiting owners. My job was to greet the owners, hand over the bill, answer questions, and make sure all the luggage was delivered to the right client.

There was a certain air of excitement about that Sunday night preparation, and the pets always picked up that something good was about to happen. They barked, jumped, and dashed back and forth in their runs in anticipation. Perhaps they were going home?

Cars arrived before five. On a typical Sunday night pick-up there might be three cars, a truck, and the inevitable brace of SUVs out in the parking lot. On this particular Sunday, lights of two more could be seen coming up the lane. This promised to be a busy night. I changed the "Closed" sign over to say "Open," and in streamed the owners. A tense moment passed as I decided who was there first.

"And you are here to pick up?" I paused, question hanging in the air. Names were often beyond me -- faces perhaps were better, though I could always remember a pet's name.. But at that moment I wanted to get the right name with the right pet – and the right bill.

"Rollo. I'm here to pick up Rollo. Hope he's not been any trouble." This was from short woman with a worried expression. What sort of trouble had Rollo caused her in the past?

Rollo, Rollo. Then I saw the dog's name, and the bill with the owner's name.

"Yes, Mrs. Jackson. Rollo. He's been great. Eaten well, eliminated regularly, and has not been any trouble on his walks. Looks like he's had a good time here."

I showed her the kennel card that recorded Rollo's behavior for the week he was with us.

Owners liked to see records like this. I collected a check from Mrs. Jackson while Louis fetched Rollo and took him by the back door to the Jacksons' waiting van.

The same process was repeated a few more times with more pets, owners, and bills. Then there was a change in the pattern. A sort of hiccup. A young woman holding a small child and with a young man standing behind her pushed her bill toward me. The young man had a bored expression that told me he didn't want to get involved in what was about to happen.

"I don't think this bill is right," she said. "You've charged too much."

I looked at the bill and knew at once what the problem

was. She didn't remember we charged for the whole day on Sundays and that the bill was, in fact, correct. There was often someone questioning this and sometimes they would get irate because no one had told them. We had notices up giving answers to what we hoped were all the questions that came up most frequently.

"We open late on Sundays – some kennels are closed the whole weekend, you know. So we open late but charge for the whole day, and it would be the same if you came tomorrow morning. This saves you coming tomorrow if you're at work." I tried to explain, but she didn't get it and turned to her husband for help – perhaps he could put me right, I didn't know. He didn't want to get involved and just said something about paying so they could all get home; he was exhausted after all the driving. She smiled as she wrote the check – the sort of smile that said we were still friends.

It all took time. Bills were given out, money collected, change given. I tried to remember who was next in line to collect their dog at the back door from Louis or the staff person of the evening. Inevitably I would get the order confused and someone would glare at me while firmly handing over their leash with a comment about keeping to the order, and that they had family waiting at home.

Another hiccup. A credit card was handed to me.

"I'm so sorry -- we don't take credit cards, just cash or checks."

There was a pause, the sort of pause that said, "What sort of business are you that you don't take cards?"

Yes, that's exactly our kind of business – one that doesn't take credit cards.

I gave them the bill and said as quietly as possible that they could mail us the check in the morning. I made a note to remind me to look for it; if it wasn't sent, we would mail them the bill at the end of the week.

Another hiccup came when someone came for their pet and we weren't expecting them for another couple of days. No problem, but I would have to run the bill, Louis would have to find the food and bedding and anything else they had brought with them, and it all would take time. I tried to explain and deal with those who were still waiting and not get everyone upset with this interruption.

Behind this couple came a line of more owners waiting for their bills and their pets. I continued to match names, pets, and bills until eventually the front office was empty for a short period and I could start entering payments into the computer, making sure we had been given the right amount and that I had entered the right amount into the computer.

We all enjoyed talking with the owners. They wanted to know how their pets had behaved.

"Did he 'go' in his run, or did you have to take him outside?" one owner asked.

"I thought he might just stay in his house and refuse to come out. Oh, you used hotdogs to tempt him – I must remember that. He's such a nervous hound dog!" a very fond owner remarked.

Someone laughed, "I knew she'd chew up that blanket. We'll use yours next time."

"Those two look beautiful with their grooming. Your groomer does a great job." A five-dollar bill was handed over with the check. "That's for the groomer."

On it went. I was always just as enthusiastic as the owners as we talked about our pets. It was hard to say who was more excited - pet or owner.

I warned owners not to give their pets any treats or anything to eat or drink for at least two hours so that their digestive systems could settle down after all the stress of the exciting occasion. The pets had all been fed and were "ready for bed," as I would put it. No one believed me. We had notices printed and given out to first-timers when they left, but of course no one read them. Sandy, the tall blonde owner of Prudence, an equally tall blonde Poodle hadn't read the notice nor listened to my warning. Both owner and pet were delighted to see each other and probably it never entered Sandy's mind that there might be a disaster in store when the hugs and kisses, licks and yips were over.

The phone call came about two hours later.

"She's vomited everything all over the rug. She's never done that before. What were you feeding her?"

I waited to see if she had anything to add. I reminded Sandy about not feeding Prue for at least two hours, and no water either, just an ice cube if she seemed thirsty.

"Yes, yes -- Mike reminded me, but she went straight for the cat's water and then dug in the cat litter box. I guess that's what did it. Sure stinks up the place."

I wanted to laugh at the picture I had in my mind of the mess on the carpet – probably a lovely pale one too. I said how sorry I was to hear of the accident. I was sorry, too – to hear about it. Sandy muttered some apologies and said they'd remember for next time. At least they were thinking that there might be a next time.

We heard all sorts of comments on Sunday nights.

"You're the best place in town." We liked that one.

"My mother said to bring her cats here and now I know why – there's no smell to the place." How we had tried to make sure there wasn't!

I frequently asked how the weekend or days away had

been for the owners, and heard many tales of skiing trips with perfect snow, or no snow, or rain. I heard about engagements and weddings, new babies, grandbabies, graduations, and sporting successes.

I asked carefully about the progress of an ill relative and learned early on not to ask "Did you have a good time?" One time I had asked that question only to learn that the pet owner had been to the funeral of her mother. With time I knew who had a relative who couldn't tolerate the dog or the cat, whose son's or daughter's soccer or swim team was in winner's circle, whose house was being renovated, and who had had this or that success or tragedy. All life's turning points seemed to involve the family pets being left behind in care of someone else. I heard we'd done a good job and I heard we should have done something more. I heard people vent their frustrations on us or on their pets, and I learned to listen and not to take it too personally.

Seven o'clock eventually came around and the last owner left with their pet, and it was time to close up, go home, and count the money!

A little later there was a phone call. Mrs. Brown had made it home early and wanted to come and pick up Boots in about half an hour – would that be all right? I made my voice sound as sympathetic as possible but said we were closed now and would not be open until nine in the morning. Mrs. Brown did her best, insisting that it was only a couple of hours after the kennel closed – surely we'd open in these circumstances? It was an emergency. She couldn't quite say what sort of emergency this was, so I repeated that we'd be open in the morning. We considered births, deaths, and emergency open heart surgery to be the only true emergencies

Even on Sunday nights Louis and I had to go out to do the

last go round for the day and take the little Front Room Guys
out for their last run on the exercise yard. Most nights it didn't
take long to do all this. At least, my part didn't take long. I just
looked at the answering machine to see if there were any messages, picked up the end of day reports and the money, and
walked around to see that lights were out, the alarm on, that
pets had water, and doors were locked. There might be one or
two dogs to check on, such as Edna the Poodle who had seizures and was on medication, Buster the Lab who wore one
of those plastic collars – Elizabethan collars – that prevented
him from reaching the hot spot on his front leg and licking it
raw. He hated that collar and did everything he could to get it
off, so I had to check on him.

Louis had the much more difficult task of taking the Front
Room Home Style Guys out. Usually this didn't take too long
– it was just letting them out of their houses, and herding them
through to the back door and out to the exercise yard. He had
his own approach to this. First he shut the door to the Front
Room before taking the top row of little dogs down, then the
next row, and finally opening the doors to the ground floor
houses. Next he opened the door and stood back while there
would be a wild rush of the little four-footed mobsters, all following one old-timer who knew the routine, past the reception
area, through the office, and out the back door. Louis watched
to see that they didn't fight, that they did their business, and
that none escaped. Things became more time-consuming if any
had messed in their houses, peed on corners on the way out, or
had messy bottoms! Then there was cleaning up to be done.

I left him out there most nights and headed for bed with
Lucy, Buddy, and Benji, the Corgis, demanding their end-of-
day treat. One night the phone rang. It was Louis, from the
kennels, desperation in his voice.

"There are three Dachshunds and they all look exactly alike – black with some red on them, but I can't tell them apart and I don't know which dog goes into which doghouse. I need a hand, help!"

It could be difficult. On this occasion one Dachshund, Junebug, was already in one doghouse but it was the wrong one – one of the others had already claimed hers and was curling a lip, ready to fight off any intruder. Could we leave Junebug where she was for the moment and put the other two into the houses they belonged in? I was fairly certain which was which of the other two, but already another intruder, a little white Maltese, Bobo, had taken possession of one of the houses. Bobo belonged on the top floor but didn't want to move from this ground floor house – she had snuggled into the blanket there. It took some time to sort out these occupancy problems.

"Try a treat, Louis -- treats are a great way to get someone to move!" I wanted to get back to bed myself, and if we could just get these little ones into a house with water and bedding, then we could sort out who was in whose house in the morning.

I thought about what I had said some time later – much later, in fact. I could hear my words echo some time later: "Try a treat, Louis – treats are a great way to get someone to move."

Are We Getting What We Wanted?

WE HAD HAD other plans for retirement besides building and running the boarding kennel, though they were put on a back burner for a long time. Louis wanted to train his English Pointers for field trial competitions. I was not sure at first what I wanted to do, but sometime after the kennel was up and running, I found myself thinking more and more of my old dream of writing stories.

Did we get to follow these plans as well as build and run the business?

We did!

Louis kept at least three English Pointers in his barn kennels, and was always on the look out for the next puppy. Sometimes there was one new puppy, sometimes two. Training started first thing in the morning, either in the barn or out in the pasture, depending on the stage of the training. Puppies came from breeders as far away as Texas, though usually closer to home. They arrived all soft silky fur, wet noses, and rough tongues that they would use to lick anyone around. We had them in the house when they were very young to get them used to being around people. Louis would take a puppy with him wherever he went. This was the best way to socialize a young puppy, getting him or her used to being around people and around other dogs, and especially around the comings and goings of daily life in the house. We would run the vacuum cleaner, bang pan lids together, and have the radio or television going. All this time, a puppy would live in a crate which would be inside an exercise pen, either in the sunroom or out on the lawn. The only problem was that these puppies grew larger, and in time could climb onto the crate and then over the exercise pen and out. Then it was time to put them into a barn kennel, and life for that puppy became more serious. Training was focused on more than just to "heel" and to "whoa," and in time they would be introduced to the birds. Louis kept pigeons for training the dogs to point and to retrieve. He also had two horses that he used to "road" the dogs. "Roading" was when he was on horseback and two dogs would be on long leashes out in front of the horse, running at a fast pace. This was a strength-building exercise for the dogs. To be competitive at field trials, a dog must be able to run for about an hour. One could call it a dog marathon event. The field trials that Louis went to took place over several days during the spring and the fall in Washington State, Idaho, and Oregon. His dogs did well. One qualified to compete in a National Field Trial back in Illinois. Not bad for an amateur trainer. Another dog that Louis trained was picked by a professional trainer for a client, and Louis sold that one. Again, not bad for an amateur. Louis still had his goal of winning a big championship. He had many wins, though the big one seemed to evade him. He just kept going, never letting up on his goal for that championship. The pups kept coming to live in our sunroom before moving out to the barn and traveling in Louis's pickup to those trials.

The barn housed not only the tractor and backhoe and other implements that go with a tractor, but also the pickup and the horse trailer. The back of the pickup had been fitted with a canopy and with crates to house three or four dogs. The horse trailer could hold two horses and all their tack.

Louis started his search for the horse he needed about a year or two after the kennel was well established. He needed one for following his dogs at field trials as well as for the "roading" training. A gaited horse such as a Tennessee Walker or Missouri Foxtrot was what he wanted. He found Ace, a pretty chestnut Tennessee Walker with black mane and tail. He was a gentle horse, easy to ride, and our children and grandchildren loved to ride him. Ace was later joined for short periods of time by two or three others before Louis decided Ace was too slow. Ace found a home with a family, and Louis found first Sonny and then Ebony.

The pastures behind the barn were pretty: green grass, weeping willows along the south end, and a tall row of pop-lars along the west. The wind set the poplars dancing in a majestic chorus line of waving green arms, with the willows forming a corps de ballet of long sweeping skirts. Standing in the pasture, I could hear the music of the wind in the trees.

The grass in the pastures grew fast -- faster than the horses could keep it grazed down. Louis could mow it, but that was taking precious time away from the time he wanted to spend with his dogs, or gardening, or answering the calls from the kennel to fix some maintenance problem.

We tried cows to keep the pastures mown. We borrowed the cows from a neighbor cattle farmer who appreciated free feed. They were pretty animals and they had calves, but they left unsightly mounds of manure that grew grass longer and thicker than elsewhere. A New Zealand cousin suggested sheep. Again, we borrowed the sheep from a neighboring sheep farmer. They had lambs. But they wouldn't eat the grass that grew tall and thick around the piles of cow manure. We tried cows again, a different breed this time. Same thing happened. Were all animals so fussy? We went back to the mower and hired Bill to do the mowing and take care of the landscaping too. That was a good move. In addition to the other heavy- duty machinery, the barn now housed an enormous riding lawn mower nicknamed The Tank.

Meanwhile, what about my writing? I signed up for a class for seniors at the local community college. I enjoyed writing about anything, though poetry was not my choice. I liked to write short stories, especially about incidents I remembered from my growing up in New Zealand. I tried my hand at fiction and completed a novel that might fall into the "horror" genre, or murder mystery. I had two friends read it and then decided it was terrible and boxed it up to lie in the closet with the suitcases and Christmas decorations. Short stories took less time, so I concentrated on them.

I went to writing seminars and to the Fishtrap Writers Gathering at Lake Wallowa in Oregon. The classes there inspired me to keep going. I sent some of my short stories off to magazines in the hope of having something published. No luck. I had a file folder of rejection slips. But I kept going. Someday I'd get something published, I told myself, even if I had to self-publish. Louis and I shared something driving us to demonstrate our competence.

"It's your hobby," someone said to me once. And I thought, *No, writing is not my hobby; it's my work.* It's work I enjoy and I do it to become proficient, just as Louis works at his dog training. But we both need affirmation that we're good at our chosen work, for which we don't get paid and to which we give many hours of our time. They could be called obsessions we are passionate about. And we're not going to stop.

Years Roll On

I READ IT was good business to be always looking ahead, anticipating the needs of the business and to plan for new ways to increase client numbers. We had survived the first five years of business without going under, and that was a sign of success. But when the ten-year mark was reached, we thought it was time to look for some ways to upgrade Sagemoor Kennels. Did we need new equipment? Repairs anywhere? What could we do to encourage and reach out to potential clients? If we were a restaurant, we would be thinking of a change of color scheme and some new menus, even some new desserts, just to keep the clients coming back.

Breakfast time was discussion time for the two of us. After we had read the paper and checked the e-mail, but before Louis took off to work with his dogs, we put our attention to some of the kennel problems.

Our manager sent over typed notes, double spaced, 14 point upper case, which made them easy to read and hard to miss.

"Light bulbs burned out on the odd side."

"We're out of coffee and paper towels."

"Please call Coco's dad about his cat's cut ear."

"Dr. V. isn't doing cat leukemia shots, do you want to talk to him?"

This was all stuff that needed our attention. Some days there were several pages of notes and I laid them out on the kitchen counter where Louis couldn't miss them as he poured his cereal.

Some notes were directed to me so I could talk to Louis first before the three of us discussed the issues.

"Time to review staff raises."

We talked about some of the difficulties staff might be having, either home problems or work problems, or most likely a combination of both. The lives of some of the staff were better than soap operas when reported by the manager. What, if anything, could be done? Sometimes it was a personality clash between two staff members. Should we just tell them to do the work and forget about it, or did they need to be scheduled for different shifts? It sounded so trivial, but it was the stuff that made for a comfortable work environment, and that would mean good animal care and happy customers.

One concern that kept coming up was the schedule and keeping enough staff on a shift to cover the work, but not too many when the number of pets was low. It was the manager's job to take care of that one. But more hours used meant less money coming in. What about raising our rates? Shouldn't the groomer raise hers? The rates went up in small increments every year, and the only one who noticed was the owner of a small Poodle who noticed she was paying more than she had the last time she had boarded.

"How long ago was that, Mrs. Bennett?" I asked.

She frowned as though searching her mind for the date.

"About three years ago. It was when my husband had his open heart surgery."

Hard to forget that date, I guessed, and, yes, we had raised our rates since then.

One concern that kept coming up was the holiday reservations. Over the years as our reputation for providing the "best of boarding care" grew, owners were making their holiday reservations as much as a year in advance. What was more, they made reservations for many more days than they would actually need, just so that they would be sure of a space when they needed it.

"Here's Mrs. H." The manager rolled her eyes as she discussed this one. "She's making a reservation for her two Labs for ten days at Thanksgiving and two weeks at Christmas. I know she is doing it because we were full last year and we couldn't take her dogs, but she won't use all this time and will cancel most of it a few days before she comes. Then it's too late to find someone even if we have a waiting list. At that time people on the waiting list will have found somewhere else."

She was right. But what to do about it? Advance deposits for holiday boarding? Go to credit cards so we could make deposits easier? Send out reminder postcards a month before boarding dates? Phone calls to confirm dates?

The simplest were the postcard reminders and the phone call confirmations. We found those worked well. But there were still the half dozen clients who caught us at the last moment with sudden changes or even cancellations.

"We've decided to stay home this year."

"We just want the dogs to come for a weekend – someone else will be wanting the rest of our time – I'm sure you'll be able to fill it." A week before Christmas? Not much chance!

We reviewed some of the ideas that had surfaced over the past few months, even years. Credit cards, different ways to advertise the business, building additional kennel space for the busy times, a soundproofing system in the main kennels, new sealing on the kennel floors – the list went on and on.

It all meant money.

Were we making any money?

Sunday nights Henry and Sandy, our son and daughter-in-law, came over for dinner. This was a good time to talk about any kennel questions. After all, these two were business people and had a better idea of what we were doing with the kennel business than either Louis or I did. So we picked their good business and accounting brains for direction.

While we were making money, we weren't making a great deal of money. Economy was always emphasized by those two. They pointed out the positive effects of taking credit cards, but we were not convinced. Few of our clients were upset by our not accepting them. The only benefit might be that credit cards would make taking advance deposits easier for the busy times like Christmas. We decided to wait a while and see if we could get away without adding credit cards. There were fees attached to credit cards and besides it might take some getting used to the process.

.

We looked around for other ways to economize. Advertising was expensive. What about cutting out some of the advertising costs by going to smaller ads in the Yellow Pages? We had three local phone books to consider, and if we cut down on our large colorful spreads in those, that would save a considerable sum each month. After this length of time we felt we would not lose many customers if we cut down there. Our best referrals were still satisfied clients and the veterinarians in the area.

We agreed that in order to stay in business, after all this time, we needed to be assured of satisfied customers, owners who kept coming back and who would pass the word on to their friends, relatives, co-workers, the person standing in line at the supermarket with a cart full of dog and cat food. We knew we gave "peace of mind boarding," as advertised in our brochure and the Yellow Pages. Why else did Daisy dance her way out to the exercise yard with her Front Room friends, or Edgar come in from the parking lot, tail held high and body wiggling with delight at the thought of the treats and tummy scratches he would get from the staff? What else should we be doing to make boarding their pets an easy experience for the owners?

Gradually we added to our community presence. Our website was an important addition, making our services more accessible. Through our site, interested people could get most of their questions answered, look at pictures of the place, study the map to find their way to us, and could even make online reservations for boarding or grooming. Although we believed that people liked to speak to a "real" person on the telephone, there was no doubt that in this cyber age, making a reservation online was easy, and when we responded in a timely manner to messages left on the answering machine, we had come a long way toward making boarding easier on the owner.

We were members of the America Boarding Kennels Association. I had taken two levels of their Pet Care Technician certification. We encouraged our staff to do the first level and several had, while others were not interested. I believed that not only did that test give staff some basic information about animal care, health, and safety, it also gave owners some reassurance that we were not only informed, but belonged to an organization that had some standards of quality in the pet care industry. The next step for the kennel would be to go through the ABKA Facility Certification. This was a long process and involved a great deal of work on our part to put together the necessary paperwork and have someone come to inspect us to see that we were doing what we said we were doing. But again, it would be a worthwhile activity if we wanted to show that we were still a developing business. I found that it was like rowing against the current to get anyone to do any of the work necessary! If I wanted that Certification for Kennels, then I was going to have to do it myself, or at least keep stirring others to help.

But a happy customer was the one who could have their pets boarded whenever they needed to. Being put on a waiting list for the Christmas holidays did not answer an owner's needs. More space would help, and many owners asked why we didn't add on some more kennels. There would be no unhappy customers that way. But Louis and I had decided long ago that we were not going to increase our facility. If we did that, we would still be faced with the times when business was slow and when there was barely enough work for the manager and one kennel worker.

Community involvement was another answer to getting our name out there where people with pets could see it. We gave support to organizations that had connections with the people who had pets and who used our services – the Humane Society, National Public Radio, and other local radio stations and the newspapers. We donated gift certificates and "pampered pet baskets" for boarding and grooming to fund-raising groups for their silent auctions.

"You should think about credit cards, you know, Mom

– no one carries cash with them these days." Henry would bring this up, but I had to point out that we tell people we take only cash and checks.

"And you know, most people remember that now!" I said.

And Now for the Rest of the Story: Fifteen Years Later

WE KEPT GOING -- like that battery bunny, we kept going and going, though not without some interesting and even exciting moments. Some of them I would call "learning experiences," which means one wishes they didn't have to happen but it was a good thing they did.

Turnover of part-time staff was often a problem, but not one that Louis couldn't fix. He was the expert at hiring and firing. I learned I was not the best at the personnel part of running the place.

Louis was able to spend more time with his English Pointers, training them for field trials. He had two horses, Tennessee Walkers, important for those field trials where the dogs are running for at least an hour and only someone on a horse can keep up. While he enjoyed those dogs, six of them, he fast became attached to the small dogs we boarded in the Front Room. I loved to watch him pick up and cuddle one of those tiny little guys, frequently tucking one inside his jacket if the weather was cold.

"Some day I won't be able to do the field trial stuff, and

then I'm going to get one of these little fellows," he would say after tucking some of them back into their houses late at night. But meanwhile he was caught in the competitive crunch of training those hard-running pointers, and I often saw him give them a pat and scratch around the ears as he fed them and said good night.

I became more and more involved in writing. I attended classes and seminars. Some were at Fishtrap in Oregon and others were online through the University of Washington, Stanford University, and the University of Minnesota mentorship program. I completed two novels, a memoir, numerous short stories, and a score of poems. I sent them off to agents and magazines, but then joined the long list of rejection letter writers. It's a difficult moment when the letter reads something about being "unable to accept your manuscript at this time." How could I claim to spend my time writing and consider it an important occupation when I had nothing to show for it? It was labeled as my "hobby" by family, and probably some friends. I didn't consider it a hobby and kept my eyes on that prize of publication. In desperation I considered the self-publishing option, but there was always that hope that someday, some publisher would see a financial value in what I wrote

I had this dream, long held, of being up on some stage, and receiving the audience's applause for something great I had accomplished. I don't know what accomplishment it woule be, but at this time, having something published might do. Did this indicate a need for acceptance? And if so, acceptance by whom?

Meanwhile I tried to make Sagemoor the very best boarding kennel possible. While Louis managed maintenance and the septic system, and the manager took care of the staff and daily running of the place, I was left to order supplies, pay the bills and do the payroll, write the newsletter and manage the website and e-mail, and deal with the difficult clients.

The website was to become one of those "learning experiences" – like stepping into a muddy puddle and suddenly finding it's a hole and you're being sucked in deeper and deeper. We updated the Sagemoor Kennels website, now ten years old, adding new information and as many photos as possible. It looked wonderful when finished, complete with drop-down boxes, but it took a while to iron out some of the glitches. Some sections wouldn't print and the online reservation form had to be redone several times before it met with both client and our own satisfaction. Now clients were filling in a reservation request only to be met when they pushed the "submit" button with a notice that said the page could not be submitted. We received one unhappy phone call after another with that one.

In the end I decided to turn the whole problem over to a local business that was familiar with our website. The pages that wouldn't print, and the reservation form that couldn't be submitted and wouldn't come through to us were fixed in a few days. The original lay-out we had worked so hard to complete now looked as good as we had hoped, and now it worked the way it was supposed to. It had taken a long time to get there but I'd learned some important things along the way. This website would stay the way it was – there are some things one doesn't have to do twice.

Emboldened by our success with the new website, we went on to consider how to deal with those clients who would make two- or even three-week reservations around a holiday time and then at the last minute cancel all but three days. We would be left with days we would be unable to fill with paying clients, and sighs and frowns when we thought about it. The only thing to do was to go to a deposit system for those busy times. Henry helped work with Louis and me on the wording for notifying clients that at certain times, now listed on website, in the newsletter and almost everywhere else, we would expect a deposit to hold a reservation – nonrefundable in the case of cancellations – but that would ensure the reservation. We expected a certain amount of argument from clients, especially longtime ones, but were delighted to find all were in agreement with the new system. Our manager put it to work with mailings, tracking the deposits and reservations, and made it work. She had some explaining to do when a long-standing client said

"But I always make this Christmas reservation! Why should I pay a deposit – you know I'm coming."

"Of course, but in the past you have changed those dates several times, and we haven't been able to fill the dates you cancelled."

End of conversation. There was no getting around our manager on this issue. We kept waiting for more complaints, but none came.

What should be next to make Sagemoor Kennels run more smoothly and give clients more satisfaction? Louis and I were examining payment by credit card. Henry, our son and a very experienced manager of a large business, assured us that credit card payment would make it easier not only for us but most important of all, for the customer.

"Happy customers keep coming back," Henry would re-peat.

Louis might say something about my not remembering some of the things I have learned – such as why it's not a good idea to change things that are working.

"It's important to be up to date," I reply.

My next endeavor to bring Sagemoor into the twenty-first century had nothing to do with the computer.

I decided the kennel needed to meet some performance goals.

Years before, when I worked for Westinghouse Hanford, we were forever faced with meeting performance goals. In a modern business operation it was important to measure performance by examining whether the organization was meeting various goals. So why shouldn't this apply to a boarding kennel? Why not Sagemoor Kennels|?

PetCare Services Association, formerly the American Boarding Kennels Association to which we had belonged since before we even built the kennel, offered an Accreditation Certification. I read the fine print and decided it didn't sound too hard and would certainly give us a method of measuring our performance. If we passed, we would be only the fourth or fifth in Washington State to achieve this goal. The blue ribbon would be eye-catching on our logo, too.

I signed up.

The UPS guy, who had been trained to give my dogs treats when he came, delivered a large parcel containing the workbook and instructions on what was needed to achieve either the Silver standard or the Gold. I went for the Gold. I saw at once that this was going to take some work, but never considered the time it would take. I looked casually at the various standards we had to meet and the criteria used to measure our performance on each standard. It was a little overwhelming at first glance.

I put the whole thing back in its packing box and decided to wait for a while. It was summer, and that meant trips to the mountains and a busy time at the kennel. There would be more time later. From the little I saw in the instructions, I could see I would have to do some writing, and that could wait.

When I eventually retrieved the box and examined what was expected if I wanted to be a Pet Care Services Gold Accredited Kennel, I saw I would have to demonstrate that we met certain standards - a great many of them. The easiest and most acceptable way was with photographs. So I took photos of everything about the kennel, both inside and out -- from the large sign out at the road, the parking lots for both clients and staff, the reception area, the kennel space, to the bathroom, the kitchen, the food storage, and even the fire extinguishers; the fences, the signs, even the one that says "no smoking" – I photographed everything. Then I put the photos in the enclosed photo holders and labeled them according to the instructions. Whew! That was a big job.

It all took a great deal of time and writing and included a visit from another kennel owner to review all the work I had sent in. Then we waited and waited.

Then it came. A phone call first, and then the official-looking envelope and certificate. We had received the Gold Accreditation Standard for Boarding Kennels. We put it up in a professional-looking frame and sent in a press release to the Tri City Herald. A few weeks later I had a phone call from one of the best editors on that paper. She wanted to do an article about Sagemoor, and would bring a cameraman with her. That article was a winner. I had it framed and it is now on the wall of the reception area for all to see and read. I felt I'd done something very special – like getting up on that stage in my dreams and receiving applause from a large audience.

Alarms and Excursions

THE NOISE WAS loud. Louis and I were both asleep when the alarm sounded almost over our heads. The alarms were placed in two locations in the house, as well as up in the apartment and over in the kennel. But the fire alarm sounded outside as well. So when the fire alarm sounded that night, it was enough to wake the dead and it blasted us out of our sleep. Somehow we were not surprised.

Earlier in the evening the last staff member to leave had talked to us about a smell in the kennel.

"It's like something's burning, an electrical smell." Louis looked everywhere but could not locate the origin of the smell. It was slight but definitely from something burning. Louis and I checked again when we went over to the kennel about nine-thirty to take the little Front Room Guys out for their evening run on the exercise yard. No clues, but still that slight burned smell. We went to bed.

The fire alarm sounded about midnight. Louis tore over to the kennel, and I called 911. Moon Security, our security folks, called us to confirm that we needed assistance, and in the midst of all these alarms and excursions my three Corgis all barked and ran madly around. I tried to get the alarms turned off but gave up until Moon Security called back to tell me to turn off the alarms by putting in my security code. Why didn't I think of that? What was it, anyway? Oh, yes -- it was on top of the control panel. Success, and I was on my way to the kennel. I put on slippers and a raincoat – I don't know why a raincoat, because it wasn't raining, but it was hanging over a chair near the back door so I grabbed it and left.

There was thick smoke in the front office and the front area of the kennel. There was a firewall between that area and the main kennel where the majority of the dogs are boarded. No smoke back there. So the fire was somewhere in the front.

Louis yelled at me to start with the cats. Our proposed plan for cat evacuation was to put cats in pillow cases and take them out that way to the barn. But most cats, thankfully, come in their own cat carriers and those are parked in the Cat Room. There were three cats, and one of them was Nicholas who was the Sagemoor cat and lived in his own two-room cat condo on the ground floor. He was happy to be let out, and streaked out the door and on out through the open front door. I remembered our emergency plan for getting the cats out, and I pulled down a pillow case from the shelf where they were stored under the label "Emergency Only" -- why would anyone want a pillow case for anything else out there? I wondered. Cat number one didn't want to go into any pillow case – no way – he made it very plain with that low growl cats can give. Then I noticed where the cat carriers were stored, and resorted to those. But this cat didn't like this idea any more than he did the pillow case. He considered this all a game, and ran up and down from one level of his condo to another. Eventually I pinned him down in the lower level and he had nowhere to go except into his carrier. I hurriedly shut the door and turned to get the other cat into her carrier. I stuffed her toy mouse into the carrier first, and she followed. She was no trouble then. Louis appeared to pick up the carriers and take them outside.

"Jenny, I've got the Front Room Guys out on the Exercise Yard, so would you herd them into the empty barn kennel so I can let the other dogs from the main kennels out there?"

So far, we had followed our fire emergency plan, except the pillow case idea didn't work too well. Now we had ten little Front Room dogs out on the Exercise Yard, running all over the place. The Exercise Yard was well-fenced with six- to seven-foot fences and was secure from dogs escaping. Our plan was to put the little dogs out there first, then herd them into the barn while we got the rest of the dogs from the main kennels out onto the Exercise Yard, and we would sort them out there. Fire Department trucks were arriving and their lights and sirens were setting off Louis's dogs in the barn kennels. Fires don't go quietly. I got all except three of the Front Room guys into the one barn kennel. The dogs already there were all lined up watching the excitement. The errant threesome was running round the corner of the kennels to see what was happening out there, or coming back to where I stood trying to get them to "kennel up," but without much luck. I was afraid if I opened the gate to that barn kennel, some of those dogs already safely in there would get out. I remembered there were emergency leashes hanging inside the kennel door, so I grabbed them. Perhaps I could leash one of these little boys.

The main kennel was smoke-free. But the front area of the kennel was full of smoke, with firemen streaming in the front door from the line of fire trucks filling the parking lot. I had never been so glad to see so many firemen with their heavy protective clothing and helmets. I was aware of my raincoat and pajamas. The sheriff drove up – not in protective clothing, but I still felt pajamas were not exactly the appropriate wear to meet the sheriff who boarded his dogs with us. He wanted to know how the fire started and that was not something I knew, so I directed him to Louis and the group of firemen, who seemed to know something about it.

Louis was taking firemen up the ladder from the food storage room to the attic. Apparently the fire had started up there. I grabbed the leashes and went back to see if I could get those three little ones into the barn. I was beginning to think if the fire was up in the attic, it might not have spread to the main kennel, where there is no attic. I felt I was in the way and would do better watching the dogs. Nicholas the cat found me and was doing the "cat twist and shake" around my legs, singing a plaintive song about how nobody ever fed him.

The firemen stood around outside. The fire had been dealt with. It was out, and a couple of firemen were doing a last-minute check with various instruments to see that all was well and we could all go home and go to bed.

Louis and I opened windows in the kennel to let the remaining smoke and smell out. The Front Room guys appeared glad to return to their own beds in the Front Room. The cats were equally happy to return to their condos, though Nicholas was now prowling around the front door to our house, probably expecting some food from there. My three Corgis spied him through the sunroom windows and barked abuse at him, making wet nose marks all across the glass. I took Nicholas back to his two rooms and gave him some wet cat food. I decided to leave the lights on. We might have to go back again. Did those firemen get all the fire out? Fires scare the whatever out of me.

Louis and I were wide awake, even if it was three o'clock in the morning,

"What about breakfast?" I asked.

"What about a drink outside on the patio?" he countered.

So we sat outside, I with a scotch and he with his non-alcoholic beer – so his heart wouldn't fibrillate. And we reviewed all the possible causes of the fire. Louis was sure he knew, but his explanation left me a little baffled. Technological details about heating and air-conditioning were not my specialty. Apparently those pieces of machinery were involved.

Passing Time - and Lucy

FIFTEEN YEARS HAD passed since we opened Sagemoor, thinking it would be a good retirement project to keep us occupied since we were not daytime soap watchers, didn't play golf, and didn't go to kaffe klatsches. So what if we wanted to play with dogs or write a few words now and then? It had been a success, however one looked at it. What did we expect? We expected to work and we expected to take on some challenges. It was an opportunity to try something new and different. We found all of that and more.

We didn't expect to meet so many great people -- clients, staff, vendors, contractors -- and so many wonderful dogs and cats. And we didn't expect to say goodbye to some of them.

Those first dogs we boarded were not all young pups when they first met us. After fifteen years, even the youngest ones are getting up there now. We've said goodbye to many dear ones – Rusty, Eddie, Sara Grace. But there were others, too many to name. Your ghosts prowl the Exercise Yard fence, chase the green ball across it, sit at your run gates. We hear your bowls rattle as though expecting food, your yip and woof from the Front Room long after we're closed, your meow from Condo Eleven in the Cat Room and no one's in it. Who took the leashes off the wall where they were hanging, opened the run gates to 32 and 11 when no one was using them, whose feet pad the hall, whose nose pushes against a hand about to lock the back door and say good night?

All of us who have worked at Sagemoor have said good-bye to some dear friends. We all know of others to whom we may shortly say goodbye. These dogs and cats become our family, as they have to their own families, and we grieve when they leave us. Somehow, though, they are always with us.

FIRST DOG LUCY

She gives a woof.
Her dark eyes hold mine
damp nose nudges hand.
It's time, she says.
Time for dinner.
Time for a walk.
Time for whatever happens next.

When her time comes
will she again give me
that woof ?
Her dim eyes search for mine
to signal again it's time?

We sit together, warmed by spring sun.
Bird sounds break the windless quiet.
A robin digs for worms in soil still feeling winter's chill.
Lucy gave up eating a few days ago.

Today her eyes are bright, nose twitches,
Those prick ears erect as ever.
I rub those ears, her legs curl, her eyes close
Her smile says to keep this up.
I read that familiar face.
Is it time? I wish I knew.

We tried
She and I
Not believing
Not admitting
The end would come.
Six months or more
We battled
Ever denying we couldn't win.

Now at peace,
She rests beneath plum trees,
Among bright flowers.
A stone marks her spot
Facing east towards the rising sun

Our Roots

IT'S 2010 AND I'm out in New Zealand for my annual pilgrimage to my roots. I keep in touch with Louis by cell phone.

Today I'm watching the waves break on that mound of rock and clay, standing alone offshore, its green vegetation clinging bravely, wind-blown shrubs and trees leaning in one direction. I think of green whipped cream on top of a small chocolate cake, surrounded by sauces flavored with the tastes of a thousand miles of Pacific Ocean, whipped by the strong easterlies to crash in a froth of spray against this coast. That small island seems stuck out there, a lone swimmer almost to the mainland -- yet if it reached out an arm of rock and clay, it still would not make it to shore. Below where I sit, there's a curving bay with plenty of room for the island to nestle in, among the pohotokawa trees bright with blossom, New Zealand Christmas trees decorated with red ornaments. Island, you might feel more secure with the land's arms wrapped around you. So near and yet so far from a safe harbor.

Mother was like that island. She never quite made it to shore, preferring, I think, always to stand a little outside, in her own space. Did she have any doubts about where she belonged? Was it England or New Zealand? Did she feel she was welcomed in New Zealand, or did she have to cope with some anti-British sentiments, unthinkingly expressed? They were there, and still can be. Dealing with the rough introduction to the country that she experienced, I think she coped by remaining true to her English background. As my cousin Janet says, "She remained the same, never changed, always that English lady doctor."

Janet, my cousin, is right. Mother never changed.

I wonder what drove her, what were her passions, what mattered most to her. I can list some items I know were important to her.

"Being a wife and mother are the best thing for a woman."

I can almost hear the clipped tones to her voice: "More rewarding than any other career. At least I found that to be so, Jenepher."

Was that a passion, something that drove her on? She had a medical degree, was a qualified doctor, taught in the Medical School for a short while, and worked for years as a School Medical Officer, examining school children, running well-baby clinics, talking to mothers about their children. I think this was another way of her expressing her passion for mothers and children. She used to tell me of some of the worries and concerns mothers would share with her. She would frequently share with them some of her experiences with her own children -- Tony and me. Sometimes a mother would share a worry that her child wasn't talking yet, and Mother's response might be that her daughter – me – also hadn't spoken a word until even later. I believe that some mothers may still believe that Dr. Fitzgerald's daughter didn't talk until eight or nine years of age, walked later, and refused to eat any vegetables – and now she was talking clearly, running a mile, and eating anything put on her plate. Mother had a great belief in reassurance that one's child was doing well and really quite normal.

Mother loved to travel. She loved not just being in another place, another country, but the whole process of getting there. She loved planes, trains, buses. I remember the time I joined Father and Mother in New York, where Father was a speaker at some international medical conference, and Mother and I went to every art gallery we could find. We went from New York to Williamsburg and on to the Great Smokey mountains and Tennessee and on south to Galveston, Texas where Louis and I were living. We went by Greyhound bus the whole way, traveling during the day and stopping off at night.

"You can see so much more from a bus," she said. She was always first in line to board the bus so as to get one of the front seats -- not the ones behind the driver, but the ones across the aisle. She loved seeing the small towns and little bus stop restaurants, where she would buy a serving of cherry pie a la mode. She always said that it was better to ask for the ice cream on the side, but still would be served the pie with ice cream on top. And she would never say "a la mode."

"That's French, Jenepher. And we're in America. It should be just cherry pie with ice cream – and I want it next to the pie, not on the pie."

She always said that, but to me, not to the person behind the counter, because as she put it, "I can't understand what they say and they probably don't understand me." She would quote Winston Churchill's words about one people separated by a common language. Or whatever it was he said.

Travel was high on her list of passions. I should add that she would never use the word "passion," probably preferring to list her "interests."

Next on her list of "interests" would be books, reading, politics, the daily news, and news analysis. She wasn't much into television, preferring to listen to the radio, especially the late- night news and "Book at Bedtime." She read aloud to Tony and me when father was away at the War, and I don't remember her ever being without a book in her hand: Jane Austen, the Brontës and Galsworthy, and especially Kipling. Detective stories were high on the list, but not thrillers or spy novels.

"I never liked anything where there was a lot of violence and killing. I liked Margery Allingham and Dorothy Sayers because they always gave you some clues so you could guess who had done the murder. And of course, they wrote so well."

I look out at that small island, so firmly anchored in its place just offshore, waves breaking and spray flying now the wind has risen. What kept Mother firmly anchored in the face of storms? When Father died, and with Tony and me married and living on the other side of two oceans, it seemed as though she lost whatever had kept her anchored to New Zealand. She returned to England to live, where she had friends who dated back to her school days. One of her passions must have been her English roots, so she moved back there. She returned to New Zealand only once, preferring to save her travel passion for almost annual trips to the U.S. to visit her grandchildren, , or for travel with old friends to France and Italy and other European countries. Once she was about to go on a trip to China, but cancelled that at the last moment.

"If I died out there, Jenepher, it would be such a mess for you. So I thought it wiser to cancel the trip."

"No, Mother," I thought to myself, "Go and enjoy, and if you die, that's just fine – it will probably be the only way I'll get to see China."

But she didn't go, and she didn't die, not then, and I have never seen China. But China may have felt too distant from her beloved England, and she needed that English bond to keep her feeling anchored.

Of course her great passion was her husband, Henry Walden Fitzgerald, truly the love of her life. Forty-seven years of marriage, separated by the war for five years, by occasional trips to England. She travelled to the U.S.A. to see us, but she never really felt comfortable in this country where she couldn't understand the language or the customs – or so she said. Her passion as a wife and mother never died – she needed to make sure her "cubs" were secure in new dens with no dangers lurking around. Later there were grandchildren, and she dearly loved spending time with them. I have the photos of her and my four children and my brother Tony's children. She read to them, played card games, taught them those famous "Pounce" and "Huff" card games... my children remember her well for time spent with them.

She even knew her great-granddaughter, the next Jenepher, Elizabeth's daughter. How she would have loved to talk with Jenny today. Jenny is in Geneva, working for a brokerage firm and spending her days off with her Italian boyfriend. Jenny, I think, prefers Italy to Switzerland, and she is determined to live in Europe. How Mother would have enjoyed time with Jenny exploring art galleries, museums, and the high-end fashion shops. I'd like to think her spirit is hovering somewhere over this great- granddaughter, who remembers her today as "tiny-grandmother-who-went-flying."

Mother never knew her other great-granddaughter, Gabrielle, Catherine's daughter, but she would have enjoyed Gabby's enthusiasm for sports, books and travelling. Gabby has been to places Mother never went to: Nepal, India, and Africa, as well as New Zealand, England, and Italy.

As I write this, I think how powerful are those genes that came from my mother, and are still at work. Her love of art, travel, politics, and reading continue to thrive. And so does her capacity for coping with the challenges.

But life wasn't always that easy for her. Is it for anyone?

We all knew she was a worrier.

"If you're not back when you say you'll be, then I'll worry."

I can see that look on her face now as she said that. Brow furrowed, a blink of the eyes, a slight sniff, lips tight, as she turned her head away to signal that's all to be said about that. No one cared to allow Mother the opportunity to worry. But if she ever worried about Walden, I don't remember her ever expressing the displeasure she voiced when others had allowed her to worry.

"We were all scared of your mother," a close cousin comments. I was scared, especially if I was late home and she would be waiting and worrying. Don't know about my brother. I have the impression he might have done no wrong in her eyes. He was the son, the boy, the man who followed the path she had chosen for him, though I am sure it was one he chose happily. She was more comfortable in the company of men than of women, probably because she had grown up with two brothers and a father who adored her. I never quite understood this, but I remember her saying something about men having more to say than women. Even years spent in a girls' boarding school, a women's college, her work with mothers and children as a school medical officer, never changed this view. There may have been some inner belief that men were more important than women. I feel sad about that. She must never have believed in herself as an important valuable human being. And she was. She gave me so much, and I discovered that only when it was too late to tell her.

I often have that "lone island" feeling. Where do I belong? What would be the best fit? Where am I most welcome? My little offshore island of clay and rock and scrubby plants sometimes disappears from view, and I wonder where I now would find a safe harbor to welcome me. Mother was sure where she belonged, no doubts there, and it was England. I am not so sure for myself. How welcome am I when I visit? Would I consider New Zealand my home, in the way Mother had no doubt about England being that home for her? Yet, I see the hills of Central Otago, the Maniototo plain and the Rock and Pillar range, the Southern Lakes and the Dunedin harbor and Blue Skin Bay and I want to steer my rocky island into the cove or rock shelter that I see would give me a good fit.

My passions are like my mother's, though I go off in new directions. While I love my books, I also like to write; I love art and music, and especially ballet. I love dogs, definitely with a passion, and I enjoy historical research. But first and foremost, my husband, my children and grandchildren, my three companion dogs and my home in eastern Washington share space when it comes to the passions of heart and head. I cannot choose among them at this time. I could not leave my house and land on the banks of the Columbia River – it has become my "New Zealand."

And yet, and yet?

That question lies still unanswered. Did Mother have any doubts about leaving the house she and my father had built close to the native bush in Dunedin, where the huge native pigeons, the korere, came to feed at the bird feeders, where the bell bird and tui chimed their daily carol to the world and the little fantails fluttered busily around the beech and manuka trees? She never said and I never asked.

I have recently read in the New Zealand *Listener* of an artist, poet, printmaker, painter, and novelist, John Pule, who comes from Niue, a Pacific Island, and lives mostly in New Zealand. He writes:

"We all share the same experience – of coming from overseas, of hardship, of trying to make a go of it."

I think he is talking about me and about Mother. He didn't know either Mother or me when he wrote those words. But they speak to me. Pule was writing more about the Pacific Islander experience, whether white or brown, small island or the bigger ones of New Zealand. His point was that when you come from somewhere else, from crossing the seas, there will be hardships not just in that crossing, or passage as I call it, but in the arrival in the new place and the need to "make a go of it" - to struggle with that which the new place presents us. Mother coped with the new experiences of being in New Zealand, of the hardships presented by economic depression and by war, of being the stranger in a large family. I too when I arrived in Texas, a married woman, but a stranger, had some difficulty finding what was the expected way of behaving.

Where did we come from, she and I? I know she came from England and I come from New Zealand, in that those were our "natal shores," to quote Kipling. But therein lie our differences as well as some commonalities. She was born at a time when England and all of Europe had been enjoying several years of "peaceful productivity," when there was time and money for travel, such as Mother's family long stay in Switzerland. However, by the time she reached her teenage years in 1914, the Great War, World War I, had been declared, to end just over four years later with more than ten million dead and many more millions whose lives were changed forever. The optimism present in European culture in the first decade of the century had ended, never to return. A small piece of Mother's dreams for her children may have come from those early childhood years when she and her family spent time traveling, attending concerts, finding time to talk, to discuss, to play together. I imagine that hidden sense of optimism found a place when it came to her decision to marry my father and sail away alone to the other side of the world. That pre-war British world before 1914 was one where people travelled to distant countries, lived in places where language and customs were different.

While English was the common language, those living in what was then the British Empire – and it was always colored pink on the world maps -- learned some new customs, met new people, learned new languages, and were introduced to new foods, all of which were described in letters sent by ship back to England, still called "Home" by those expatriates. Mother's cousins, Kitty and Francie, lived in China for several years as teachers, and other cousins emigrated to Canada. Even her grandfather had been captain of his own sailing ship, journeying between the Orkney Islands, England, South America, and India, a captain of a merchant ship carrying corn, cotton, possibly coal and fabrics. Her grandmother and several uncles accompanied him on occasion to those distant places. New Zealand wasn't such a new country, and in one sense not that far off, but it took a long time to get there. At least the new inhabitants came for the most part from the British Isles and spoke English in all its dialects. Travel might be slow, either by train or boat, but it gave time to talk, to read and to write letters. Those letters were written with a good understanding of good grammar. No telephones, no television, no internet, and no cell phones! I think Mother would be horrified by the way I rely on e-mail for most of my correspondence and my cell phone for communication.

It was a slower time, even after the end of the Great War. Mother finished high school and went to university. The only reference I remember her making in regard to the Great War, as it was called back then, was than her two brothers volunteered and served, one in the Navy and the other in the Air Force, both as reservists, which meant they were not in the regular service. She never mentioned whether they were drafted, though I know there was conscription in England during the last year of the war. She also mentioned one great friend who had been at university with her and whose fiancé had been killed in France.

"A whole generation of young men were wiped out in France."

If she didn't say that, then I'm quoting someone. There was much censorship of information in the newspapers about the action in Europe – and no radio or newsreels to bring the war back to the home folks. I know Mother must have read about it, and probably she heard her parents, especially her father, discuss what they knew about what was going on. No bombing, no planes overhead, no news reports – it might have been hard to imagine horrors that were happening over the Channel in France or on the Eastern Front or out in the Atlantic where the German submarines were wrecking havoc with the shipping. Mother never talked about it, not even when the Second World War came along. Still, she was a child of war. As I am.

Life in New Zealand those first few years after my birth was a period of economic depression, but also a period of peace prior to the Second World War. I was much younger than Mother had been when war hit her early life. I was only six years old at the time the war broke out. Father left for overseas almost immediately. Like Mother, I grew up during a world war and it had its effect on me. I was frightened a great deal of those years, terrified it would come to New Zealand, afraid my father would be killed. I remember the nightmares still.

Why else am I so passionate about war? I am perhaps trying to fix something that cannot be fixed. I read mostly about the first and second World Wars in particular, but also about medieval wars. At the same time I am a child of an immigrant, and am myself an immigrant. So I read about migrations, people on the trail, on the high seas, in search of their dreams. Motivations, what makes people move from one place to another, how to they move, what happens to them personally, inside themselves, when they do move. What do they bring with them, what leave behind, what is too heavy to carry and is it left behind somewhere on the trail, buried deep in the ocean? What does one generation of migrants pass on to the next? Is it picked up and again passed on? I am still seeking answers to those questions for myself.

While Mother loved art, music and beautiful china, furniture, rugs, both antique and modern, she never tried any artistic expression herself. On the other hand, I have tried almost everything that has been offered in an art class or pattern book. Father had some skills at watercolor and I picked up his paints and tried my hand at watercolor. There were one or two artists on the Fitzgerald and Walden side of the family. I took whatever classes were available to me. I would not put myself in the same class as those family members who became well-known New Zealand artists. Like Father, I found it easier to use my camera to record the places and people that caught my eye and my imagination.

Once children were settled in school and I had more time I took classes in fabric art, and found embroidery, knitting, weaving, quilting, and appliqué gave me much more satisfaction. I love the interplay of color against color, fabric against fabric, wool against silk, the feel of the fibers twisting through my fingers, the pattern developing as I progress one row after another, one piece next to another, small and large.

There are patterns in the sweater I am knitting, the shawl I wove that now hangs over an old rocking chair, those Oriental and Navajo rugs lying on my hardwood floors, the half-finished rug on my loom, the quilts I have pieced and quilted, especially the one hanging on the wall. That's a quilt that I look at often, and wonder why did I ever put that piece of turquoise- green fabric in the center? The color doesn't really fit in, but I just liked it and thought it matched. Only later, looking at the whole thing – and it's not a large quilt – hanging where it is, did I think I should try replacing that green piece with another one that matches the other colors, that fits in. But it would be a complicated task, taking a great many stitches out and restitching, so I haven't done it. There's a tradition among quilters, I believe, that there should always be one little fault, a small one, because only God can do "perfect" and we mortals should leave perfect up to Him. Perhaps that piece says something about Mother and me – we never quite fit in, but at the same time, we stand out in our own way, making our own special contributions, not wanting to be missed or overlooked.

There are patterns everywhere we look. Large patterns, like the seasons, or the procedure for making a cake or a dressing. Then there are the details that go into those patterns that make one season, or recipe or rug or quilt differ from another that may look the same at first glance. Last winter may have been colder than the previous one, the spring windier or wetter than this, but overall, winters follow the same general pattern and are followed by spring with its green shoots and summer with its blooms and autumn with its fruits. General patterns -- but the differences, the things we remember, are the details. One knitted Aran sweater, full of cables, will not be the same as another. One Two Grey Hills rug may not be exactly the same as another, even by the same weaver; my recipe for chicken cacciatore may be different from my daughter's.

Our lives have patterns, though we may not always know we're following one, becoming aware of it only over time. There is Mother leaving England, marrying a doctor and living in New Zealand, a far-off country, going back to school for graduate medical work later on and then working in her chosen profession. Then there is me. I marry a doctor, leave New Zealand and live in a foreign country, go back to graduate school and get two graduate degrees in mental health that enable me to work in that field.

What are the details of our lives? So much depends on our circumstances, the context of our lives. Do we seize the opportunities offered, or do we not? I think Mother seized those available to her through her marriage. Walden was well-known in the medical field, and he and Mother travelled to international medical conferences and entertained some interesting people from overseas. But perhaps there were not the opportunities offered her that were available to me when I came to the States.

I dove right in almost as soon as I arrived in Galveston, Texas. Louis had a very low salary as a surgery resident, and so I quickly looked for a job. My first one was as secretary to the Dean of the Medical School and Director of the University Hospitals. I had a boss with a high-sounding title and an administrative assistant with whom he was very close, but not a great deal of work for me. I think I got that job because I had shorthand in three languages and spoke with an accent. I never used the shorthand, and didn't talk much to anyone. But one day I was asked to give a lunch time talk on New Zealand to the local Kiwanis. In attendance was the director of the local public library. He offered me a job as Young Adult Librarian in the public library. I seized that opportunity. That was much more interesting, and I read books and went to schools to talk about those books to students. I soon found that people listened when I spoke – it was the accent. I learned not to be put off by the remark: "Oh, how I love to hear you talk!"

I have Mother's old recipe book. There is her recipe for marmalade, another for baked custard, ones for curried lamb (using leftovers from the Sunday roast lamb) and highly spiced chutneys to go with the curries, and some others, including one for Christmas cake that I know she never used, preferring to buy one from the bakery. I still use the tomato chutney one and the one for marmalade.

Mother and I must have been working from the same recipe book. It might have included one for "Immigration" or "A Medical Marriage" or " Raising Children in Another Country" or many other titles. But we followed such similar paths. I didn't have to deal with a war and an absent husband, but I found the United States was a country with very different customs and language than New Zealand. Mother and I both went back to graduate schools when our children became teenagers and then we both worked for many years. We found different flavors to spice our lives: Mother was involved with community activities, and I explored fabric arts as well as women's issues. We communicated at long distance, mostly by letter, sometimes by cross-ocean visits.

Significant changes came for us both about the same time in our lives My father died at seventy–one, leaving Mother to decide whether to stay on in New Zealand or move back to England to live. She chose to move back to England. I, on the other hand, had to deal with retirement, both mine and Louis's. Our retirement brought us to build a new life together, building a business and building a new house. To do all that meant leaving the house we had built and where the children had grown up and starting over in a new location, with a new business and a new flavor to our relationship, definitely adding spice to our lives.

It's been fifteen years since we moved across the river, built our timber-frame home and opened Sagemoor Kennels. And it's all still going strong.

I had promised myself two things when I retired. One was to get back to writing. I had let that slide over the years, except for letters, a journal that I kept up only now and then, and all the mental health records I kept daily. Now I was going to do some writing for myself. I wanted to write a novel. And the other thing I wanted was my own dog. So I got a Welsh Corgi like Mother had so many years ago when I was a teenager. And then I got another and later a third. My corgi herd. I discovered writing courses, both locally and at the wonderful organization called Fishtrap.

Mother bought an apartment in Cambridge and lived there for twenty-five years. We visited her there as often as we could. She came out to us every Christmas for three weeks until the Christmas of 1994, which was her last visit to us. That time she was ill and had to be hospitalized, much to her disgust. Illness was something she thought she could deal with by just being strong-minded and "getting on with things," as she would put it. But this time she was slow to recover, and when I took her back to England after almost three months with us, it was obvious she needed to live somewhere with some nursing care on hand. My brother and I found her a very pleasant residence where she had her own bed sitter and bathroom and could have her meals either with other residents or in her room. Catherine and I visited her several times and always shared her meals with her in the elegant dining room, where everyone was served sherry with their meals and the food was excellent. She watched the news every day, listened to the news on her radio and to "Book at Bedtime" and read her Jane Austen and the *Guardian*.

Was she content? She missed her beloved Walden; his photo sat next to her bed and another on her desk. She had some of her favorite pieces of furniture with her, her grandmother Catherine Tutin's dresser, her mother's desk, a small bookcase from her home in Wallasey, and her father's chair and a beautiful old dressing table with mirror that she and Walden had bought in an antique sale in Dunedin. She never stopped missing her independence. If she could, she would have liked to have had one more trip, one more flight across an ocean, perhaps to stay with us.

I don't live in New Zealand today. I live in Washington State. Even though I find much in this state that reminds me of Dunedin's grey stone buildings, the Otago coastline, its ribboned rivers and bouldered hillsides, my internal compass points south across the oceans and, like the albatross that nests at the Taiaroa Heads, my sense of who I am wings to the place I still call home. So much has changed out there, yet so much stays the same.

I lean forward to peer out the window of the plane. Thin clouds slide past for a while, cutting off my view of what is below. Then they separate, like theater curtains when the show is about to begin. There is the sea, deep blue green touched with white, where the long Pacific rollers crest gently before making landfall. The Waitaki River pours its wide fan of silt into the ocean, only to be absorbed into the heaving blueness. The map below is familiar. In my mind, I give name to those steep volcanic cones shaded with forests or velvet smooth with tussock grasses, the rocky promontories cutting slices from the sea's smoothness, rivers and streams etching patterns across this patchwork of greens and yellows. The little towns spin past as I turn my head to take note of each: Palmerston, Waitaouiti, Karitane, Warrington, Waitati, with Blueskin Bay and my grandfather's summer home. Then we're over the long arrow of the sandy Spit, pointing to Taiaroa Heads and the Lighthouse and the entrance to the narrow Otago Harbor with the peninsula on one side and the railway line out to Port Chalmers on the other. A second later and the plane sinks low over the hills, and Dunedin is below me. I want the plane to slow down, to stop for a few moments so I can identify all the familiar streets, the buildings, and the Town Belt of native bush that swathes itself across the city.

The sound of the plane's engines changes to a low growl, and then comes the clattering of its wheels being lowered. Clouds roll in, but for a moment I can see the slopes of Saddle Hill and the beaches beyond. Then we're crossing fields of cows and sheep, then the winding Taieri River, and ahead is the Maungatua Range with Central Otago hiding behind its lowering ridges. The plane's wheels bump, and engines give a final roar of greeting before we roll to a stop.

It's January, it's summertime, and I've come home again.

I'm back on familiar ground, walking streets I have known so long, the same but not the same, old buildings now dwarfed by new. I turn around to look at the city nestling between hill and harbor. For me it's more than the closeness of family out here in these antipodean islands, it's this closeness of the country I grew up in. My favorite poet, Brian Turner, himself a native of Dunedin and Central Otago, writes:

"and finally, it's the where
you know, that refines
the who you are."

There's something about this place that I know so well, even after being away for a while, that when I hear the familiar words, the accents, see the houses, and turn the corners without thinking whether I am driving on the left or the right side of the road, it's like putting on an old favorite sweater that still fits and it warms me.

It's not the streets, and it's not the houses, and it's not the students who no longer wear gabardine raincoats and "Cambridge blue and old gold" hand-knitted scarves wound round their necks, but it's something else that tells me this is where my roots are still firmly embedded. I can feel it when I drive out to Waitati or up past Middlemarch into the Manioitoto and see the Rock and Pillar Range where as students we skied weekends instead of writing history papers, and the Rough Ridge and the Lammermoors, and that sky that is nowhere else in the world so clear. I'd like to say that my roots tingle, that I want to just stand still and stretch out my arms and hold it all tight to me.

And so I keep coming back.

Today I watch the water break on that island, still in place, and I soon will return to my other roots on the banks of the Columbia River.

It's Been One Heck of a Ride!

"ONE OF THESE days we're going to have to give this up!" Louis's words sent a shiver through me: not of excitement this time, but of apprehension. Give up the kennel? Sell the place? Surely he didn't mean we'd move somewhere else?

If treats were helpful for little dogs, what would it take to get me to move? What had it taken in the past to get me to move? The prospect of something new, something exciting, shared with Louis, the promise of a new house, shared interests – any and all of these, but I had lost interest in moving from where we were; changes were not a priority for me now. Besides, that nightmare of being left alone, floating unattached in some dark empty space, had never left. It took just a few words to unleash that free- floating anxiety.

"Someday we'll have to sell this place. It'll be too much for us," Louis said.

"I'm not leaving here – you'll have to carry me out in a box. Better still, you can bury me here – I'll pick my spot." I couldn't tell anyone of my fear of moving from the place in which I felt so well- rooted. I had ownership in the kennel business and I loved the house and the land around us. What did Louis mean? If the kennel were too much, why not lease

it out to someone who wanted to run it? A veterinarian, perhaps?

Louis saw it as a whole parcel and that someone might
want to buy kennel, house, barn, pastures – the lot. It would
be a pity to pass up such a possibility. Where did he think
we would go? Not to one of those retirement villages? There
had to be a way to stay here, have someone else do some
of the heavy work. But Louis was not one to give up doing
something that he saw himself doing well. No one, in his es-
timation, could do the garden, the maintenance, take care of
the pasture, the sprinkler systems, and septic tanks as well
as he did. He was right, of course. He was a perfectionist in
his own way – just as I was in mine. I had learned to give up
some tasks. Perhaps he could pass some of his on to someone
else?

He'd set a date – another ten years, five years…time was
passing far too quickly. He hadn't slowed down at all – sped
up, if anything. It would be the same as when he set his date
for retirement – one day, he'd announce that this was it! I re-
solved to do it differently this time. I just wasn't moving.

Traditionally a personally owned business is passed on to
the next interested person, often a family member, a son or a
daughter, who has seen the business grow, been involved in its
development, and looked forward to someday stepping into
Father's or Mother's shoes. I had a hunch that this was becoming a less popular option, but I kept thinking which of our children might like to take on the kennel, perhaps build their own
house on one of the pastures, enjoy the potential the barn and
the other pasture offered, and we could stay on in the house,
still enjoying the view and the space, and even having family
close by. But I had no idea how to make it happen. The last
thing I was good at doing was discussing such difficult things

as the future. I sat on challenging problems, waited to see what happened, but did not take any initiative – at least not until the last moment. There had been times, of course, when I had put some plans into place, and then announced what I was going to do. Marrying Louis was a good example, and going to graduate school was another. I think my decision to sit down and write was the same. That was about it

I reviewed these thoughts on my early morning walks down our lane. First thing in the morning was my time to walk with my dogs to get the newspaper. It was just the four of us -- and the birds and other wildlife to keep us company. As we turned down the lane, there in front of us to the west flowed the Columbia River with Rattlesnake Mountain and the Horse Heaven Hills in the distance. Behind us, to the east, irrigated farmland spread out like a quilt patched with the changing colors and textures of the crops season to season. We had driven up this lane all those years ago to see what the sign "Ranch for Sale" was all about.

In the summer, the sun rose over the eastern edge of the farm at about five o'clock, though the surrounding hills had been touched with a pink glow that also filled our bedroom, signaling my dogs to come and put their paws and noses up near my face to see if I was aware of the time. Lucy grunted her warning while Buddy and Benji uttered sharp barks.

"It's time," they were telling me, "to get up and go get the paper." The dogs sat quietly while I dressed and started the coffee. Then we headed out the front door on our morning exploration.

The sides of the lane, where the gravel was thin, showed the tracks of any early morning passers-by, quail or pheasant and deer, the occasional pawprints of cat or coyote. The dogs sniffed, to see who had entered their territory; their noses dripped with excitement as they checked even the smallest stone for messages from an intruder.

Juniper, sage, and rabbit brush grew up the sloping sides lining the lane, and from deep inside the bushes came the sounds of movements and rustlings. Buddy disappeared and within seconds there was a violent shaking of juniper limbs to mark his progress. A quail flew up from further down, never in any danger, but if I were the quail I would never be sure. The covey was still small. About a dozen birds flew out with a whirr of wings, startling the dogs standing still for a moment before making a team play to catch any slow risers. They had never caught a quail, but lived in hope.

It was the same every spring and early summer when the sun was low and the quail crowed their nesting success. One year I saw a rooster quail escorting twelve little downy golf balls of babies and I could only hope that a hawk had not caught his lady friend. Another year we saw a pair of red foxes herding five pups up the lane to disappear into the field. I wasn't breathing a word about them to anyone.

With the summer came the seagulls to the islands out in the river, taking over from the Canada geese and the ducks who had headed north for the summer. High above came the plaintive cry of the sandhill cranes, their slender shapes disappearing into high drifts of cloud. The seagulls screamed as they circled higher and higher, following the trail of bugs born up on the thermal currents. Soon, those master plasterers, the swallows, moved in to build their nests in the eaves of our house and the kennel.

The three dogs were on watch for the little rabbits, who lived in the juniper bushes and sat like statues waiting for the dogs to catch their scent. The rabbits teased the dogs into chasing them, seeming to know they were never in any danger.

As the seasons changed, so did the sun's entry into our world. In the summer it rose at the eastern edge of the farm, while in the fall its large red globe struggled over the neighbor's cherry orchard further south at a much later hour.

In the long summer evenings, when winter was only a memory or a thought for the future, Louis and I walked around the house, the yard, pausing to survey the river below where yet another house was springing up. When we first came to here I had jokingly said something about hoping for a gas station that sold milk closer than a fifteen-mile drive. Over the years the gas station had come and so had a supermarket, banks, fast food places, a Starbucks, a WalMart, and a movie theater. Houses, condos, and apartments surrounded these icons of civilization.

"Did you ever think we could do it?" I asked Louis on one of these walks.

"I never knew what to think. But it turned out well," he replied with a grin.

"We never really planned anything, though – not long-term goals, that sort of thing?" I was fishing for something more definite that I could get my teeth into.

"I've really only had two goals, Jenny. Getting into medical school, and marrying you." Perfect. I'd heard it before. And I believed it.

"Me too," I reply. "Just two. Marrying you and getting into graduate school."

"I guess retirement was a sort of goal." Louis stopped walking before adding, "Mostly I've just fallen into things -- drifted, you could say." I'd heard that before and it was partly true. The kennel and house building were a long time in coming, but we had thought out every step of the way very carefully, making sure we could make it a success.

Sagemoor Kennels had done so much for us both, providing us, not only with an interesting and challenging business, but also giving us the opportunity to learn so much more about each other. I knew Louis was much better than I was at managing people, doing the training of new staff, and hiring and firing, as well as being the one to take care of the septic system and broken hoses and irrigation systems. I had learned how to run the computer, do payroll, order supplies, and pay the bills. I was more inclined to keep records of all transactions than he was, and I surprised myself, as well as him, with my embrace of the new technologies, such as cell phones, the Internet and later, the automatic irrigation system. We learned to respect our individual skills as well as our differences.

Our children too were all great resources. When we needed an answer to how to fix a clothes dryer that wasn't working, our son Michael said "Google it" and he did and found the answer. He was the technician who could fix technology's breakdowns. Henry told us how to run our business, Sandy told us how to keep the business books straight, Catherine explained how to keep staff happy, and Elizabeth explained the finer points of marketing.

"We must have done something right," I said to Louis on one of our walks.

"It's being a great run for our money," he replied.

As summer moved into fall, the colors changed and the air became heavy with the scent of the late-blooming roses. Our lawns were smooth and green where once lay dead twigs, dried weeds, and even the bones of some long-dead animal.

"I can't imagine we made all this happen." He shook his head in disbelief.

I grabbed hold of his hand. We had had our moments

when we weren't sure we'd make it. I wasn't sure what lay ahead for us now.

All too soon it was fall. The sun came up just that much later and the air was beginning to feel cool as I walked down the lane with my three companions to get the paper. The sky was not as clear, and the light softer. The annual batch of forest fires that plague the state had left a haze in the air.

The lane had changed little since we first drove up in search of that "Ranch for Sale." It had been widened after the New Year's Eve flood to allow for the increased traffic and to make room for better drainage. The junipers still climbed the hillside and the same Dutch elm dropped a limb or two in the strong winter gales, but it was firmly rooted in the dry sand and rock. A rope swing dangled from one limb, installed by Louis for grandchildren. An oriole's nest, no longer protected by a curtain of leaves, hung lonely from another branch. A notice had been added a few yards up the lane from the mail box asking drivers to watch out for the quail, pheasants, rabbits, and dogs -- "yours and ours" -- and even approaching cars. People still rushed up the lane in a hurry to get on with life. The dogs and I took our time on our daily walk.

The colors of the leaves of the trees around the house and kennel soon changed and the yellow, gold, red, and purple of fall replaced the bright greens of summer. As the leaves dropped, more birds' nests showed up, though they too would be blown away later with winter's rough untidy weather. The dry blooms of the roses, dulled and shriveled, rattled in the cold breeze. The quail covey grew to more than forty. The dogs gave them a half-hearted hurry along and they all, heads down, topknots aquiver, scurried to the safety of the sumac.

With the change in seasons, the seagulls left the river and the migrating ducks and geese took their place. As the days grew shorter, we were met on our walk with the sound of beating wings from a formation of Canada geese, their wild calls announcing the arrival of winter. Like a squadron of bombers on a mission, they circled before gradually sinking, undercarriages lowered, to land with a final beat of their wings. The wind from the river blew chill in our faces as we picked up the paper before turning our noses back up the lane in the direction of the warmth of the house. Sometimes we were greeted by a thick fog rising from the river, and if there had been a frost, there would be a crystalline cover to all the twigs, dead leaves, and sprays of asparagus growing wild in the field.

Winter mornings were dark, and the wind whipped tears to my eyes as we started down the lane – I didn't know about the dogs' eyes, but they looked like they closed them! The chill sank through my down jacket, but never seemed to bother the dogs with their thick double-layered coats. The Dutch elm was leafless, its limbs creaking and rattling in the wind. Snow came soon enough together with freezing rain, grey skies and clouds reaching to the ground.

There would be mornings when the sky was a silvery grey with a hint of blue and the sun, still hidden behind Earth's curve, would light the snow on Rattlesnake Mountain to a rosy pink.

"Red in the morning/Shepherd's warning."

I remembered that old chant as I watched the sun paint the clouds in the east with vivid hues of red and orange, then fading to a grey with a forecast of snow later on. The dogs loved to race through the snow, leaping over and plowing through the drifts. Like skiers with fresh powder, these three delighted in being the first to break a trail through the clean white surface.

Coffee and breakfast waited, and as we turned toward the

house I heard a dog bark in the kennel. The business of the day was about to start.

Fifteen years ago I had had my apprehensions about starting out on a new road, leaving behind something I loved. There had been no mail box, no house, barn, kennel, or Corgies, just the lane and the view. I had joined Louis in his dreams so that they became my dreams too. What new challenges were waiting for us both?

I thought of my mother, who, like an erratic rock, had moved from one place to another, always managing to take something of the past with her. I thought of Eddie. Changes bring endings, and endings mean saying goodbye. I wasn't ready to say goodbye. This erratic meant to stay a little longer in her niche on the Columbia River before digging into another piece of dirt and sand. Staying here would mean some changes.

I thought of the lists I had made when I started out on this road. The lane had been rough and narrow when we first drove up it, but with the years it had widened and become smoother. Were our opportunities narrowing at this time?

Perhaps it was time to start another list.

We do a great deal of talking and also a great deal of sitting and reading, either in the sunroom or outside the sunroom on the patio under the cedar trellis and the shade of the locust trees. It's a great place to review what's going on in our world of dogs, clients, staff, the river we look over, and the farm at our back. We planted those trees fourteen years ago and now they are tall, with thick trunks and branches that shade the patio and are in need of some pruning.

Fifteen years ago we moved in, on one hot windy Fourth of July. We had no lawn, no sprinklers, and no shade – not even a small tree. But Louis had a plan for it all, and in fourteen years the landscaping has taken shape. Trees, shrubs, roses, the lavender and lilacs are all mature. The lawns are a soft velvet that are mown twice a week to a lush smoothness. There is always change in the yard – or the garden, to use a British term we prefer. Daffodils and tulips give the first color, the rhubarb and the asparagus in the vegetable garden, the flowering plums and pears, the lilacs...we watch their progress. In March and April Louis's time is taken up with the early pruning and planting the vegetable garden. Pruning and weeding are constants, and all are taken to the burn pile. When the wind is right, Louis will set fire to the burn pile. Any day, if the wind is right, he will spray for weeds, either with a heavy backpack spray or with a small squirt bottle with which to do in the odd dandelion or tumbleweed. Annuals are planted for more color, and each year another twelve roses are added. In the fall we look for the color changes. Maples, flowering pears, vibernum, spireas, burning bush, sumacs have all been chosen for the brilliant colors their leaves present in the fall. Other shrubs have bright berries, and some roses have been chosen for their bright red hips.

We walk around almost daily to watch the changes, and Louis describes what his next landscaping detail will be. This shrub should be taken out and something else put in its place. It's his great novel, still unfinished. He sees where it needs editing, which sections must be rewritten, what additions will make his meaning clear. It is a work in progress and we both love it. Once we thought we would move from here, sell the kennel, find someplace easier to keep up. That is no longer our plan. Neither of us can move from this place that bears our signatures.

Those words "The End" have not yet been written.

CPSIA information can be obtained at www.ICGtesting.com
Printed in the USA
BVOW011705231011

274292BV00001B/1/P

9 781432 769291